Case Studies in Curriculum Change

Great Britain and the United States

Edited by

William A. Reid
School of Education, University of Birmingham

and

Decker F. Walker
School of Education, Stanford University

Foreword by Professor Joseph J. Schwab

Routledge & Kegan Paul
London and Boston

First published in 1975
by Routledge & Kegan Paul Ltd
Broadway House, 68–74 Carter Lane,
London EC4V 5EL and
9 Park Street,
Boston, Mass. 02108, USA

Set in Monotype Plantin
and printed in Great Britain by
Western Printing Services Ltd, Bristol

Copyright Routledge & Kegan Paul Ltd 1975

ISBN 0 7100 8037 9 (c)
ISBN 0 7100 8038 7 (p)

Case Studies in Curriculum Change

Contents

Foreword

Many books have been devoted to studies of the strategy of curriculum building. Though this volume does not ignore the strategic perspective it makes a much needed contribution to the understanding of how human agencies, through day to day involvement in planning and implementation, translate ideas, visions and theories into programs and practices, and how, in the process, the ideas themselves are recreated. Curriculum building, like literature, can be approached and interpreted on many levels: of these the least understood, but perhaps the most critical for confronting practical issues in innovation, is that of deliberation and tactic.

Deliberation and tactic (or the lack of them) are the factors above all other factors under our control which determine the course of our lives, our happiness, our satisfaction. It is through deliberation and tactic that we shape difficulties into problems we can recognize. It is through deliberation that we generate alternative solutions to our problems. It is through deliberation and tactic that we consider consequences of alternatives and test these consequences against our hopes and wishes. Finally, it is by deliberation and tactic that we initiate and maintain action toward our chosen ends and means.

The arts of deliberation and tactic serve these important purposes in both our private and our public lives. In our private lives they work to help us know whom and when to marry and how to make marriage work; where and what to do as our work, and how to rear our children and support them over the rough spots in their growing lives. In our public lives, these arts operate at every level from the international to the village. It is through these arts that we weigh and take the steps we must to deal with our friends, competitors, and potential enemies abroad; to maintain amity, peace and prosperity at home; to obtain or prevent a zoning restriction in our neighborhood; to determine and to undertake the what and the how of teaching our children in our schools.

These arts are, in brief, the brothers of logic and strategy. What logic and strategy do for us in the realm of the 'theoretic' and remote, deliberation and tactic do for us in the realm of the 'practical,' the immediate. Where our problems are problems of coming to conclusions and ultimate goals – detecting and formulating the *general* truths about nature, moving from premise to conclusion, or setting the major goals for a lifetime or an era – logic and strategy are our great means. Where our problems are problems of arriving at choice and decision about ends-in-view, of selecting and taking of actions, of dealing with what is here – now, the similar means are deliberation and tactic.

If, however, deliberation and tactic be the brothers of logic and strategy, they are the younger brothers. Where logic and strategy have received large and successful study down the ages, yielding the most powerful canons and instructions for their use, the more particular arts of deliberation and tactics have been given little more than honor for their function. From Aristotle to Dewey and Peirce, they have been recognized for what they do, honored for their contribution to our lives, but given little or no attention in their own right.

The reason for this neglect is not hard to find. It stems from the virtual absence of record and the impossibility of a verifying repetition. In theoretical works, whether esthetic, ethical or scientific, the argument is presented for all to read. The experiment can be repeated. But deliberative and tactical work take place by word of mouth behind closed doors (even behind the closed door of a single mind) and they deal with the unique event. Moreover, the memoir of deliberative and tactical judgments tends to be misleading by virtue of the orderliness which memory tends to superimpose on the waywardness of the processes of deliberation and tactical judgment.

For these reasons the recovery and report of deliberations and of tactical judgments constitute a labor of great importance. Only a large and growing body of them will provide us with ground for testing our views of what constitutes better and worse in these critically important arts. When such reports concern education, which is to say, when they concern the decisions and actions by which we determine preparations for the living of human lives, such a work is of special importance.

No more need be said in praise of the materials of this volume except the plea that philosophers and psychologists, as well as teachers and administrators in education, give them the attention they deserve.

JOSEPH J. SCHWAB

Preface

The preparation of this collection of case studies came about in a way not dissimilar from that described by some of our contributors when they try to characterize curriculum building. Central to our 'platform' was a belief that prescriptive theories of course planning and implementation have tended to be based on a false, or at least limited notion of how curriculum designers (including teachers) could or should behave; that dissatisfaction with such theories shows signs of becoming widespread, and that the way to point up new directions for thinking and conceptualizing is to go to descriptive case material which, while it is not plentiful, is certainly less hard to come by than it was a few years ago. Our ideas are not original; like curriculum builders we owe much to the work of others. Especially we would like to record our indebtedness to the work of Joseph J. Schwab, whose series of articles in *School Review* (Schwab, 1969, 1971, 1973) has stimulated new ways of thinking about the curriculum and has emphasized the importance of collecting data on the curriculum as it exists.

An opportunity of translating our 'platform' into 'deliberation' came at the 1973 American Educational Research Association Conference. Once the decision had been taken to put together a collection of case studies, progress was rapid. We were agreeably surprised by the amount of good case material which we were able to find – though, for busy people as most teachers and curriculum developers are, the process of tracking it down in unpublished papers, theses and dissertations can be a burdensome task.

In selecting studies to bring to a wider public we were guided by the beliefs already outlined: at the same time we hoped to avoid dogmatic adherence to a particular point of view. The studies speak for themselves; each author, individually, tries to deploy the perspectives which seem most useful to him in analysing what he has documented. What ties the studies together is a common view of the intricacy and complexity of bringing about change; but also of the effectiveness of human capacities for dealing with complex phenomena – capacities which, in our opinion, have tended to be underrated by many theorists. Traditional curriculum considerations, such as objectives, planning and evaluation, are not forgotten, but they take their place alongside more mundane issues – personalities, limitations of time, money and energy, conflicting interests and competing enthusiasms – to form a wide-ranging account of how the curriculum changes.

The studies offer descriptions of a variety of phases in planning and implementation, and represent serious attempts to reflect on what has been documented, and to discern general propositions which respect the complexity of the innovative process. Abstraction, when it is used, is invoked to help in the understanding of practical experience, not to provide *a priori* rationalizations. It is acknowledged that successful change demands flexibility, the ability to adjust to circumstances, redundancy in the face of variability.

The decision to include studies from both sides of the Atlantic was based on the proposition that, if descriptive curriculum studies are to be a subject of academic concern, they cannot afford to develop within parochial boundaries. Our confidence that conclusions could emerge that transcend national frontiers seems to us to have been justified, and we have been encouraged in our belief that the wider perspective is more conducive to fruitful theorizing.

It is hoped, therefore, that the studies and the commentaries on them will provide for student and practitioner alike a fund of information and ideas which will provoke them to think productively about the perennial issues in curriculum studies. What do we mean by curriculum? How and why do curricula assume the forms they do? How do they change, and how can we evolve more effective tactics and strategies in planning and implementing change? The material of the studies should be set against a re-reading of some of the better known and influential accounts of curriculum change and curriculum development, such as Tyler's *Basic Principles of Curriculum and Instruction,* Taba's *Fundamentals of Curriculum Development,* or Wheeler's *Curriculum Process,* in order to raise questions about the extent to which these seem consistent or inconsistent with what is described here, and about what might be gained and what lost by an approach to planning which built on the norm rather than the ideal. In education the relation between these is always problematic. To underestimate the potency of the idealist position is to accept too modest an ambition: to overestimate it is to run the risk of misdirecting valuable energies and misusing scarce resources. The ability to choose the right stance can only arise from a fruitful interaction of theory and practice. And to this we hope these case studies will make a worthwhile contribution.

Each study has a brief introduction summarizing the issues which it raises and pointing to connections with other contributions to the collection. The first paper takes a very broad perspective, looking at some aspects of the high school curriculum in an American city over a period of thirty years. Subsequent papers deal with particular facets of curriculum change in a sequence which moves from the planning level, through the level of administration to classroom implementation. The final contribution is not a case study but a discussion of some major themes in the theory and practice of curriculum design and implementation, drawing in part on the case studies for illustration. Extensive references are given in the chapter notes, and works which are frequently cited, or which seem to offer a major contribution to the understanding of change and innovation, are gathered in a select bibliography.

Our thanks are due to many people who have helped and encouraged us. In particular we should mention Mrs Audrey Witherford of the Birmingham Teaching Research Unit who prepared the typescript, Brian Holley of the University of Hull who advised on the editing of the study by Herbert W. Voege, Ian Westbury of the University of Illinois who was an indefatigable correspondent and always full of good ideas, and Philip Taylor of the University of Birmingham whose wide interests in the curriculum field were an essential catalyst in bringing together the people and ideas gathered in this volume.

WILLIAM A. REID

DECKER F. WALKER

The Editors and the Contributors

N.B. DICKINSON was recently appointed to the headship of Greatfield High School, Hull, having previously held a number of posts as assistant and head teacher in secondary schools. He took his first degree at the University of Manchester and received the degree of Master of Education from the University of Birmingham in 1972.

DAVID HAMILTON is lecturer in education at the University of Glasgow. After taking his first degree at the University of Edinburgh he taught in an English secondary school and then returned to Edinburgh as a research student in the Centre for Research in Educational Sciences, where he took his Ph.D.

W. LYNN MCKINNEY is assistant professor in the Curriculum Research and Development Center at the University of Rhode Island. He has taught in schools in Denver, Colorado, and holds a Ph.D. from the University of Chicago.

WILLIAM A. REID is lecturer in education at the University of Birmingham. He took his first degree at the University of Cambridge, and has taught general subjects in secondary modern schools and languages in a boys' grammar school. He has directed two Schools Council Projects in the field of sixth form education.

K.E. SHAW is principal lecturer in education at St Luke's College, Exeter. Prior to this appointment he taught in secondary schools in the North of England. He holds the degrees of MA and Ph.D. from the University of Bristol, and his main research interests are in the sociology of education and in management and organization theory as applied to schools.

HERBERT W. VOEGE is professor at Ferris State College, Michigan. Following graduate work at Ohio State University, he served for ten years on the faculty of Adrian College, Michigan, where he became chairman of the Division of Social Sciences. He is a certified public accountant and holds the degree of Ph.D. from the University of Michigan.

DECKER F. WALKER is associate professor in the School of Education, Stanford University. He received his Ph.D. from Stanford in 1971 and has remained on as a member of the faculty since, with the exception of one year spent at the University of Illinois. Previously he taught science in secondary schools in Pittsburgh, Pennsylvania.

IAN WESTBURY is associate professor of secondary education in the University of Illinois, Urbana-Champaign Campus. He previously held posts in the Ontario Institute for Studies in Education and the University of Chicago, and has taught in schools in Australia.

I
Stability and Change: the Public Schools of Gary, Indiana, 1940–70

W. Lynn McKinney and Ian Westbury

Editors' introduction

Few people today are interested in discovering how to maintain curricula as they are. Yet the attempt to understand how to bring about curriculum change would seem to be hopelessly incomplete unless it also includes an investigation into the factors which tend to perpetuate existing practices. McKinney and Westbury argue that maintenance and change 'are the two primary functions of the administrative and governing structures which surround the schools', and that an appreciation of the interrelationship of these twin functions is a prerequisite of planning for curriculum innovation. Their perspective entails an extension of the sphere of curriculum theory to include the institutional framework within which curricula are devised and mounted: it also suggests the utility of engaging in case studies which extend over a long-time period – possibly several decades – as well as those which focus on the few months or years which cover the planning and introduction of a single innovative programme. The school system chosen to test out their ideas presents a number of features which make it suitable for a study of this type. In particular, as a result of its unique history (which is summarized in the early pages of the paper), it was twice subjected in the period under review to formal surveys by *ad hoc* commissions which produced comprehensive documentary accounts of the schools. These, together with other archives, provided the authors with many valuable data which they were able to supplement at critical points by interviewing some of those who participated as teachers or administrators in the events which are described. It is not possible to present all this material within the compass of the present volume, and the major focus of attention has been directed towards three areas of the curriculum – social studies, science and vocational education. These are studied against a general background of developments in the school system over a thirty-year period, and the results reviewed in the light of conclusions presented by other researchers in the field of curriculum theory.

Note

The research reported herein was performed, in part, pursuant to a grant No. OEG-5-72-0039(509) from the National Institute of Education, US Department of Health, Education, and Welfare. However, the opinions expressed herein do not necessarily reflect the position or policies of the National Institute of Education and no official endorsement by the National Institute of Education should be inferred. In addition to acknowledging their gratitude for this grant, the authors wish also to thank Dr Gordon McAndrew, superintendent of schools for the School City of Gary and his staff for the assistance they provided. Earlier versions of this paper were read and criticized by Charles E. Bidwell, Robert Dreeben, Dan C. Lortie, and Robert L. McCaul. It is much the better for their assistance.

I

In this essay we wish to explore the most fundamental problem that faces all of us who wish to think about, and prescribe for the improvement of schooling. The curriculum of the schools must be, we believe, relevant and adaptive to needs, self-renewing and emergent; but, as we all know all too well, the reality of the schools falls far short of this ideal, often so far short that we are reduced to despair by the schools as they are. And, given our commitment to a different kind of reality, we all too often react to our despair by condemning the schools either as a whole or in one or another of their aspects – their organizational structures and styles, their clienteles, or their teachers – and arguing that, if only our chosen aspect could be changed, things would be different. There is, of course, some merit in this argument, but perhaps less than we are wont to claim – we tend not to face the possibility that it might be the ways in which *we* see innovation and adaptation that is the source of *our* failure to effect the reforms we wish for in school practices and programs.

This last possibility is the issue we wish to address in this paper. We do not argue against the aspiration for improvement which lies at the heart of thinking about education and the curriculum; instead we wish to suggest that this aspiration will, and can, become real only if we see schools in more complex ways than have been traditional. Thus we wish to follow, on the one hand, Taylor and Sarason[1] in emphasizing the constraints which must inhere in the school setting if the school is to function effectively, but which by their presence inhibit ready changes in practices and, on the other, follow the directions suggested by, for example, Clarke, Giaquinta, Smith and Keith, Sieber, and Young in stressing the need for formulations of the process of educational change that acknowledge these constraints.[2] We believe that if we can understand them and, in so doing, acknowledge their power as both positive *and* negative forces in the schools, planning for systemic changes in educational practice can make a difference.

This point of view and this conclusion are grounded in an assumption that must be made explicit. We assume that the goals of the nineteenth- and early twentieth-century founders of universal public education in Europe and America were carefully considered and carefully executed.[3] We believe that these goals have been, in the main, amply fulfilled. While one may question both the ultimate validity of the goals of our founders and some of the means they chose to pursue them, we are convinced that we must acknowledge the difficulties they faced and their achievement in creating the systems of schools we have today, and ask *how the system works*. It is, we believe, only hindsight and familiarity that make the organization and structure of the schools appear relatively simple, obvious, and malleable. Only if we recognize that the simple and the obvious are not necessarily commonplace will we have a basis for seeking ways in which we might enact a new charter of purposes.

To answer the question 'How do the schools work ?', we must subject the obvious to analysis and ask, at least initially, such simple questions as 'Why don't the schools teach such subjects as dance, engineering, or Russian history and why do they teach, almost universally, such subjects as history, science, algebra, and the like ?' The first, speculative section of this essay attempts to answer questions of this kind by sketching a conceptualization of the character and functions of subjects, the pervasive and fundamental building blocks of the curriculum. We argue that we will understand what subjects are and how they function only if we see them as social institutions that work to order and direct the form of the intellectual experience that schools offer their students.

The emphasis on control that emerges in the course of this analysis leaves a problem inasmuch as it highlights the difficulties inherent in the task of changing the curriculum. Clearly change in the curriculum of the school has taken place. This inconsistency between the conclusions of our theoretical analysis and the seeming reality of curriculum change led us to undertake a study of a concrete case in the search for a way of reconciling the conclusions of our general argument with the facts of at least one particular situation. Our ultimate conclusion, to be developed in the last pages of this essay, is perhaps paradoxical for, in a sense, it is possible to view the changes that took place in the curriculum of the schools we examined, those of Gary, Indiana, as supporting rather than disconfirming the focus on the institutional ramifications of the curriculum that emerged from our initial speculations. Indeed, institutional constraints and institutional supports played a major and central role – more central than we had expected – in the change process as we observed it in Gary.

Our concern with the problem area we are venturing into in this essay, and the first glimmerings of the ways in which we now see its dimensions, had their beginnings in two research studies and one attempt at innovation we participated in that seemed to sum to the conclusion that curriculum change is awesomely complex. Let us begin this discussion with these experiences as a backdrop for both the thesis we will develop in this section and for the study of Gary that follows:

During an attempt to introduce Italian as a foreign language for Italian immigrant students in an Australian high school, we were met by the school administration (and defeated) by the simple (and, given hindsight, correct) argument that we could not guarantee that the one Italian teacher we knew would remain at our school for long enough to provide a continuing program in Italian over the school lives of the cohorts of students we anticipated teaching. We were told that such a program could not be introduced in our school until the state university could and would provide a flow of qualified and certificated Italian teachers. Our task, if we wanted our innovation, was to persuade the university to create a program in Italian that would provide such a flow of potential teachers.

Five years ago, in the course of a status survey into the teaching of Canadian history, we found that, despite the jealously-held prerogative that all provinces claimed to develop programs that were adaptive to regional differences and interests, there were in fact only two Canadian history programs in the country – one common to all English-speaking provinces, and the other taught only in Quebec. The program common to the English-speaking provinces had been developed originally in the 1920s and reflected the concerns of

English-speaking academic historians of that decade and was, of course, far removed from the concerns of Canadian historians of the 1960s. Needless to say, the course had been revised, but such revisions consisted of units added onto the program which brought it up to date temporarily – and we found that these units were seemingly rarely taught. Most teachers found it very difficult to escape the temporal and intellectual boundaries of the old course.[4]

In the course of an evaluation of an experimental program in social work, we found that the faculty teaching the program experienced considerable difficulty as they sought to generate a content that they could use as a basis for their day-to-day teaching that reflected their goals and aspirations for both social work practice and their program. They found it almost impossible to escape from the pull of concepts, content, and methods that they had long taught and used. The task of inventing a content that went along with and could be the basis for delivering on their visionary goals about what they might do defeated them.[5]

All of these experiences suggested that curriculum change is complex, more complex, and certainly more problematic than most conventional views of the process would imply. And there are many instances reported in the literature that can be taken as supporting at least the burden of our experience.

Before turning to the task of exploring how our experiences might be understood as a representation and manifestation of some fundamental structural characteristics of schooling, let us offer a rapidly sketched sample of references by others to incidents of the kind that we have been describing in the hope that we can assert at least the relative generalizability of our reading of the problems and difficulties that face those who wish to reform schooling.

M.P. Smith reported a three-years-after follow-up of a local primary school science development project in England. He found that the program had persisted in the schools in which it had been initiated only for as long as the original developers remained in their schools. However, the program spread to new schools as the original 'activists' moved and initiated development at new sites. In this case grass roots development failed to have significant and lasting effects in the schools in which the work had been initiated because heads and teachers who had not wanted to work with the project at its beginning permitted the curriculum to lapse when its proponents left. This lapse of the program is reminiscent of the lapse that our administrators feared when we wished to introduce a new subject in one high school without support from the state's major teacher training institution.[6]

There are many examples of innovative programs being defeated by more explicit opposition than that implied by our examples. Wilkof describes the downfall of the University of Chicago 1940s experiment in liberal education at the hands of faculty who regarded the demands of traditional graduate education as the primary justification for any under-graduate program: Gallie reports a similar defeat of the curricular initiatives at Keele University in the same decade by faculty who believed in the unassailable rightness and educative power of the traditional disciplines.[7] Young and Goodlad describe a different aspect of this power of vested interest: the domination by the traditional disciplines of most of the resources for curriculum development in England and the United States over the past twenty years. Minimal funding had been devoted to either development projects in new subject areas or to redevelopment projects in less central subject areas, for example, the arts, industrial arts, and the like.[8]

A common thread seems to run through all of these anecdotes and examples. In all cases the curriculum can be seen as an *idea* that becomes a thing, an entity that has institutional and technical form. In the case of our experience in curriculum development in social work, the translation of an idea into a functioning curriculum required the invention of ways and means, and the task of communication of these ways and means to the teachers who were to work within the new idea was overwhelming – and older curriculum ways and means inhibited both the search for new means and the ready communication of new means to those not actively involved in the initial development. In the case of the battles at Chicago and Keele, different ideas and concomit-ant sets of ways and means become the foci of essentially political battles between factions with differing, and often incompatible investments, in old and new. In the case of Canadian history, we see a curriculum sur-viving long after its original rationale in ideas has lost its force; the curriculum was a tradition which survived because it was embedded within an institutional structure, not because it had any independent intellectual vitality. Finally, in the case of our attempt to introduce Italian, and in M.P. Smith's study of the failure of one attempt to introduce a new primary science program, we see the converse of the inertias that this last observation attributes to institutionalization – the necessity for explicitly institutional structures of support and control if a given idea is to be enacted competently and with a continuity that transcends the life of a given teacher in a given school.

It is these institutional and technical characteristics of the curriculum that we have been emphasizing that we see almost all curricular enquiry neglecting, or else treating unsympathetically. Perhaps these aspects of

the curriculum are too obvious or too obtrusive to be seen as problematic and so worthy of serious attention. However, something of this
obviousness and/or objectionable obtrusiveness appears in a new light
when we invoke, on the one hand, our initial concern with the effective
delivery of schooling to masses of students and, on the other, Kuhn's
term *paradigm* and ask whether or not the curriculum, at least in the
aspect we have been exploring here, has functions similar to those we
can associate with the forms and structures that control and make
possible scientific enquiry.[9] Thus, viewed sociologically, scientific
activity is work, the creation of potentially consensual knowledge; the
means of science, its methods and technologies, are designed to facilitate
the creation of knowledge by *groups* of scientists and to validate such
creations. As Ziman writes:[10]

> The whole procedure of publication and citation, the abhorrence of
> secrecy, the libraries full of periodicals and treatises, *Lernfreiheit* and
> *Lehrfreiheit* – freedom to learn and freedom to teach – cosmopolitan-
> ism, internationalism, abstract journals and encyclopedias – all are in
> the service of the mutual exchange of information. . . . But merely to
> point this out tells us very little about the nature of Science itself. I
> want to go further and suggest that the absolute need to communicate
> one's findings, and to make them acceptable to other people, deter-
> mines their intellectual form. Objectivity and logical rationality, the
> supreme characteristics of the Scientific Attitude, are meaningless
> for the isolated individual; they imply a strong social context, and
> sharing of experience and opinion.

Yet, while this potential analogy between science in its social aspects
and the curriculum in its social aspect does serve to direct attention to
some aspects of the curriculum that have been given too little attention,
the analogy only carries us so far. Thus, although the interests of the
schools connect with those of science inasmuch as both science and the
schools are concerned with intellectual, abstract, and conceptual matters,
and although scholars, intellectuals, and teachers frequently share a
common role as cultural guardians and subject matter experts, and
although the schools are institutionally contiguous with the university,
the recognition of these similarities must not blind us to the fact that
the mission of the universities as research institutions and the mission
of the schools as teaching institutions diverge in fundamental ways.

The task of the schools as organizations is the systematic and routine
induction of large numbers of students into valued aspects of the human
experience. Within the schools the curriculum specifies the scope and
forms of this valued knowledge in so far as it specifies the knowledge
that it is thought students of given ages and kinds can and should learn,

the manner of the teaching of this knowledge, and the conditions under which teaching will take place. The problems and considerations which flow from concerns of this kind have, in the main, only the remotest connection with the problems and considerations which vex scholars.

One example can serve as the basis for an elaboration of this claim. Latin *qua* classical studies is a set of problems inhering in the corpus of texts written in Latin. *Qua* the schools, however, Latin is a smaller collection of texts and procedures (prose composition and the like) organized in the interests of 'educative' potency and pedagogic communicability and efficacy. When Latin is considered in the context of schooling, it is its curricular aspects which come to the forefront; for the schools and for teacher training institutions Caesar's *Gallic Wars* is a text chosen because of its accessibility to students with limited facility in Latin. It is a text which is to be taught to teachers because they will teach it in schools, and it is a text which is to be explored inasmuch as it is educationally and pedagogically, rather than intellectually, problematic. Teachers must know the text's potential for the 'education' of their students, they must know and be able to anticipate all the difficulties that it might present the students they will teach, and they must have at hand methods and procedures which can be invoked as necessary to obviate any difficulties, anticipated or unanticipated, that might occur when a particular class encounters Caesar. Inasmuch as the mass teaching of Latin requires that many, many teachers have these competencies and capabilities, structures of teacher training, credentialing and the like have been designed to minimize possible variance among teachers in their competence and capability to teach, at least adequately. The existence of many teachers teaching one or a small number of known texts to students of known kinds permits and makes possible collective attention to these same problems: it is this collective and public concern for the problems in teaching a bounded and known universe of content that makes possible school texts, published aids, and the like.

Similar tasks and similar structures are found for all of the discourses (mathematics, art, and so on) which make up the components of the school curriculum. Intellectual discourses which are thought in a given period to be of cultural or instrumental value for the young, become, in the school, *subjects* which, in their turn, offer the intellectual organization for, and the vehicles by which teachers of known character and quality are deployed to teach their knowledge systematically to millions of students for the twelve or so years they are in school. Teachers leave the schools but students remain – it is the existence of a program organized in routinized ways that makes it possible for one teacher to pick up where another leaves off, whether in mid-year or at year-end.

It is the existence of these social institutions with their known character that makes possible the common endeavors of a school system – the training of teachers, the writing of texts and examinations, the construction of apparatus and buildings and the like. In other words, subjects and the forms of schooling which surround them are structural frames which specify the conditions and the meaning contexts within which teaching will take place and are the foci and the means of institutional collaboration by the agencies of schooling for the furtherance of their work. Subjects are, in this sense, the educational analogies of the formalized collaborations that institutionalized scientific enquiry has developed as it has sought to transcend the limitations of one man and his experience.

Mastery of the contents and the means of the subjects of the school curriculum takes many years. Every teacher, whatever his subject, must know how he can teach the skills and contents his students are learning. Teachers learn the complex sets of skills that make up their competence not through formal courses in education, but instead through mastery of the subjects that make up their own schooling, through modeling on their own teachers in school and college, and through practical experience in teaching.

All professions and crafts rely on informal learning of this kind and all professions and crafts have elements of their work that involve flying by the seat of the pants – however, few professions or crafts have their ways and means so little codified as does education. As a result of this circumstance, education has been characteristically unable to evolve procedures or methods that point to or evaluate single clusters of behaviors which might, or must be modified, in the interests of more effective, or qualitatively different teaching. Neither successful teacher training nor meaningful supervision of teaching have been successfully institutionalized in most school systems; as a result the only control that a school or a school system has over the nature or the quality of its teaching is its ability to determine who will be appointed to its staff and who will be retained – and, given the teacher shortages that have plagued public education through much of its history, this has been a minimally effective power.

The problems inherent in training for or controlling performance within an occupation with so many ambiguous and uncodified elements have been further complicated by factors associated with teaching within most formal educational institutions. Thus, typically, teaching is an occupation with limited positive attractiveness to many, if not most of its recruits; the maximum of five years many teachers spend in teaching inhibits sustained experiential learning and craft mastery; the characteristic egg-crate social organization of schools has inhibited either collegial or supervisory contact between teachers and the resulting opportunities for learning of new classroom behaviors. The reward and incentive systems that are typical of most school systems give only minimal incentive for investment by teachers in either development or learning of new practices and procedures – with the result that those teachers who, whether consciously or subconsciously, calculate rates of return for investments of time and energy in both curriculum development and learning of new ways see only a limited return deriving from such investment.[11]

Teaching is, then, a complex task, made more complex and less open to analysis and appraisal by virtue of organizational forms within which it is embedded. The consequence of this interaction between the problems of the task and the structures which surround the classroom but give only minimal support to the work of the classroom has been the development of adaptive sentiments within the occupation that emphasize the relationship between the teacher and her class and the uncertainties that are an omnipresent part of that relationship and minimize the role of supervision and control of outcomes, and the significance of educational agencies external to the school and classroom. Effective teaching is usually viewed as requiring that teachers be emotionally invested in their students and their classrooms; and reward and satisfaction are seen as coming not from collegial or supervisory recognition of work well done but from the responses of their students to their efforts. Curricular change, with its inevitable pressure for new habits and practices, must have only limited appeal, at best, for most teachers.

A tacit *modus vivendi* between the demands that might be made on an educational system and the interests, desires and capabilities of teachers can be, and usually is, achieved by a compromise. Teachers can be given autonomy to teach the subjects they know in ways they know in the hope that the student will reach adequate levels of proficiency while administrators can grapple with problems of recruitment and finance, with instructionally irrelevant issues like community relations or accounting, or with decisions with consequences that do not impinge too fundamentally on the major concerns of the teacher. Traditionally the curriculum has fallen into a confused area between these tacitly accepted zones of responsibility – and instruction has been firmly incorporated within the zone of responsibility of teachers. The time alloted to a given subject may be expanded by a period or two a week – but the use of that time cannot be determined by an administration. Teachers can be expected to produce given levels of achievement on tests of one kind or another, but only if it is acknowledged that standards can be trivialized by permitting teaching for the test.[12] But, while compromises of this kind work out reasonably well in any short run, what happens when a whole subject faces anachronism, not in the schools where it may have a life of its own, but in relation to changes of one kind or another in the world outside the school? Or what happens when a new subject or new conception of an old subject is thought worthy of incorporation in the curriculum? The examples we cited earlier, and our argument, suggest that this is a real problem. Change can occur only when there are individuals who have themselves learned some new methods or new content in the course of their own experience. But these individuals can only effect lasting systemic change if their innovations become institutionalized, that is, when structural support of the kind that we have been associating with the institution of a subject, is offered them – but the diffuse organization of the schools and the needs of teachers we have identified suggest that these structural supports are difficult to establish. In short, our analysis of the curriculum as an institution gives us a way of accounting for both the failure of innovative efforts and the persistence of old forms – but it gives us no way of accounting for change when such institutional support is not given or is not available. We can only say that change takes place when a new generation of teachers' demands change – but this begs our question!

It was this problem of explaining the processes of change in the curriculum of the public schools that led us to a study of the curriculum of the Gary, Indiana, secondary schools between 1940 and 1970. The 1940s and early 1950s were marked by ferment at the ideological level about the goals of the American schools, the late 1950s and early 1960s by unprecedented investment at both the local and national levels in curriculum development. This effort appears to have had somewhat less dramatic effects than the proponents of ideological or practical reform could have hoped for. As we would expect, the most significant change during this period was by way of the development of new courses within the traditional subject areas rather than by the addition of new subjects.[13] Yet while change in the range of subjects offered by the high school has been more or less minimal, change has taken place in the content taught within these traditional subjects, in the availability of subjects within particular schools, and the like. To the extent that this is so and to the extent that our analysis of the difficulties that face proponents of change in the curriculum is correct, we do have the question: 'How did the changes that did occur in the schools happen?' Our goal in our case study was to search for a way of answering this question. We will summarize our findings about the process of change as we saw it in Gary in the next section and turn, in the final section of this paper, to an attempt to explicate where our findings have led our thinking.

II

Gary, Indiana, stands, as one commentator on Chicago put it in 1926, 'where most people, except for Chicagoans themselves, think that Chicago stands: at the southern end of Lake Michigan,' twenty-six miles from Chicago's downtown loop.[14] It is an industrial city, carved out of the sand dunes that surround the Lake Michigan shoreline in 1906 as the site of a steel mill. Six months after its incorporation, Gary had 10,000 inhabitants and was a company town, dominated by a mill that separated the town from the lake and marked by row upon row of jerry-built frame houses standing on sandy lots in which no grass would grow. By 1940, the city had over 100,000 inhabitants and was one of the largest satellite cities in the Chicago metropolitan region. Gary is one of the few school districts in the Chicago region that has had a large school system through most of its history: as such, it is one of the few school systems in the Chicago region with an archive of committee reports and the like that covers the period in which we were interested.

The availability of an archive is an essential condition for, not a justification of a study, particularly when the archive offers us data about a place as untypical as Gary. But, happenstance made Gary a more logical place for a study of the kind we wanted to undertake. In 1940, the Gary Plan, one of the major American experiments in the design of alternative forms for the delivery of schooling, was still operating in the city while today the Plan has gone. This death was gradual: as late as 1955, elements of the Plan still existed and were still being attacked by those who wanted to bring Gary's schools into conformity with what was seen as desirable and normal school practice. This shift, from being the exception to conformity with the norm, is of course the converse of the problem that is our focus. Our hope was that perhaps this extreme case could illuminate the problems that one school jurisdiction faced as it underwent almost total change in at least its forms and structures. The question is, of course, whether this extreme case has any relevance to the problems that face conventional school systems which wish to undertake more or less conventional reforms. Hindsight has convinced us that the problems that Gary faced are similar to those that all school systems must face when they undertake change, or have change thrust upon them – but we recognize that that is a judgment that may well be questioned.

In 1906, William Wirt, then superintendent of schools in a small town in rural Indiana, visited the new city of Gary. Tom Knotts, the president of the local school board, met him during a Sunday morning stroll among the sand hills where the city was later built. Knotts discovered that the young man was a schoolteacher, and set out to find what the stranger knew about education. Before they parted, Wirt was asked if he would consider a proposition to head the new school system.

This chance encounter marked the beginning of what could have been, had the place been more propitious and the times less dominated by universalizing concerns, a significant exploration of possible alternative forms for the delivery of schooling to America's rapidly developing cities. In common with many of his contemporaries, Wirt did not believe that the traditional school systems were adequately meeting the social needs of the then developing industrial city. Wirt had a concrete plan, and presumably it was this plan that impressed Knotts, by which the schools could meet the demands of the new order and do so economically. Gary offered Wirt the opportunity he craved to enact his vision: the city had virtually no schools and needed them; it had no constraining traditions of plant to inhibit his development for new forms, while the city's immigrant population had no clear ideas about what American schooling should be like and had, therefore, little interest in inhibiting him or capacity to do so.[15]

Wirt had one educational goal: eliminate the pernicious influence of the city so that children could learn:[16]

> Pedagogy has long tried to educate children by the intensified use of the few short hours in the study schools, by highly developed teaching methods and devices, and by a correlation of subject matter in a curriculum of subjects to meet the needs of children. It is now generally recognized that the proper development of the child in the modern city is more of a social problem than it is a psychological or pedagogical problem. Psychology and pedagogy cannot do much for children as long as they are left to the crowded unsanitary tenements for their home life, and to the gangs of the streets and alleys for their activities.
>
> The teacher who has a social service viewpoint in regard to his work no longer depends on pedagogic nostrums and devices for the development of the souls of his charges. Rather he now attempts to give nature a chance to work the marvelous changes that come irresistibly and naturally in the growing child under fit living conditions.

Wirt's plan for urban education, as it evolved in Gary between 1907 and 1915, had three features, the platoon plan, the lengthened school day and year, and the unit organization, which together summed to effect a pattern for schooling which he believed would minimize the evil effects of the city and provide a positive educational experience for children – economically. Four kinds of instruction were offered in Gary schools: (1) academic, which included reading, spelling, grammar, writing, arithmetic, geography, and history; (2) special work, which included drawing, science, cooking, and manual training; (3) auditorium, which provided for singing, movies and drama; and (4) physical education and play. In order to provide all of these experiences and still keep school construction costs within reason, Wirt devised the platoon plan. Each school would have academic classrooms for only half of the students in the school. While one-half of the student body was using these academic classrooms, the other half would be using the shops, gymnasium, auditorium, and laboratories. Halfway through each day the two platoons would switch places. The money saved by building only half the usual number of classrooms was used to construct the extended, and occasionally elaborate, 'special' facilities.

Wirt's curricular ideas were not particularly unusual. What was unusual in his plan was that these special activities were added to the regular school program instead of being squeezed into it. He lengthened the school day and year to keep children busily and constructively engaged for as long as possible. In this way the social purpose of the school in the city, to keep children occupied under 'right conditions,' could be met. The lengthened day, of course, was the only way to provide the variety of educational experiences Wirt prescribed to each student on a daily basis. From the earliest days of the Gary schools until 1941, the school day was eight hours in length, from 8:15 to 4:15, with one hour for lunch. In addition, until the early 1930s, the schools were open on a voluntary basis from nine o'clock until five o'clock on Saturdays, and there was a ten-week summer program.

The third feature of Wirt's schools, the unit form of organization, describes the composition of the student body of Gary schools. All students from kindergarten through twelfth grade living in a given geographic area attended the same school. Each unit school was to be a community center for schooling as well as other activities, much in the manner of rural schools. A sense of community identity was to grow around the school.

This unit form of organization aided the fulfillment of the social purpose of the school because it dictated that the school, like the world around it, should be composed of a variety of individuals of differing ages and interests. It also removed the artificial 'breaks' found in the traditional school. Wirt argued that the Gary schools had greater holding power because the completion of sixth or eighth grade did not signify 'graduation'. There was continuity in the Gary schools, not a series of 'completions' any one of which might serve as a stopping point for students dropping out. As important, Wirt's concerns for economy were served by the unit plan of organization. The construction of the extended facilities such as shops, laboratories, and swimming pools was justifiable only when it could be shown that these facilities were used to their maximum capacity. In order to so use them, a large number of students was needed in each school. Large extended schools built to serve just high school students could have served the same purpose, but students would have had to travel farther to school, and the other benefits of the unit organization, its social purpose, and its educational continuity would have been lost.

III

William Wirt died in 1938. In his thirty-one years in Gary, he had constructed a school system that in the 1910s had won national acclaim, but which, by the 1930s, had become only an interesting part of the history of American education as far as most schoolmen were concerned. However, in Gary the Plan persisted, marking its schools as anomalous in the eyes of most observers. Wirt himself declared in 1935, that the objectives of Gary's schools had not changed at all in the preceding thirty years and, as if he were proving the correctness of his affirmation, he proceeded to plan what were to be his last schools – two unit schools that were to be completed in 1937 and 1939, and were to be built along exactly the same lines as the six schools that had been built between 1909 and 1922. Wirt had not only built, but also maintained a system of schools that was no longer responding to the social and intellectual currents of a new and different era. In 1939, America had a higher goal for its schools than any but utopians at the turn of the century would have thought possible: but Wirt no longer distinguished between his goals and his means, and rejected notions of adaptive evolution of ways and means under the control of an intellectual impulse. The Plan was fixed and immutable.

Wirt's death faced the Gary School Board with the problem of deciding what it should do with its, in many ways, anomalous school system. It could not bring itself to face this issue head-on, and, instead, perseverated by, on the one hand, commissioning a survey of its schools by faculty from Purdue University and, on the other hand, appointing Charles Lutz, then the principal of its Horace Mann school and a teacher in the system since 1924, as superintendent. Lutz's appointment foreclosed the system's response to the recommendations of the Purdue faculty; he was Wirt's man and a believer in the Gary Plan – but he did not have the capacity to renew Wirt's original work or search for alternative forms for the American school. A process of gradual erosion of the Gary Plan began soon after Lutz assumed the superintendency as the outside world, which Wirt had for so long ignored successfully, demanded that Gary fall into line with the dominant patterns of American education. In 1970, when our study terminated, there were no remains of the Wirt Plan in Gary.

This essay does not have as its central theme the erosion of the Wirt Plan, although inevitably the Plan and the organizational saga that the Wirt years created in Gary become major sub-themes in our analysis. The Plan, the opposition to the Plan and its erosion are themes which should be handled for their own sake – and that was not our intention. Our concerns were simpler: we wanted to see how the curriculum of one admittedly unrepresentative school system changed over a thirty year period. And even that focus proved larger than we could cope with, with the result that we will present here only an analysis of three subject areas from the Gary schools, social studies, science, and vocational education. Even within these subject areas, we were forced by the constraints of time and availability of sources to limit ourselves, in the main, to change at the formal level, at the level of the approved curriculum; we recognize, of course, that at best this gives us only a partial view of developments and changes in Gary and that a complete study would require us to understand, much more completely than we were able to, what teachers were doing in classrooms.

We should say, to offer an extenuating circumstance to mitigate the charge that our study is too incomplete, that we did try to secure data about teaching – and at times we were successful: we were able to interview some informants who had participated as teachers or administrators in some of the events we will be describing. But mostly we had to rely on formal documents and formal minutes. We were lucky in our search for such formal evidence: Gary, because of its unique problems (in part a legacy of the Wirt years) was subjected twice in the period we were exploring to formal surveys by *ad hoc* commissions (the Purdue Survey of 1942, and the Public Administration Service Survey of 1955)[17] charged with the responsibility of examining of the city's schools on behalf of the Board. These surveys were, of course, somewhat mixed in their value as historical sources: they were created to assist the Board in its attempt to cope with concrete administrative and managerial problems and an administrative perspective dominated their reports: they were written by outsiders who were unsympathetic to the Gary saga and as such tended to highlight features of the Gary schools that were, from the viewpoint of a proponent of conventional schools, unfortunate to say the least. And finally, when they discussed curricular matters they tended to be vague and exhortatory rather than explicit and analytic. Yet, in spite of these clear shortcomings, these reports do offer comprehensive accounts of the Gary schools. When used in conjunction with the minutes and other papers of the Board they gave us the basis for at least an overview of the dynamics of curriculum change in the city.

IV

In the early 1940s, racial unrest in Detroit and a number of other cities stimulated American teachers and curriculum developers to turn their attention to the problem of what role the school might play in relieving racial tensions. One response to this concern was the idea that programs stressing intercultural relations might assist integration; and despite the press of war, a number of national organizations of teachers and school districts picked up this theme and launched committees to study the problem. Gary was one of these cities; in December 1943, it engaged the Bureau of Intercultural Education, a New York consulting firm, to begin working with representatives of the school system in designing an intercultural curriculum. In September 1945, a racial strike broke out in Gary's schools. The strike gave an explicit motivation for the school system to move rapidly with its program development and almost immediately an active attempt to design a curriculum was undertaken. By 1947, the strike had been settled, an integration policy for the city's schools had been adopted, and an intercultural curriculum had been designed. In 1955, the integration policy was firmly in effect, but the intercultural curriculum was being used by no more than a handful of Gary's teachers. What happened to the curricular initiative during the intervening years?

On September 18, 1945, a majority of the white students at Froebel School in Gary went out on strike protesting the integrated nature of the school. The initial demand of the striking students was the reassignment of all black students to 'their own' school. The issue facing the school system was racial prejudice. Gary civic and school officials viewed this potentially explosive situation as two separate but related problems, one short-term and the other long-term. The short-term problem was always seen as primary. Striking students had to be returned to their classes, and strikes had to be contained in one school. In other words, the schools had to be kept continually operating, and the threat of their closing had to be eliminated. A long-range solution to the racial unrest was thought to lie in addition of an intercultural component to the social studies program.

This idea went back two years in Gary. After the 1943 Detroit race riot, the Gary Chamber of Commerce had appointed a race relations committee that included several school employees as members. As if in concert, the Board of School Trustees in December 1943 engaged the Bureau of Intercultural Education, a New York-based consulting firm, to begin working with representatives of the schools in designing an intercultural curriculum. Although several meetings of bureau and school people had been held by the time of the first strike, no curriculum had been designed. With the advent of the first strike, bureau assistance was actively sought both to keep the schools functioning and to plan a curriculum.[18]

However, because the strike naturally seemed to be the immediate problem facing the school system, in September 1945, the most intensive efforts were directed toward its solution. Numerous statements were released by civic organizations condemning the strike. Meetings were held involving the Board, school personnel, striking students, and their parents. Enforcement of the truancy laws was threatened. By December 1946, the Board felt that the situation was sufficiently calm to pass a resolution affirming the principle of geographic attendance areas for all schools. For the first time in Gary, black students would not be forced to attend the all-black elementary and secondary schools.

Work on the long-range problem of creating programs in intercultural education continued during 1945 and 1946. A city-wide committee was appointed with the task of designing an intercultural curriculum. Despite scant resources (no released time was provided, and materials about intercultural relations were not easily found) the committee built on work that had been done in 1943-4 to complete the writing of a program by the end of the 1945-6 school year. One teacher in each school tried the curriculum during the 1946-7 school year. The program was allowed to end with the end of this one-year trial; it did not spread system-wide or even throughout any one school, and at no time during the remainder of the period under study was there an attempt by the school system to revive the intercultural curriculum. By 1955, only vestigial remnants of the program remained in isolated class rooms.

The strike that began at Froebel School on Tuesday, September 18, 1945, continued until the following Tuesday when the strike leaders suspended it, acquiescing to a demand by the Board of School Trustees. Had the strike continued, the Board would have refused to hear the pleas of the strikers at its regularly scheduled meeting that night. The strike resumed, however, the next day because the Board refused to act on the demands of the striking students.

Feeling that the Froebel principal was pro-black student and anti-strike, the striking students demanded his replacement. This demand was partially agreed to with the hope that the strike would be ended and Froebel kept integrated if the principal were sacrificed. Instead of immediately replacing him, however, the Board asked a committee to look into his administrative practices; accordingly, the principal was given a leave of absence. On the first day of the principal's leave, October 1, all students returned to their classes. On October 23, the investigating committee reported favorably on the principal. Enraged by this seeming betrayal, the strike committee, this time backed by many of their parents, called a second strike to begin on October 29.

The second Froebel strike started on October 29, and ended on November 10. The parents' committee which had emerged during the second strike had traveled to Indianapolis, the state capital, to present its demands to the State Superintendent of Schools. He was unsympathetic to their cause and asked that they help end the strike. The State Superintendent's rejection combined with the fact that no further support for the strike was developing in the city brought the second strike to an end.

Yet a third strike was called for March 5, 1946, with the demand again for integration of the school system. However, before the strike could occur, the combination of the efforts of organizations and individuals and the threat that truancy laws would be enforced convinced the students that their efforts were in vain. The strike teams that the strike committee had dispatched to other schools met with little sympathy and support. Although there had been no clear directions about integration from the Board, the strike threat had been effectively ended 167 days after it began. School was again operating smoothly with no threats of closing to concern it. The city's success in achieving this point of relative calm was the result of a combination of many efforts.

The actions of all the individuals and groups involved in ending the strike would fill a book; representative selected examples will have to serve here to indicate the range of efforts. The first official action of Superintendent Lutz was to ask for strong anti-strike statements from community leaders and organizations. His request was responded to by the superintendent of the US Steel Mill, the police chief, the mayor, four members of the Board of School Trustees, and by the *Gary Post-Tribune*. Yet, despite the individual statements of the Board members, the Board was unwilling to take an official stand on the strike; thus, in its first statement issued on September 21, 1945, it was unclear what the Board planned to do. The next step by the superintendent was a series of face-to-face and telephone conversations with as many local leaders as could be reached, asking them to speak against the strike at the September 25 board meeting. Again, response was good.

By October 4, additional statements condemning the strike had come from the League of Women Voters, the YWCA, the United Council of Negro Organizations, and the teachers' union. In October, 150 different local organizations were represented at a meeting called by the mayor. Again, the intent was to formulate plans for ending the strike and to demonstrate overwhelming community condemnation of the actions of the striking students. The Julius Rosenwald Fund, the Bureau of Intercultural Education, and the schools combined resources and efforts to sponsor an appearance of Frank Sinatra on November 1, 1945. Sinatra sang and severely criticized the strike. The additional voices of Edna Ferber, Carl Sandburg, Bill Mauldin, Clifton Fadiman, and William L. Laurence were heard pleading for an end to the strike at a Victory Bond rally on November 4.

Several local organizations started programs of their own. The League of Women Voters, with the help of some high school social studies teachers, sponsored a series of studies of delinquency, recreation and housing. The Urban League and the Downtown Methodist Church offered tours for high school students through the area around Froebel School so that students could see the living conditions there. The YWCA, Women's Forum, Urban League, and the League of Women Voters conducted a workshop to train human relations leaders on April 1 and 2, 1946. The American Council on Race Relations had field workers in Gary helping local CIO leaders plan educational activities which would develop interracial understanding among union members.

Once the strike and the threat of strike had ended and the new Board policy on integration had been approved, efforts to educate the community about the policy were undertaken. Superintendent Lutz and several other school administrators explained the reasons for the policy and its likely effects to groups of parents and various civic organizations. Between September 1946 and August 1947, when the integration policy was to go into effect, school officials participated in over two hundred different meetings.

As was feared, several school strikes occurred when school opened in the fall of 1947. By this time, however, the community programs had had their effect. The Board acted quickly to cancel athletic events, to apply truancy laws, and to notify parents of striking students that they were breaking the law by encouraging truancy. As a result, the strikes did not gain momentum, and the school was operating smoothly within two weeks.

While the strike situation was being settled and the Board was moving toward an integration policy, it seemed as if the parallel attempt to develop an intercultural education curriculum for the Gary schools would meet with success. However, as we have already suggested, this developmental effort failed and a program that would be taught in all Gary schools never in fact emerged. Hindsight, however, suggests that some of the purposiveness of the developmental activity that took place between 1945 and 1947 was illusory rather than substantive. In the words of Dana P. Whitmer, then an administrator in the Gary schools:[19]

There has been much activity in the Gary schools regarding race relations. A considerable amount of this has been related to the Intercultural Policy and means by which it should be implemented. A lesser amount of emphasis has been related to the educational aspects of intergroup relations. The city-wide Democratic Living Committee has devoted thought to intergroup education and has served as a means of communication among schools. A considerable number of short workshops, conferences, and meetings have been held in which intergroup education has been considered. Individual teachers have attended summer intercultural workshops. One experiment in intergroup education involving the several schools has been carried on. Bulletins to teachers from supervisors have included considerable material on intergroup education. A seventh and eighth grade science curriculum has been developed in which a strong emphasis on intergroup relations appears. Individual schools and teachers have engaged in special projects designed to influence the intergroup attitudes of children. These all may be characterized as influences which undoubtedly have resulted in special efforts by some teachers and schools toward the provision of learning experiences in intergroup relations. These have, however, only been influences. There has been no planned program through which the majority or even a large number of teachers have worked toward common ends in intergroup education. The programs of intergroup education which have been developed, while being influenced by those above mentioned activities, have depended largely on the individual interests, initiative, and enthusiasm of the principals and teachers in the schools.

In the absence of organized effort on the part of the system and individual schools, teachers were left on their own. And these individual efforts were neither numerous nor extensive. Whitmer reports that, in 1947, 40 per cent of all Gary teachers acknowledged feeling that intergroup education was important, but only 17 per cent claimed to be providing appropriate experiences as an integral part of classroom work.

In the subject matter areas of science, social studies, and English, only 19 per cent of the teachers above the primary level reported using teaching units that were somehow concerned with greater understanding of intercultural problems. There were almost no attempts to use minority group speakers in classrooms, to arrange for discussion in classes between white and black students about intercultural relations and problems, or to visit local organizations concerned with minority groups. No teachers were involved in in-service programs, only 9 per cent of Gary's teachers worked on the committees planning curriculum, and only 25 per cent were involved in study groups concerned with intercultural relations.[20]

Yet Gary did devote some attention to intercultural education. A curriculum was developed, and it was tried by a limited number of teachers for a year. Most of these teachers had served on the various committees in existence during the 1945–6 school year. They used, refined, and used again the materials they helped develop and some of these teachers were, we were told, still improving and using their units in 1955. To say, then, that no attention was paid to intercultural education would be incorrect; in fact, it received considerable attention. A curriculum was written, and efforts were made to include it in the secondary social studies program. But these efforts were at best only partly successful. Why was the curriculum not widely used?

The initial demand for the creation and use of an intercultural curriculum came from the civic elite, the Board, and the superintendent. Yet despite this early demand for an intercultural curriculum, those individuals making the demand soon withdrew their support in the face of community resistance. The Board and administration were not quick to act directly to end the Froebel strike, and a school integration policy was a year and a half in the making.

Yet the continued functioning of the schools was highly valued and this value led to action to end the strikes. But this was an immediate issue for the administrators of the school system and could be readily joined without engaging the deeper problem. Inevitably the school administration were heavily involved with the strike, much less so with curriculum. The principals and teachers in Gary appear to have, with a few notable exceptions, involved themselves neither in ending the strike nor in designing an intercultural curriculum; and their lack of engagement in either issue undermined the ambitions of the developers inasmuch as the deeper convictions of the city's teachers about non-involvement in vexing community problems (and, presumably, their latent racism) remained unchallenged by an involvement in the problems that faced the city.

Thus, Whitmer reports that, of the principals of the eight unit schools, only four felt that direct attention should be given to intergroup relations. Seven principals did not approve of school involvement in community problems of any kind. The attitudes of the teachers were similar to those of the principals. Five hundred of the 650 Gary teachers were polled in 1947. Of the teachers questioned, 62 per cent stated that they felt good intercultural attitudes would result naturally from 'a good basic education;' 27 per cent felt that they opposed stressing inter-cultural education because it would stir up trouble.[21] Of the teachers Whitmer polled, many offered reasons to justify their feelings that an intercultural education program could not be conducted. Forty-five per cent cited a lack of time, 46 per cent said that classes were too large; 21 per cent said that the course of study was already too time consuming; 19 per cent had too many home and school responsibilities already; and 14 per cent said that they did not know what to do.[22]

In summary, the two aspects of the intercultural problems that faced Gary between 1945 and 1947 received different treatments, and, as a result, were not equally successful. The superintendent, Charles Lutz, had been instrumental in recognizing the race problem, in retaining the bureau, and in establishing the committees, but when the strikes began, he withdrew his support from these activities and gave his attention to efforts to end the strike. Given the pressure of events and given no support from the community, the only groups wanting an intercultural curriculum were some teachers and the Bureau for Intercultural Education, an outside agency.

The problems faced by these committee teachers and the bureau were numerous. National societies and organizations began to devote atten-tion to intercultural education in the middle and late 1940s, but despite this concern for the *idea* of intercultural education the curricula they needed were only in their embryonic stages, and as a result neither abun-dant nor easily available. But, more important, the support needed for this curriculum development undertaking was not available. The com-mittee was obviously aware that over two hundred meetings were held for the purpose of ending the strike and smoothing the way for the integration policy. And it was certainly aware that Lutz was a driving factor in setting up and participating in these meetings. But they were given no released time to develop curriculum, were given no money for materials, and were not kept informed by Lutz of what he was doing about the strike and the integration policy. Support for the pilot project lasted only one year and was then withdrawn without an evaluation of the project. The contrast, of course, is between the way in which the strike situation was handled and the way in which the designing of a new curriculum was handled. Efforts directed toward maintaining the operations of the school were considerably more extensive and successful than were efforts to implement an intercultural curriculum. More meetings were held, more people were involved, and certainly more money was spent in maintaining the service than was done in changing the nature or improving the quality of that service.

V

In 1956, the science program of the Gary high schools was similar to the science programs found in most schools in the United States at that time. One science course was required for graduation; most students took either general science in grade 9 or biology in grade 10. A few students took physics which was offered, like general science and biology, in all eight of the Gary high schools. Chemistry was also available, but in only four schools. No advanced courses were offered in any of the sciences. Two schools in Gary had laboratories; instruction in the other six unit schools was confined to the classroom.

By 1968, much had changed in Gary, yet again, Gary's science program was typical. All Gary schools in 1968 offered, in addition to courses in bio-physical science, biology and physical science, first and second years of physics and chemistry. Courses were differentiated as to method and purposes so that students could select from among them according to their own wishes. An earlier conception of science as a body of fact had changed, at least in terms of the rhetoric of the curricula, to science as a process of enquiry. As a result, science classes in Gary as often as not met in the new or remodeled laboratories found in all of the city's high schools. The number of topics to be 'covered' in each course had been reduced, permitting exploration of a selected few in more depth.

In 1956, a curriculum committee was formed in Gary, for the purpose of improving the secondary science program and courses within it. The efforts of this committee resulted in a new curriculum guide which listed an expanded course-offering and outlined content, outcomes, and materials for each course to be offered. But while ambitious in scope, the new curriculum guide had no discernible effect on science teaching in Gary. Yet, between 1960, two years after the guide became available, and 1968, science education in Gary began to change; several new courses were added and approaches, anticipated outcomes, and methods of teaching were different. In short, the Gary school system was unable to produce change by its own efforts between 1956 and 1960. However, without direct effort of the school system, the changes mandated earlier began to occur after 1960. New programs and new resources became available from outside the school system after 1960, and produced the changes sought earlier. Curriculum change, then, occurred in Gary not as a result of local initiative, planning and effort, but as a result of national initiatives and national planning. Why did events follow this course?

Gary initiated a major attempt at revision of its science programs in 1956. Two interconnected events precipitated this development, the first such undertaking in the history of the city. The Public Administration Service Survey had been released and had included criticisms of almost all subject areas in its trenchant castigation of the system. The report had led to the dismissal of Charles Lutz, Wirt's successor as superintendent, and had prodded the Board into both hiring a superintendent from outside the system, Alden Blankenship, and giving him a mandate for change. Blankenship quickly turned his attention to a reform of the system's curricula. Planning for a *Gary Curriculum Guide, Grades 7–12* began in 1956 and it was ready for use when school opened in the fall of 1958. Before undertaking our examination of the sections of this guide concerned with science, let us explore the background both of the guide itself and the work of its science committee.

As we have indicated, the Gary science program in 1956 consisted of only four courses, each a year in length: general science, biology, chemistry, and physics. Students attending the schools not offering chemistry were usually permitted to enroll in the course at another school. The teaching of all of these courses was handicapped by inadequate facilities. Yet, despite this rather uninspiring picture of science education in Gary, the city's program was typical of that in other schools. During the 1930s and 1940s, science curricula had received little scrutiny or care. In 1956, only one in twenty high school students took a physics course; barely half of American high schools offered such a course. General science and biology were the only two courses widely offered and the only two taken by many students.

The science program that was typical of the schools of the mid 1950s differed markedly from the ideal program envisioned in the science education literature of this period. One widely prescribed change was the scheduling of classes a year earlier than customary so that enriched, advanced courses could be offered. In grade 9, for example, it was widely felt that general science, general physical science, and biology should be offered. A second common prescription focused on the manner of teaching, inasmuch as it was felt that the essential goal of science education was to foster enquiry rather than to master content. Ultimately, it was hoped that science programs, when changed in prescribed ways, would appeal to a larger percentage of students because science was seen as having growing importance in all areas of life. The logical methodological change to accompany these prescriptions was to move instruction from the classroom to the laboratory. Only by experimentation could students begin to understand how scientific knowledge was discovered and ordered.

The Public Administration Service Survey of the Gary schools, although critical of the city's programs, gave little guidance to the subject matter committees they began to meet. Nevertheless, a series of organizational arrangements which had curricular ramifications were cited, and did lead to the structures within which the guide was developed.

Wirt had, from 1906 to 1938, headed a centralized school administration. To correct the excesses of this administration, Lutz, his successor, radically decentralized the system. Curricular revision became the responsibility of principals and their faculties. This arrangement resulted in the near-total absence of curriculum evaluation and revision in the Gary schools. In the words of the survey,[23]

> In Gary, curriculum development machinery at the secondary level exists largely in name only. Vital parts are missing. . . . There is an urgent need for additional supervisors or consultants in the central office. . . . With an enlarged staff of this sort, it would be possible for the secondary school teachers in several fields to effect a complete evaluation of their programs at least once every three years and to make those changes which such an evaluation proved to be needed. Supervisors must, of course, devote a portion of their time to instructional development. In the work of curriculum planning and evaluating, it is essential that more and more teachers out in the schools initiate and participate in the process and that principals likewise assume leadership in performance of this function.

Correction of the faults pointed out by the PAS survey was begun as soon as the report was received. A curriculum committee structure could be created easily; since 1956 was a year in which a textbook had to be adopted, some committee structure was needed to make text selection anyway. Subject supervisors were also hired; although adding personnel in form of supervisors for several subject matter areas would increase the budget, some changes in the administration of the schools was inevitable.

Work on the *Gary Curriculum Guide, Grades 7–12* took two years. At its regular meeting on April 22, 1958, the Board was presented with the document, and Board approval was given on May 13, 1958.[24] At the same time the Board was reviewing the guide, it was revealed that two school administrators had[25] presented the *Curriculum Guide* to the State Department of Public Instruction where it was seen as '. . . a complete and detailed piece of work.' The officials of the State Department of Public Instruction also described it as '. . . a very tangible contribution to the progress which is being made in the program at Gary', and added that the various committees who served in preparing this *Curriculum Guide* are to be congratulated for their efforts and thoroughness.

In the face of such praise, let us turn to the work of the committees generally, and the science committee in particular, to see what was done.

Each subject matter committee working on the *Curriculum Guide* was asked to consider four questions in drafting its curriculum. First, what is the best program in secondary education for boys and girls? Second, what courses should be offered? Third, when should they be offered? And, fourth, in what order should they be offered? These four questions became the two tasks that had to be undertaken by each committee. First, they had to establish the structure of courses in their field. Second, they had to describe each of them. Each course description was to be written in terms of (1) the major areas or topics to be covered; (2) emphases or outcomes; (3) typical activities; and (4) aids for instruction and evaluation. To expand the information given in the resulting charts, a one-paragraph description of each course was also to be written.

By January 1958, after working nearly a year and a half, the science committee had decided on its focus – the courses that should be offered rather than on their content. It recommended that the schools[26]

(1) increase minimum graduation requirements in science for all students from one to two units, (2) enable students with special interests in science to get more training, and (3) establish a science program for students with outstanding abilities.

The course sequence designed by the committee is shown in table 1.1. In addition to the sequence chart, each course was outlined.

New curriculum guides are usually a mixture of what is real and what is ideal. The science committee had no more access to or control over the hiring of additional teachers or of the building of additional rooms to provide for the new courses than they did for building new laboratories and equipping them. That part of the new guide that called for additional courses, then, was taken thin-covered from the literature of science education as a goal for Gary's schools, but there was no reason for the committee to think that the new courses could actually be offered in all schools within the next ten years. In fact, the full program of courses was not offered in all schools until 1963, and this, as will be shown later, was the result of the availability of resources from outside the school.

TABLE I.I   Course sequence in science

Grade 9	Bio-physical science, parts A and B
	Biology
Grade 10	Bio-physical science
	Biology
	Chemistry $\Big\}$ only for students in advanced programs
	Physics
Grade 11	Physics
	Physical science
Grade 12	Physics
	Chemistry
	Physical science
	Advanced chemistry $\Big\}$ prerequisites: biology, chemistry, and
	Advanced physics physics

Source: School City of Gary, *Curriculum Guide*, 1958, not paginated.

Since the curriculum committee had merely to hope that provisions could be found for the new courses, the question of their effect on the curriculum of each course is of interest. Since they could not command the necessary resources for the number and sequence of courses, could they change the content and focus of any single course? The answer again is no. The committee members did the easiest thing they could do. They simply copied the chapter topics into the major areas column of the guide for each course from the primary textbook for that course. The guide for the physics course to be offered to eleventh and twelfth grade students was typical. Six topics were to be covered. They appear in both the guide and the table of contents in the text in the same order. They are, of course, the conventional topics dealt with in physics courses of the time. Moreover, the new text that was selected was traditional. Although the unit titles of the physics series that had been used in Gary for more than fifteen years prior to the 1956 adoption were slightly different to those in the new, the topics to be covered were the same as in the *High School Physics*, and the approaches of the old and the new textbooks were the same.[27] The outcome of the work of the science curriculum committee was, then, insignificant. The curriculum consisted of two things: a hoped-for sequence of courses which would or would not be realized through conditions and actions over which the committee had absolutely no control, and a faithful reworking of the chapters of the textbook, a series of possible activities that could be used to reach the goals, and a list of books that could be used. The science committee, created to bring about change by program improvement, had changed nothing.

By the time the *Gary Curriculum Guide, Grades 7–12* was completed, in 1958, there were movements at the national level which would result in considerable change in Gary's science program. Conventional wisdom says that the successful launching of the Russian Sputnik in 1957 resulted in a massive concern for science. In fact, a concern for science and mathematics education had begun several years before 1957, and had gained considerable momentum by that time. We have already discussed the prescriptions from the literature of the 1950s; beyond these prescriptions, however, several concrete actions were taken to strengthen school science teaching.

The National Science Foundation was established in 1950 and throughout the period under study increased the scope of its activity and its funding. In 1956, President Eisenhower established the National Committee for the Development of Scientists and Engineers, 'in view of the nation-wide critical shortage of scientific and engineering manpower and the need for such manpower in expanding programs involving national security.' All departments and agencies of the government were directed to work with the National Committee in support of its programs and to re-evaluate and strengthen their own contributions in helping to solve the science 'problem.' In 1954, 72 per cent of the 664 private philanthropic foundations were either expressing an interest in or actually contributing to educational projects. Out of this effort came a series of curricular packages, a federally funded set of National Defense Education Act (NDEA) institutes for teachers and science, and ultimately federal funds for rebuilding and re-equiping science laboratories and classrooms.[28]

These developments quickly came to the attention of Gary's teachers. The text, *High School Physics*, that had been adopted by Gary in 1958, was used in all of the physics courses in Gary during the 1958–9 school year. However, in the summer of 1959, one teacher attended a Physical Sciences Study Committee (PSSC) summer institute; he was enthusiastic about what he had heard and persuaded a colleague both to use portions of PSSC *Physics* during the 1959–60 school year, and to attend a winter institute. Gary's science supervisor, Floyd Flinn, also became aware of PSSC *Physics* during the summer of 1959 while on a travelling program to Michigan State University. He returned to Gary enthusiastic about the program but felt that before teachers should use it, they should want to use it and should attend an appropriate institute. No encouragement was needed to get teachers to apply for and attend the institutes. Tuition and materials for the institutes were free. In addition, the National Science Foundation (NSF) paid, tax free, $75 per week for the teacher attending plus $15 for each dependent for each week the institute lasted. The Gary schools accepted attendance at institutes as course work which would advance a teacher on the salary schedule, and some teachers were able to get master's degrees in their subject matter fields through the institutes. *Physics* spread quickly throughout the Gary schools. In the 1960–1 school year, it was in use in two schools. The following year two more schools offered it, bringing the total to four, half of the Gary schools. In 1966, the text-adoption year, *Physics* was selected to be used by all physics teachers.

The Biological Sciences Curriculum Study (BSCS) materials had a similar history in the Gary schools. Again, teacher by teacher, beginning in 1963–4, BSCS materials began to be used. But there was less agreement among teachers about the usefulness of the BSCS materials than there was about *Physics*. The adoption year was 1966. No clear mandate for the adoption of a BSCS text emerged from an informal polling of Gary's biology teachers. As a result, biology teachers were asked to vote. When the results were tabulated, it was found that half of the teachers wanted the BSCS blue version, and half did not want to use the BSCS materials at all. But the blue version of the BSCS text had been the object of controversy because of its strong evolutionary orientation; this difficulty swayed the department heads and the city to choose the BSCS yellow version as the official text despite its lack of support among the teachers.

Chemistry teachers likewise slowly began to use the CHEM Study materials after this text became available in 1963–4. But by 1966, when the new official texts were to be selected, comparatively few of the city's chemistry teachers had had an opportunity to become acquainted with the materials. As a result, teachers were permitted to select the materials they wanted to use within each school. Four schools chose to use CHEM Study, four chose other materials.

By 1967, then, the Gary science program had changed, much in the same way that science programs across the country had changed. In Gary PSSC and BSCS were used in all physics and biology classes while CHEM Study was used in half of the classes. However, as Herron has suggested, although from a different perspective, teachers did not feel comfortable with the new materials once they were in use.[29] Only when Supervisor Flinn taught a course using the new materials was he aware that there were problems in using them. Upon expressing his amazement at the difficulties he found, he was quickly inundated with complaints from the other science teachers. They really did not like – or did not know how to use – the new materials, and in 1969, new, more conventional texts were adopted.

Contrasting the two periods of 1956–60 and 1960–70, several interesting differences and similarities emerge. In the earlier period there was a strong local demand for change – but in the absence of any basis for an exercise of choice about what the character of that change might be, the reforming impetus became translated into symbolic terms and left unsatisfied such yearning for real change as the work of the curriculum committees symbolized and created. This demand may have reasserted itself in the latter period, but the changes that came about appear to have been more directly linked to demands for particular kinds of change which originated at the national level and filtered, in non-directive fashion, into the classrooms of Gary – to be picked up not by a committee which had no greater wisdom available to it than that possessed by the ablest of its members, but instead, by individual teachers and a supervisor who could channel and support individual teacher initiatives. This national press became, in Gary, however, a quite traditional curriculum, a text which could be adopted or rejected by teachers and resources to build the laboratories and buy the equipment that had been long needed by the city. And, in the absence of the necessary skills that made their use of the national programs easy, Gary's teachers ultimately rejected the new national curricula in favor of more traditional approaches that were more compatible with their existing skills and competences.

What does this suggest about curriculum change? When change was demanded, no changes occurred. Gary did not add new science courses or change the content of the courses already in existence despite the demands for change and the *Curriculum Guide* of 1958. Resources for adding teachers to the faculty, for building new programs, for purchasing additional equipment, and for building and remodeling laboratories could not be commanded by the science curriculum committee. Instead of producing change, then, the Guide was successful only in describing the status quo.

Moreover, the creation of the organizational structure for change did not guarantee that it would occur. The curriculum change mechanism was elaborately articulated in 1956, but change did not come about until textbook and fiscal resources were made available from outside the system. The availability of new funds and new programs after 1960 produced change – but not of the kind that had been anticipated by the sponsors of the new programs. The national concern had focused, at least in its rhetoric, on the quality of science education in schools; this interest, itself a response to almost thirty years of neglect of school programs, both created and resonated with concerns in the schools for this same interest – but the fundamental interests of Washington's reformers and the schools went in different directions. The preoccupations of the schools were simpler and less ambitious than were those of the national bodies: they wanted an opportunity to do something about their own problems as they saw them; they wanted new equipment, new labs, and more courses. The new texts, facilities, equipment, and materials that the national committees and national funds provided could be used equally well with new or old teaching skills – or so it seemed at first. The national concern for quality science education and scientific manpower was, in a sense, only epiphenomenal when looked at from the vantage point of the teachers of Gary and of other systems like Gary, but the funds and programs that were provided by the national bodies did permit local jurisdictions to give attention to their budgets of needs. Science programs in Gary changed then after these new funds and new programs became available because these funds and programs struck at and went to the heart of the local problem, a problem that up to that point local communities and school districts had not been able to address. And to the extent that they served this function their achievements became less grand and more subject to the capacities and the abilities of teachers whose own training and own interests had not prepared them to participate in a goal of fundamental curriculum renewal. In a direct, although less dramatic sense, the ambitions of those who wished for profound change in science teaching in Gary fell foul of the same resistance that had defeated the Gary campaign of a decade earlier for a meaningful program in intercultural education.

VI

Until 1968, Gary had an inadequate vocational education program. Several times during the period examined, 1940–70, the deficiency was noted and recommendations to correct were made. The Purdue University Survey of the Gary school system, released in 1942, criticized the existing vocational education program and recommended that the first priority for building construction be a vocational-technical high school.[30] But between 1942 and 1955, the schools in Gary, and also the vocational education program, changed very little. As a result the criticisms made of the vocational education program in 1942 were made again in the 1950s. A US government pamphlet in 1954, the Public Administration Service Survey of the Gary school system in 1955, and a National Education Association investigation in 1957, all castigated the city's vocational education program.[31] Recommendations of possible solutions were offered to alleviate the difficulty; the school system, however, was able to put only a few of the recommendations into effect before the middle 1960s. By that time, the earliest recommendations for reform were over twenty years old.

Yet, the school system in Gary did not totally ignore the recommendations; effort was made after each survey to respond to evaluations of the vocational education program. In 1942, after the release of the Purdue Survey, the Board of School Trustees resolved to rename the shop at Froebel School the Gary Trade and Technical Center. The new center apparently did not function according to intentions, for in 1944, the Board resolved again to establish a technical school at Froebel.[32] The effect of these two decisions, however, was to narrow the vocational education program because shops at the other unit schools were closed in anticipation of the operation of these centers. By 1955, the vocational education offering in Gary was almost non existent.

As we have already seen, one response of the Gary school system to the recommendation of the PAS (Public Administration Service) survey of 1955, was the appointment of curriculum committees in each of the subject matter areas. The vocational education committee, like the other twelve committees, spent two years preparing its new *Curriculum Guide*. This guide recommended establishing three centers, one each for distributive, business, and industrial education and the creation of several new shop courses. The three centers were put into operation – in so far as no funds were needed for remodeling or equiping the existing facilities – but the new courses were not offered until 1968. The practical effect of the 1958 *Curriculum Guide*, then, was minimal.

Suddenly in 1963, the Board of School Trustees passed a resolution calling for the construction of a new technical-vocational high school. Plans for the new building were to embody many of the recommendations from the earlier survey reports. Although ground breaking was delayed for two years, construction did begin in 1965. The Career Center, Gary's new area technical-vocational high school, opened in September 1968. After twenty years of sporadic attempts by the school system to provide an adequate vocational education program, success was finally achieved. Two factors brought about this success: first, the technical-vocational school had at long last become top priority for construction, and second, money from outside the school system, from the federal government, became available to help finance the building. It is no coincidence that the Gary Board of School Trustees decided to build a Career Center in 1963, the year of the passage of the Vocational Education Act. The Act did what the surveys, the prescriptions, and the efforts of a few individuals in Gary between 1940 and 1963 could not do – provide resources for a vocational program for the school system.

Wirt's program has been discussed above. Vocational education fell under the work aspect of the Work-Study-Play Plan. The early emphasis was on practical experience, building and repairing desks, tables, and chairs, setting type and printing books and school forms, and raising a garden. By having students engaged in 'real' tasks such as these, it was thought that the offerings were truly vocational.

Wirt's intention for shop courses was neither to expose the student to occupational categories nor to prepare him for specific jobs; rather, he wanted to keep students busy with 'real tasks.' But the confusion as to the goals of the offerings which resulted from this ambiguous purpose led to an increasingly chaotic and diminishing array of courses. Between 1906 and 1938, the emphasis on maintaining and furnishing the schools decreased. Nothing replaced this emphasis. The decreasing concern for shop courses was evident in 1937 and 1939, when the last two unit schools constructed, Edison and Wirt, were designed and built with no shops other than for mechanical drawing. In the other six unit schools at this time students could take different shop courses, but they had little opportunity to receive directed pre-vocational experience.

The first major assessment of the Gary school system in our period was the Purdue Survey of 1942; the criticisms of the vocational education program paralleled the more general criticisms of the system as a whole and were similar to the criticisms made by the PAS survey of thirteen years later. The report first took note of the history of the schools and the relationship between the schools and the city. Whatever the virtues of the Wirt Plan in its earlier years, the report implied that they were no longer present. It was suggested that there was no provision in the Wirt system for keeping up-to-date.[33]

> As time has gone on, there has been a tendency for the program [vocational education] to become narrower instead of broader; the unparalleled advancements that have come about in our industrial society have not been accompanied by similar advances in the Gary school program.

> If the industrial city of Gary is vitally concerned with its own needs and welfare it cannot afford to be disinterested in the kinds of pupil services which it can guarantee to its present and future citizens. An important part of this service may be found in the school's industrial arts program and in its vocational trade and industrial education program.

While these comments of the Purdue Report only foreshadow the more specific criticisms that were to follow, the fact that the vocational education program was not adequate was strongly implied. One reason for the deficiency was found to reside in an organizational feature of the Wirt system with which later generations of administrators and teachers had to contend. The first six high schools in the Gary system had been built during the Wirt years and according to Wirt's specifications. One component of each of the schools was the unit shop. With a shop arrangement of this kind, only one kind of activity could be carried on in any shop. Each shop was so designed and equiped that to use it for purposes other than those intended by the creator would have required remodeling. 'While many school systems utilize the unit-shop system with varying degrees of success, a number of undesirable practices are apt to result from this type of organization, particularly in the lower grades.'[34]

The unit shop organization created problems for both industrial arts and vocational education. An exploratory program in industrial arts was very difficult to conduct without an elaborate scheduling of students whereby classes would rotate from shop to shop over a nine or eighteen week period. On the other hand, to justify the shops for vocational purposes, classes had to be larger than just a handful of students. In order to make up large classes, students for one class had to be drawn from several different grade levels. These classes occasionally contained students ranging from grade 5 to grade 12. Teachers in these classes were then faced with the problem of teaching this variety of students. And, of course, no fifth grade pupil could be considered as enrolled in vocational training. As a result of this organizational difficulty, most classes were designed to be industrial arts rather than vocational classes. The scheduling of the classes also tended in this direction.

Following its criticism, the Purdue Report made recommendations for changes it felt desirable:[35]

The survey staff has attempted to demonstrate through an analysis of the present program . . . that the present situation in Gary in trade-preparatory or pre-apprenticeship training is not adequate; the staff has also tried to show that the general educational objectives of Industrial Arts are not being met adequately. It is, therefore, proposed that any changes or developments at the secondary level in the future consider four more or less separate and distinct areas: (1) the Industrial Arts program in the unit schools; (2) the trade-preparatory program to be housed in a separate building; (3) a special or opportunity school to be housed separately and apart from the trade school; and (4) a vocational distributive and commercial program.

The recommendation for a separate vocational school was made again in greater detail: 'A separate Vocational and Adult Center [also to house distributive and commercial programs] should be set up and students who expect to enter apprenticeships in the skilled trades and who expect to enter semi-skilled areas should transfer to such a school.' Details about a cooperative program were offered, and it was suggested that a Distributive Occupations Coordinator be hired.[36]

The state of vocational education as it existed in schools throughout the country was reviewed, at the same time as the Purdue Survey was written, in the National Society for the Study of Education's 42nd yearbook, *Vocational Education*. The findings and prescriptions of the yearbook provide a standard with which vocational education in Gary can be compared; the concerns of the yearbook are very similar to those found in the Purdue Report.

According to the yearbook, World War II was beginning to stir an interest in technically-trained manpower.[37]

The urgent demand for technically trained workers for the war industry has made everyone conscious of the importance of vocational education. New schools have been developed and the programs of existing schools have been expanded to meet this demand.

We have never before witnessed as great an effort to strengthen and to extend the program of vocational education in the schools of this country.

Yet while the yearbook implied that schools were beginning to be viewed by industry as potential training grounds for future employees, it suggested that the question that industry was asking itself was whether it would be cheaper to train new employees after they were hired or to help the schools provide the shops, teachers, and equipment to do the task. The main argument against permitting the public schools to do the task was that keeping shops up-to-date both in equipment and practice was expensive. Industry always had the necessary equipment on hand and could, in a short period of time, train an employee specifically for the task he would be doing. And, as of 1942, industry was still opting for training their own workers and encouraging the schools to concentrate on 'citizenship' education. In short, despite the emerging concerns for the area, vocational education was not a major emphasis of most school systems. In Gary, as elsewhere, the focus of the school was not on vocational education but on preparation for college.

In 1955, a PAS investigation of the schools was commissioned by the Gary School Board. Inevitably, this survey included criticisms and recommendations similar to those of the earlier Purdue Report. The PAS survey, like the earlier report, took cognizance of the philosophical roots from which vocational education in Gary had sprung. The PAS survey found it fortunate that by 1955 the emphasis on repair and maintenance of building and equipment had almost disappeared from shop classes. However, they found that insufficient progress had been made in changing from the kindergarten through twelfth grade organization of the schools. Elementary classes were still using the shops, and students of widely ranging grade levels were still scheduled into the same class.

The root cause of the inadequacy of the vocational education program was stated and found to be the same as it had been thirteen years earlier.[38]

Evidence of the existence of this outdated philosophy which views the secondary school as an institution predominantly devoted to preparing youth for college is present in the Gary public schools. Such evidence takes the form of a preference for students who will enter college and an apathy toward all others.

There were few vocational education courses offered in Gary in 1955. 'The present program provides arc and gas-welding and machine shop at the Froebel School and auto mechanics at the Emerson School. That is the extent of it.' 'The absence of day-trade training programs in the Gary schools is almost tragic.' PAS went on to state just how tragic the situation was.[39]

In general it may be stated that the Gary school system program in vocational education is almost nonexistent, in spite of the fact that the community provides greater opportunity for conduct of such a program than almost any other city in the United States.

PAS offered five specific criticisms of the program: (1) there was a lack of facilities and no drive to create them; (2) there was insufficient personnel to promote the programs; (3) there was a lack of adequate guidance personnel; (4) there was a lack of good industrial arts programs to permit interested students to explore the field; and (5) there was still the problem of the unit school organization. Given these criticisms, the survey found little difficulty in making recommendations. These bear a strong resemblance to the ones presented by the Purdue Survey in 1942. Two general curricular patterns were suggested:[40]

(1) the addition of day-trade programs in those schools containing grades ten through twelve, conducting them as part of the so-called comprehensive high school.
(2) designate and establish a central vocational-technical high school to house all of the day-trade vocational programs now operating and those that should be added at the earliest possible date. Such a technical high school should, of course, include the basic general education program as well as the vocational program.

Additional day-trade programs should be developed as the result of study of the occupational needs of the city, county and metropolitan area.

Consequently, it is recommended that Froebel School be converted by the fall of 1956 into a vocational-technical high school and that all-day trade programs be concentrated there as soon as possible. All Froebel students other than those enrolled in the vocational high school program should be transferred to other schools.

Again the Gary Board appeared to take the PAS criticisms and recommendations as a mandate for change:[41]

Discussion was held in regard to the recommendation of the Public Administration Service report pertaining to a city-wide vocational high school and the construction of new buildings. It was moved . . . that the Board authorize discussions with the Superintendent, architects, and the Public Administration Service survey staff, of the matters pertaining to a vocational high school, new building construction, and the business and financial operation of the School City before taking any action.

But authorizing discussions was an old and familiar technique in Gary as it is in all school systems. The pressing problems for the Board were business organization and buildings. The Gary schools were far from having adequate space for all enrolled students, and the assistant superintendent for business affairs had departed with Superintendent Lutz when the PAS report was released. The entire business department had to be completely reorganized and the Board was rightly concerned that the results of the overhaul would be superior to the system discarded.

Nevertheless, vocational education was included in the work of the Curriculum Committee preparing the new *Gary Curriculum Guide*. And in addition to the change in organization for curriculum revision and the work of these curriculum committees, a cooperative vocational program was launched. 'A cooperative vocational education program will be launched with the opening of the second semester of the school year in accord with the policy adopted by the Board of School Trustees at their meeting of December 23.'[42]

'Louis A. McElroy, director of adult and vocational education, called the [cooperative vocational] education project the first step in a program which will culminate in the building of a full-time vocational high school for Gary.'[43] But the reasons for this minimal immediate reform in vocational education are apparent. 'The school administrator [McElroy] said that the Cooperative Vocational Education program is natural for Gary because facilities are limited and there are no finances or facilities available for vocational-technical school functions.'[44]

The vocational education sub-committee working on the *Gary Curriculum Guide* was, however, more ambitious. The guide outlined a program which was to expand from just machine shop and arc welding at two schools to one which included first and second years of printing and two years of technical training in each of the areas of appliance repair, engineering, auto mechanics, and electronics, with these offerings to be available at all schools. But the fate of these plans was the same as that which befell the plans of the science committee. The Gary school system did not offer the expanded number of courses until after outside funds became available. The only real expansion in the vocational program between 1958 and 1968, was into the three cooperative programs, and these could be offered with a minimum of expense.

From 1958, when the Board accepted the curriculum guide, until 1962, vocational education was not discussed at Board meetings. On January 9, 1962, discussion was opened again, and approval for construction of a technical-vocational school was urged by one Board member. Final approval, however, did not come until over two years later, after the Vocational Education Act of 1963 was passed. At the March 24, 1964, meeting of the Board, a new superintendent, Lee Gilbert, cited a new ruling on vocational education from the State Department of Public Instruction calling for a curriculum allowing for at least one vocational education major for all schools of 1,200 or more students. He told the Board that Gary did not comply at this time, but assured it that the city probably would when the anticipated technical-vocational school became a reality. The United States Congress, by virtue of passing the Vocational Education Act in 1963, had suddenly changed the picture. In the fashion of the earlier NDEA, funds were to be provided for remodeling and/or new construction. In 1968, a vocational school was opened for juniors and seniors who qualified, offering programs in building construction and maintenance, business and commerce, communications, extractive industries, health and personal services, mechanics and metalworking, textiles and leather, special services and technology.

From several points of view, it can be (and was) argued that Gary should have provided a good vocational education program for its students; to encourage students from working-class homes to complete high school and because of the local need for trained workers. But whatever the theoretical importance of these arguments, the fact is that the vocational education program was notoriously inadequate (by nearly all standards) between 1940 and 1968. Despite criticisms of the program in 1942, 1954, 1955, and 1957, the program grew narrower until 1958. And, despite several attempts to improve the program after 1958, the addition of three cooperative programs in 1958 was the only change to come about until 1968 when the Career Center opened. Built and equiped partially by federal funds provided under the Vocational Educational Act of 1963, the Career Center fulfilled the earlier recommendations, some of which were twenty-six years old.

For several reasons the vocational education program in Gary received little attention for many years. There was no discernible demand that it be improved coming from the community; a vocational education program was expensive. Until the middle 1960s, the Gary schools were unable to provide buildings and desks for all students. The rapid growth in student population and the difficulties in securing building materials that followed World War II were problems with which the school system had to contend long after the war was over. When the school system did begin to spend money to change curriculum, it was the academic curriculum that received attention first. The changes that were attempted in the vocational program before the Career Center was built cost nothing. In 1942 and 1944, the Board simply renamed the shop facilities at Emerson and Froebel. The cooperative programs begun in 1958 cost the school system very little because the training facilities were located out of the schools in the community. By the middle 1960s, however, the system had housed its students and significant federal money was available to help build a technical-vocational school. Almost immediately Gary built such a school.

VII

In general, the findings from our case study of Gary support the general thesis we saw embedded in our experiences and which we found we could sustain from our readings of the literature on curriculum innovation, sociology of science, and the institutional organization of schooling. Events in Gary lacked, of course, something of the clarity of our own examples, but that was to be expected.

A failure of will brought the Wirt Plan to an end, but this change was gradual, despite the pressure that the city experienced as it confronted the opinions of outside experts about its schools, and despite the push to adopt new patterns that came from those teachers in the city's schools who preferred conventional classroom and curricular practices – both the saga of the Wirt years and the architectural forms that he had imposed on Gary's schools constrained for ten or more years the easy adoption of these conventional patterns. Expectations about what might be taught and how it might be taught did change over the twenty-five years we explored, but when these new expectations required new subject forms and new structures for their enactment, Gary's schools failed to find for themselves the new ways and means that these new aspirations required. We saw this failure writ large during the reforming period of 1956–8: despite the ambitions projected by the superintendent (and granting due allowance to the public relations aspects of his publicity about his endeavors), the best his teachers could do in the way of redevelopment of their science program was to copy the table of contents of a 1951 text into their new curriculum guide. These teachers could not escape, at least when they turned to the ritual of course-writing, from the control of old forms: and change in these forms did not emerge until new, externally developed forms were made available by PSSC and BSCS – and even then it seems that many teachers experienced considerable difficulty as they struggled to enact the forms embodied in these new programs in their teaching.

Our findings, therefore, support the general thrust of our expectations. However, there were three constants in the Gary setting which our earlier thinking had not led us to anticipate – although hindsight makes them obvious. We had not expected plant to become so significant a constraint on the curriculum; we had not expected resources to loom as large as they did as Gary sought to introduce new programs in its schools; we certainly did not expect that establishment commissions and their reports would become a major source of demands for change of the practices of Gary's schools. Let us summarize a version of the history of Gary's schools which captures our present thinking about the role of these three constants in curriculum change in Gary.

Through the efforts of the commissions which appraised it periodically through the thirty years we explored, Gary was made aware of what was thought of (at the time of each commission) as desirable practice. At times, too, Gary's superintendent and its teachers showed themselves well aware of initiatives which might be undertaken in their schools – but this awareness did not lead to any real action on the systemic level. In the case of the continuing preoccupation of the school surveyors for vocational education and in the case of the 1950s concern for new approaches to the teaching of science, resources were not available to remodel classrooms and laboratories or to build a vocational school; and in the 1950s, Gary schools did not have at their command the intellectual resources that were required to build the new science programs that the system felt it wanted. The system did not have the power or the will to persuade the teachers of a then recently

desegregated city to involve themselves actively in the teaching of intercultural education: the resistance to this initiative was not active or
overt, rather a reflection of the pervasive professional and community
attitudes which we can presume the Gary teaching force shared with
their colleagues in other cities and their neighbors. And none of these
curricular issues or demands secured the serious attention of Gary's
school board; it had no time, it seemed, for matters of this kind, or for
the curricular issues raised by its survey commissions, as it struggled
to cope with clear and pressing demands for new accounting systems,
and as it sought to house its students, man its classrooms, and contain
such threats as the strikes of the 1940s. Only in the late 1950s did we
see any indication that the board was interesting itself in curricular
issues. In short, during much of the period we explored, the board and
its superintendent devoted themselves to the task of delivering the
services that their schools were charged to provide.

The problems that the Gary School Board faced in the 1940s and
early 1950s were pressing and real. Enrollment rose from 19,212 in
1939–40, to 19,677 in 1949–50, to 34,230 in 1957–8, and 37,586 in
1959–60. The city entered this period of increasing numbers with plant
that was regarded by a 1947 buildings survey as dilapidated and somewhat overcrowded,[45] but it built only six new schools with space for
approximately 3,500 students between 1945 and 1955.[46] Throughout
this period, Indiana state law limited the bonded indebtedness of a
school district to 2 per cent of its assessed valuation and the tax rate for
retirement of bonds to $1·25 per $100 of that valuation. Gary entered
the period close to its borrowing ceilings; and it experienced no relief
from the press of this limit by increasing valuations – in 1950 the city's
total assessed valuation was only 65 per cent of what it had been in 1930
when these valuations are adjusted for the change in purchasing power
of the dollar over those twenty years. In 1955, the total valuation was
only about 73 per cent of the 1930 figure. Similar problems were
experienced with operating budgets during those years: to meet its
commitments in the face of a declining (in real terms) tax base, the
school district had to resort to constant increases in its rates[47] – but this
inevitably led to political difficulties for the board. Given problems of
this scale and kind it is not surprising that Gary had little interest in or
inclination to act upon curricular matters. Overcrowding, double shifts,
teacher shortages and the like were real problems clearly more pressing
than essentially abstract concerns about the quality of the programs or
peripheral matters like the absence of a vocational school.

Relief from these pressures came in 1956. The Public Administration
Survey brought the attention of local decisionmakers to their local

problems and contributed to the climate that brought relief from the limitations imposed by the state legislation that governed the Board. And with relief came a new building program (in 1957–8, eight new schools were opened for approximately 6,000 students)[48] and the opportunity to consider both the budget of needs that had been laid before the city again and again over the previous twenty-five years and some of the issues that were troubling all American schools in these years. Both of these clusters of concerns came together in the person of Alden Blankenship, a superintendent appointed from outside the city to succeed Lutz, Wirt's successor. Blankenship came to Gary with no commitment to the system, and with a mandate to initiate major reforms in administration and program; he dispassionately permitted the lingering remnants of the Gary Plan to be swept away and brought to the city the norms and ideologies of conventional American schoolmen of his period. The developing concerns of American schools for their programs was rapidly brought to the attention of the city by way of the appointment of a city-wide high school curriculum committee, Gary's 38 per cent high school drop-out rate became ideologically (if not

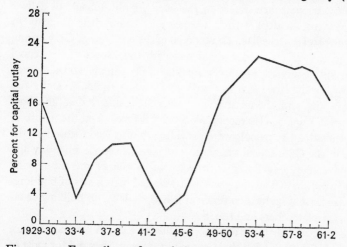

Figure 1.1   Expenditures for capital outlay as a percentage of total expenditures for school purposes in US schools, 1929–30 to 1961–2

Source: US Department of Health, Education and Welfare, Office of Education, *Trends in Financing Public Education 1929 to 1959*, circular No. 666, OE 22015, chart 87. The trend line has been extended to 1959 using data reported in US. Department of Health, Education and Welfare, Office of Education, *Digest of Educational Statistics*, Washington, DC, 1971, table 32.

practically) anathema, and the success of the city's high school graduates at college became an issue to be discussed.

But in his concern for curriculum, Blankenship was a representative American educator of the late 1950s. Between 1954 and 1958, relief from the building and staffing problems of the early 1950s came to the schools across the nation as new plant was built (see figure 1.1), and new teachers were trained. This relief made some attention to curriculum possible, a problem area that had received little financial support since the early 1930s. And in these years, the high school curriculum came to the attention of the academics as they faced the cohorts of students they were and would be teaching, graduates of the self-evidently troubled high schools of the early 1950s. Their concerns for academic quality and up-dating of subject-matter captured the ears of both their constituencies in Washington and of parents who wanted college education for their children.

The gradual emergence of an interest on the part of the schools in curricular renewal that occurred in the late 1950s is, then, a reflection of an interplay between what we now believe are the two primary functions of the administrative structures which surround the schools, *maintenance* and *change*. The first, and more fundamental of these functions, maintenance, refers to the need for the schools to deliver their services, to deploy their teachers, to house their students in adequate plant and the like. The concern of the residents of Gary during much of the period we examined was with this aspect of the school system and its service. The preoccupation of the parents who addressed the board in the late 1940s and early 1950s was with double shifts and overcrowding, with the unsatisfactory church basements that the school system was using as classrooms. None of this focused on the nature of the service that the schools were providing, but instead focused on the failure of the Gary school system to provide that service smoothly and equitably. The Gary Board spent most of its energy and time facing similar issues in these same years as it wrestled with issues of buildings and finances and spent such funds as it had available on building classrooms, hiring teachers and the like.

The ten post-war years of almost exclusive concern for maintenance problems of this kind had their reward in Gary, as they did for most of the nation's school districts, in the mid 1950s. And, as maintenance problems eased, the district was able to give some attention to its other function, to keep itself as modern and as current as possible, i.e., to *change*. The surveys of 1939 and 1955, had told the Board what it should be doing if it wished to provide adequate schooling for its children – but no real resources were available until the 1960s for any action on these recommendations to be possible. But it took federal funds (appropriated by Congress in response to an awareness of the gap between aspiration for the schools and reality) to make it possible for Gary to provide an adequate vocational program, to rebuild its laboratories, and to retrain its science teachers. In short, only when the provision of basic school service had been assured could the Board face the task of considering possible changes in that service.

The identification of *maintenance* and *change* as two different functions of a local school jurisdiction and our implication that these functions should be seen as hierarchically interdependent gives, we believe, a way of understanding many of the findings and prescriptions about curriculum change that are commonplace in the literature of curriculum. The conception of maintenance needs and the concomitant issues of the availability of resources for maintenance suggests why adaptiveness and innovation are so closely related to such fiscal matters as tax base and per pupil expenditure.[49] The wealthier a school district is, the more likely it is to have resources above and beyond those required for maintenance; these additional resources can be invested in plant, materials, and activities that produce change; these resources, in their turn, attract teachers who see themselves as innovators or who respond to concerns of one kind or another that transcend the locality. Such communities are, moreover, by virtue of their socio-economic characteristics, likely to have populations making their own ideologically derived demands on their schools.[50] The range of such socio-cultural communities and the range of resources available to districts which can be used to give flesh to the differing demands of such communities produce by their interaction a gradient of levels of innovativeness in which individual school districts locate themselves as they look at the ways in which they can concretely embody the differing kinds of prescriptions about what the schools should be attempting. To put it simply, wealthier school districts (those with resources over and beyond those needed for maintenance) can afford and can undertake innovations and, in so doing, serve as both experimenters with change and as examplars for less wealthy districts.

We would suggest that the connections we have identified between availability of financial resources and the socio-cultural turbulence and demand-making that we have been associating with such resources is firmly determined. Of course, small scale changes can take place in individual classrooms (as they did in Gary), as individual teachers experiment with new ideas or respond to their environments – although such changes must not breach dominant forms and norms too severely and must be adaptive to the constraints of existing organizational and physical structures. But, whenever curriculum change calls for the expenditure of significant resources of time, expertise or money, such resources *must* be available if change is to be carried forward. And, if fundamental systemic change is sought or required, the problems associated with changing the repertoires of habitual behavior of many, many teachers must be faced. Local districts rarely have any resources available for such tasks inasmuch as they are organizations designed, in the main, to deliver the schooling that is conventional, not develop new patterns for this schooling. At best new programs may be picked up haltingly as they were in Gary, by one teacher at a time, in different ways and in different degrees.

The literature of curriculum development has only rarely considered this issue of resources, and where it has done so has sought simply to link quality of program with high resource base. This is unfortunate for we now believe that when we overlay our conception of the costs of innovation on our initial conception of the social system that is the curriculum, we have a plausible (albeit undeveloped) way of accounting for both the conservatism of the school program as well as for change. Let us put this thesis in its most general form.

The human and monetary costs associated with systemic change of the programs within a school jurisdiction ensures, to a considerable extent, that real change in a school system will take place slowly. Plant cannot be rebuilt quickly, teachers cannot be rapidly re-trained *en masse*, and real and effective support for large-scale change cannot be readily mobilized both within and from without a school system. However, *within* a country or jurisdiction communities differ in the expectations they hold for their schools, in their ability and capacity to impose their wishes on a school, and in their ability to support such an inclination with money and other forms of social support. By virtue of these qualities such jurisdictions or communities can recruit individual teachers who are cosmopolitan in their outlook and responsive to intellectual turbulence in their, and their community's environments. This combination of factors makes such school districts responsive, both intellectually and practically, to demands of one kind or another made on them by the wider community. This predisposition to respond both encourages and supports school- and teacher-initiated exploration and installation of new curricular possibilities.

However (and the caveat is crucial), even districts or schools of this kind face limitations on what they might undertake. Definitionally, their teachers are teachers, and as such are disenabled by virtue of their experience and socialization from participating as creators in the design of radically new curricular forms; resources are not, even in districts of this kind, infinitely elastic and plant is not infinitely flexible; and the traditionally elitist, college prep orientation towards schooling of such communities inhibits what the schools might undertake and the curricular possibilities that teachers (who themselves share such elitist orientations) might explore.

The task of fundamental design and exploration of new curricular possibilities, therefore, rarely takes place within schools, institutions which are, to some extent, captive of their teachers and their milieus. Originality of insight and approach is reserved as a right and prerogative of universities or other training and developmental agencies. Characteristically, therefore, curricular initiatives come from such institutions and it is the creators of such initiatives within such institutions who meet intellectually-grounded resistance of the kind we saw at Chicago and Keele about the relative virtues of new and old forms. If such innovators succeed in overcoming their opponents, or meet no opposition – which can occur only in new institutions – and succeed in institutionalizing their innovations, their developments and ideas filter slowly to other places as disciples with legitimacy as proponents carry these conceptions to new places.

At some point and given environmental support, an innovation becomes a clear possibility, one that all schools and/or colleges might explore; and at some later point such innovations become something that *must* be adopted – and, at that point, colleges, accrediting agencies, inspectors, and pundits carry this message to all school systems. But, at the point at which an innovation must be adopted, new problems arise, centering not so much on the virtues of the innovation as on the feasibility of adoption – more often than not a question of resource availability. Are there teachers who can teach the new program? Are there funds for the new equipment, plant, etc.? At any given time some districts have the opportunity and the resources to recruit new kinds of teachers or build new plants and can therefore adopt the new. But other districts only have such resources at times of upturn in economic circumstances, while still other districts require considerable external subvention of one kind or another before they can seriously contemplate any change. Gary was (and is) such a district: from 1940 onwards, it knew what conventional wisdom said it should be doing; it made halting efforts at different times to face its responsibilities, particularly in the area of vocational education. However, an unresponsive tax base made any significant expenditures over and beyond those required for maintenance of a minimal school program impossible; indeed during the crisis years of the early 1950s the city was more or less forced by demands of and for its core program to withdraw resources from its more marginal programs.

As we have suggested, we believe that it is unfortunate that curriculum planners and policy-makers have not seen their problems in the ways we have been advocating here and have not explored systematically the interactions we have postulated between the human and fiscal resources that are required if meaningful systemic change in programs is to be undertaken. The public policy problems that arise from this form of analysis are both challenging and intriguing. For example, what kinds of linkages exist between developments in teacher training institutions (and support of developments within training institutions) and change within schools? Can funding policies speed up or facilitate these linkages? Why do the kinds of categorical grants that the US government has used in recent years to encourage school change too often produce *ad hoc* innovation that rarely has lived beyond the funding period? Are there support policies of different kinds that can more effectively liberate the creativity of educators and permit a more efficacious institutionalization of their ideas? Does investment in plant promise greater long-term influence on programs than does investment in training?

Questions of this kind are not usually thought of as curricular, and, of course, one study cannot demonstrate their salience to curricular planning. However, considerable support for the form of our findings about the connections between human and fiscal resources and the course of curriculum change is found in the work of Dahllöf, Lundgren, and Kallós in Sweden.[51] They argue that the events in classrooms cannot be considered as autonomous; the range of possible classroom events is, in given cases, always circumscribed by prior decisions made at higher governmental levels about such matters as streaming practices, funding levels, time allocation and the like. The general validity of this perspective on teaching has been decisively established at least so far as streaming decisions effect classroom processes in Swedish schools. However, it has been suggested by one North American commentator on Dahllöf's work that his approach is less appropriate for the understanding of curriculum development as it is practiced in the United States than it is for the comparatively centralized school system in Sweden.[52] Our study blunts, if it does not refute, this claim, in so far as it established that decision-making at state and federal levels did in fact profoundly influence the course of curriculum development in Gary and so the nature and kinds of teaching in the city. The form of Gary's program was, in part at least, determined by state curricular requirements. The city was clearly subordinated to, and captive of state authority as it sought the funds it required to sustain its program. It was federal funds that enabled the School City to rebuild its laboratories and build a vocational school. And the unwillingness of the city to seek the higher valuation of its property base that would have enhanced its taxing capacity was a function of local assessments of the relative good of better schools versus lower taxes. And, clearly, the School City's conception of what it might realistically achieve in its schools was determined in part by the more general parochialism of the city.

So much is clear and is consistent with the thrust of this recent Swedish work. And to the extent that we can argue that these factors influenced events in Gary, a case is made for the essential validity of the view that sees decisions made at higher systemic levels influencing in a fundamental way events at the micro-level, that is, in the classroom. And perhaps the historical dimensions of our study allow us to go further than Dahllöf to point to the hand of the past as a generic *macroframe* having profound effect on the functioning of the schools at any given point in time. The idiosyncratic plant that was one of Wirt's primary legacies to Gary influenced the character of the program in some schools in the city until the mid 1950s, long after the saga of the Wirt years had faded from significance in the city. And plant was only a physical legacy; a memory of the greatness and significance of the city's experiment with educational forms, inhibited, it seems, a realistic appraisal of the problems that Gary's schools faced at least through the early 1950s.[53]

Thus, the validity of the general orientation toward curriculum policy-making suggested by Dahllöf holds for the United States, despite a tradition which emphasizes the importance of local control in school decision-making. Our study also suggests perhaps a conception of what local control means – the right and prerogative that individual communities have to buy and sustain one kind of schooling from the array of possible kinds. To put this in a different way, there is a gradient of kinds of schooling potentially available to communities in the United States; the doctrine of local control simply asserts that individual communities have the right to determine for themselves where on this gradient of kinds of school services they will locate themselves.

So much is perhaps commonplace. It is less obvious perhaps what this gradient really consists of. In practice the range of choice about the kind of schooling that individual communities might support is carefully circumscribed both in practice and by law and is in fact choice only between varieties of *one* basic form. We saw this in our study: Gary's experiment with a different form of schooling could be sustained by the force of Wirt's will, but it could not be sustained by his successors in the face of the insistently applied demand that they experienced to conform to the dominant pattern of American schooling: and the Purdue Survey, and the Public Administration Survey were the instruments by which this demand for conformity was brought home to the citizens of Gary.

In this situation the reality of curriculum change becomes a series of successive attempts to approximate one ideal form. The problems that any community faces in delivering the service they desire has tended to obscure the reality of this limited real choice. But this conclusion brings us back to our starting point. A commitment to education commits us, as R.S. Peters has suggested, to a search for ways in which we might actualize the aspirations that the ideal of 'education' connotes.[54] If we read this observation in a minimalist way, Gary's travails can be seen as a part of an attempt to actualize one ideal. But if we read this observation as making a more profound point, it has no meaning in Gary, except in so far as Gary's troubles remind us of the problems that any institution faces in actualizing any potentiality. And to the extent that the sources of Gary's problems – the absence of adaptive openness in Wirt's conception of his schools, the hand of tradition, and the absence of human and fiscal resources required for the reforms that were sought – will surface in any school system, we must acknowledge that a commitment to an exploration of what 'education' means requires that we give attention to *agency*, to an exploration of the ways and means that will permit us to effect reform in a social system as complex as public education.

In education change must always take place within the enveloping context of organizational structures, and development and renewal are only meaningful notions inasmuch as they are embedded in structures. The ideals that 'education' connotes demand that we distinguish between the kinds of one-shot updating of program that we have been exploring here (responses, when it is all said and done, to twenty years or more of resource-induced inaction on the part of the schools) and the task of self-renewing change that has been, we suggested on the first page of this essay, the goal that we have properly clung to. The goal requires that we think about the structures within which such self-renewal might take place and the costs of such an aspiration as carefully as we think about the possible forms that such structures might take – but it does make clear, we hope, that a concern for goals without a concomitant concern for organizational matters addresses only a small part of the problem of conceiving new designs for schools.

Notes

1 Taylor, 1973; Sarason, 1971.

2 Clarke, 1968; Giaquinta, 1973; Smith and Keith, 1971; Sieber, 1972; Young, 1972.

3 See, for example, the discussion of the problems associated with the creation of a secondary school system in the State of Illinois in Henry C. Johnson, jr, and Erwin V. Johanningmeir, *Teachers for the Prairie*, Urbana, Illinois, 1972.

4 Hodgetts, 1968, ch. 2.

5 Ian Westbury and John Korbelik, 'Evaluation of a goal-focused program in social work,' paper presented to annual meeting of the American Education Research Association, New Orleans, February 1973 (ERIC ED 074 136).

6 Smith, 1971.

7 See Neil J. Wilkof, 'History and the grand design,' unpublished master's thesis, University of Chicago, 1973; W. B. Gallie, *A New University: A.D. Lindsay and the Keele Experiment*, London, 1960.

8 Young, 1972; Goodlad, 1966.

9 Kuhn, 1970.

10 John Ziman, *Public Knowledge*, Cambridge, 1968, pp. 143–4.

11 For these arguments see Lortie, 1969; Dreeben, 1970; and M. Olson, jr, *The Logic of Collective Action*, Harvard Economic Studies CXXIV, Cambridge, Mass., 1965.

12 See Lortie, 1969, pp. 12–14.

13 See US Department of Health, Education and Welfare, Office of Education, *Patterns of Course Offering and Enrolments in Public Secondary Schools, 1970–1*, Washington, DC, 1972.

14 Robert Shackleton, *The Book of Chicago*, Philadelphia, 1920, quoted in Harold M. Mayer and Richard C. Wade, *Chicago: Growth of a Metropolis*, Chicago, 1969, p. 241.

15 For Wirt's conception of the tasks and forms of the schools see William A. Wirt, *The Great Lockout in America's Citizenship Plants*, Gary, Ind., 1937; see also Frank Seymour Albright, 'A critical study of the organization of eight thirteen-grade schools in Gary, Indiana,' unpublished Ph.D dissertation, University of Chicago, 1956; Jack A. Jones, 'William A. Wirt and the Work-study-play schools,' unpublished paper, Valparaiso University, 1968; William Paxton Burris, *The Public School System of Gary, Indiana*, Washington, DC, 1914; Abraham Flexner and Frank P. Bachman, *The Gary Schools, a General Account*, New York, 1918; and George D. Strayer and Frank P. Bachman, *The Gary Public Schools: Organization and Administration*, New York, 1915.

16 Wirt, op. cit., p. 33.

17 Purdue University, Survey Committee for the Gary Board of Education, *Final Report*, Lafayette, Ind., 1942; Public Administration Service, *The Public School System of Gary, Indiana*, Chicago, 1955.

18 This account of events in Gary between 1943 and 1950, is drawn from James H. Tipton, *Community in Crisis: the Elimination of Segregation from a Public School System*, New York, 1953, pp. 18–24; and Dana P. Whitmer, 'Education in the public schools of Gary, Indiana,' unpublished Ph.D dissertation, Ohio State University, 1949. These accounts were supplemented and enriched by our discussions with Dr Marie Edwards, supervisor of social studies in Gary public schools.

19 Whitmer, op. cit., pp. 39–40.

20 Ibid., pp. 228–399.

21 Ibid., p. 310.

22 Ibid., pp. 421–2.

23 Public Administration Service, op. cit., p. 81.

24 Minutes of Meetings of the Gary Board of School Trustees, April 22, 1958 and May 13, 1958.

25 School City of Gary, *The Reporter*, January 17, 1958.

26 School City of Gary, *Gary Curriculum Guide, Grades 7–12*, 1958.

27 Oswald M. Blackwood, Wilmer B. Herron, and William C. Kelly, *High School Physics*, Chicago, 1951; our judgments and the narrative of the following pages reflect the view of Floyd Flinn, supervisor of science education in the Gary public schools from this period to the present.

28 National Society for the Study of Education, *Rethinking Science Education*, 59th yearbook, part I, Chicago, 1960; Arnold B. Grobman, *The Changing Classroom: the Role of the Biological Sciences Curriculum Study*, Chicago, 1960, *passim*.

29 Marshall D. Herron, 'The nature of scientific enquiry,' *School Review*, 79, 1971, pp. 203–11.

30 Purdue University, op. cit., p. 277.

31 National Manpower Council, *A Policy for Skilled Manpower*, New York, 1954; Public Administration Service, op. cit., p. 17; National Education Association, Committee for the Defense of Democracy through Education, *Gary Indiana, a Study of Some Aspects and Outcomes of a General School Survey*, Washington, DC, 1957.

32 Minutes of the meetings of the Gary Board of School Trustees, May 12, 1942 and December 12, 1944.

33 Purdue University, op. cit., pp. 21, 227.

34 Ibid., p. 281.

35 Ibid., pp. 285-6.

36 Ibid., p. 287.

37 National Society for the Study of Education, *Vocational Education*, 42nd yearbook, part I, Chicago, 1954, p. 33.

38 Public Administration Service, op. cit., p. 74.

39 Ibid., pp. 17, 92.

40 Ibid., p. 93.

41 Minutes of the meetings of the Gary Board of School Trustees, October 11, 1955.

42 *The Reporter*, January 9, 1958.

43 *Chicago Tribune*, January 19, 1958, part 3, p. 2.

44 *Gary Post-Tribune*, January 21, 1958.

45 University of Chicago, Department of Education, Committee on Field Services, *Survey Report, School Buildings and Sites, Gary, Indiana*, 1947, mimeo.

46 This estimate is calculated from data on school sites and plant made available to us by the Office of the Superintendent of Schools, Gary, Ind.

47 Public Administration Service, op. cit., pp. 192-5.

48 See note 46 above.

49 See, for example, Paul R. Mort and Francis G. Cornell, *Adaptability of Public School Systems*, New York, 1938, and Paul R. Mort, *Principles of School Administration*, New York, 1946.

50 We owe this observation about the relationship between wealth and ideological turbulence in the environment of the schools as a factor in curriculum change to Charles E. Bidwell.

51 Dahllöf, 1971a, 1971b; Lundgren, 1972; Kallós, 1973.

52 'Editor's comment,' *Curriculum Theory Network*, 7, 1971, p. 97.

53 For an assessment of the role of history in determining the character of a college, see Clark, 1970; Stinchcombe, 1965.

54 R.S. Peters, *Education as Initiation*, London, 1963.

2 Negotiating Curriculum Change in a College of Education

K. E. Shaw

Editors' introduction

Like McKinney and Westbury, Shaw takes as his starting point the curriculum decision system as it actually exists. The focus here is on a particular institution – an English college of education responsible for the pre-professional training of intending teachers – and how it reacts to the need to adjust its curriculum to changing demands. By limiting the study in this way, the author is forced to grapple with the problem of characterizing and interpreting the machinery for policy-making at the tactical level. Curriculum decisions are seen to result not from the application of well-defined rationales enabling pre-specified ends to be realized through uniquely appropriate means, but from a quasi-political process which allows policy to be 'discovered' through negotiation, objectives to arise when choice points are reached, and accommodations to be found which enable competing belief systems to achieve a *modus vivendi*. Does this state of affairs result from an unnecessarily primitive level of knowledge and sophistication among those involved, or is it inherent in the nature of institutions which must design and implement curricula? Depending on the answer to this question, what is the role and scope of 'management' in curriculum planning, and how might its exercise be made more effective? These are the substantive questions which this case study raises and attempts to answer.

Though the study presents many points of difference from that of the Gary schools, in respect of time scale, level of education, focus of interest, research technique, and national context, nevertheless a common theme can be discerned – the basis of curriculum decisions in a system of human relationships which must adjudicate on matters of desired ends and available means through adjustments both within itself and with a wider social and political environment, at the same time allowing consensus to be preserved and the formal machinery of decision-making to be maintained.

I

The concurrent course method of educating teachers makes college of education staff especially aware of the importance of group decisions in curriculum planning and implementation. Academic, professional, and theory of education courses have to be brought into some kind of balance, and this balance has to be readjusted with increasing frequency. New tasks are set for the colleges by changes in policy and practice in schools or by directives from central government, whilst new courses – the Bachelor of Education degree and in-service work – offer new opportunities. The academic board of the college provides the machinery for reappraisal and adjustment of curriculum balance. Negotiations take place amongst peers with the principal in the role of chairman.

This chapter tells the story of the negotiations involved in one such curriculum adjustment. From the early 1960s the then Ministry of Education had made clear to colleges responsible for teacher-training that the bulk of their students would teach in primary schools and should be trained with this career in view. For historical reasons some colleges, amongst them St Luke's, had been heavily secondary in orientation. During the decade of expansion when they were in a sellers' market they had maintained this preference for secondary work, encouraged by the shortage of certain categories of specialist teachers such as mathematicians and scientists, and by the academic specialisation fostered by the B.Ed. degree. But at the end of the decade the Department of Education and Science, in its customary discreet way, showed its teeth.

The policy on the 'balance of training' was now to be enforced. For St Luke's this meant a substantial change in the curriculum. What took place as the college attempted to adapt to this new requirement will be recounted in the following pages. But in describing this major piece of reprogramming in the curriculum of the college in the years following 1969, I want to draw attention particularly to the way in which decisions were made and implemented. I am concerned to make the behaviour of the people involved in the decisions more understandable by putting it in a wider context, and not merely to relate what they did. Because of this, I have not stinted description, comment, analysis and interpretation along with the narration. We still know, after all, very little about how large educational enterprises really work, still less about how crucial curriculum decisions are arrived at.

Let me begin, however, with a prologue, devoted to some special characteristics of schools and colleges.

II

Educational enterprises have been characterised in all seriousness, and in a journal of the highest repute, as organised anarchies (Cohen *et al.*, 1972). Of course it is clear enough that compared with organisations at the other extreme, such as continuous flow industries like oil refining, which once on stream must continue through a rigid cycle for long periods, or closed prisons where there is much regimentation, and the territorial location of inmates is very highly regulated, schools and colleges are loose and flexible. They often have a high occurrence of non-routine procedures and an interpenetration of formal and informal groupings and processes. Internally at any rate, they tend to be bureaucracies of low constraint. Their members' roles as employed professionals often have a quite limited prescribed element (being in the right place at the right time) and a rather large discretional element (personal choice of method and approach to the work, individual code of priorities, instant modification of procedures, etc.). But a reader who thought that Cohen and his associates have given way to a journalistic desire for a gripping first sentence would rightly want rather more than this. Cohen defends his choice of phrase by drawing attention to the following characteristics of educational establishments:

(a) *Problematic preferences*, which are inconsistent, undefined and discovered in action rather than used as the basis for action.
(b) An *unclear technology*, predisposing to trial and error methods, and reliance on experience and pragmatism.
(c) *Fluid participation*, that is, the members vary in the time and effort that they put into different activities, such as teaching, research, planning and administration.

Pursuing their argument the authors stress the need for progress towards a normative theory of decision-making under circumstances such as these, where goals are unclear or unknown. They also press for a revised theory of management in such conditions.

Cohen's article appeared when I was bringing to a close a study of organisation in a large college of education. It had taken more than four years. Much of my work had been concerned with the attempt to examine processes of decision-making. The results made Cohen's analysis seem very plausible. Group decision taking as a medium and means of change in organisations remains relatively unstudied and has no theoretical framework. Psychologists have concentrated on changes in judgments, attitudes and perceptions with respect to the effect of influence, including the effect of information. What is less understood is the effect of appraisal, evaluative discussion and the like; though processes which lead to convergence or promote polarisation are the most obvious starting points.

Educational enterprises are shielded from rapid and drastic change by the length of their production cycle. The time taken by students from recruitment to final departure from college may be three and a half years. Schools and colleges do not depend upon a machine technology for their transformation process. Hence they are free from sudden and unforeseen technological innovations such as occur, say, in the electronics industry. In manufacturing, too, efficient technological processes compel major producers to accept organisational change or lose their leading position. For this reason many studies of industry have drawn attention to the problems which stem from the need to change social relationships amongst workpeople from those structured by the obsolescent technology to those required by the new (for example the classical study by Jacques, 1951, or Fensham and Hooper, 1964). In educational enterprises, by contrast, the central problems have been more commonly seen as those of goal identification and the attempt to co-ordinate into a meaningful and cumulative sequence learning experiences which are offered in a variety of choices to a broad range of students. A good deal less attention has been paid to the perceptions, values and beliefs of the staff members, presumably under the influence of the idea that educational enterprises function as normative institutions. This implies that objectives, and the behaviour intended to lead towards them, are to be regarded as being governed by a common set of values shared by the participants, which act as imperatives in directing the course of operations. But Harris (1969) has pointed out that even where strong normative values to which all members assent might seem to control behaviour and create a consensus, the facts are that differently placed members of complex organisations see things differently. The teachers, in a sense, are the technology and we must start from them.

Lawrence and Lorsch (1967) bring evidence to support the view that internal differentiation is a key determinant of belief and perception systems in complex organisations. My findings agree with this. In educational settings much short term internal change stems from developments in what Hickson *et al.* (1969) have called the 'knowledge technology'; that is, changes in the sum of what is known in any area of human endeavour, in the structure of that knowledge, as conventionally embodied in courses, and the value put upon an area relative to other areas. Each discipline represented in the college has its own academic sub-environment, the 'world of English' or the 'world of mathematics' to which it responds according to the amount and frequency of contact its members make through reading the journals, attending conferences, pursuing research and so on. Though there is, clearly, incomplete sampling of what the world of the discipline has to offer, and each member of the departmental staff has presumably his own mental filters at work, the departments nevertheless adapt to changes in the knowledge technology more or less steadily. One of them speeds from traditional divinity to moral and religious studies, another largely abandons computational skills for the 'new' mathematics, whilst yet another goes on virtually unchanged like the rock of ages. Differentiated views arise about what the 'real' goals of the college are. Partially competing codes of priorities within the goal cluster develop. These are the problematic preferences to which Cohen refers. Curriculum design is heavily concerned with clarifying them and reconciling them.

It is, indeed, precisely the flexibility of the technology upon which colleges depend which emphasises the importance of the fact that varying staff belief systems about what should be done are as important as administrative constraints such as facilities or finance. Strategic decisions – those concerned with goals – are the outcome of competing priorities, values, meanings and interpretations, explored in meetings or made to prevail by such other means as lobbying, bargaining, manipulating rewards and exercising influence and power. Within this strategic area there is plentiful room for political manoeuvre.

In older institutions there is the influence, finally, of 'tradition' to be considered. It is hard to pin down, and severely eroded by new attitudes imported by large numbers of newly recruited staff during periods of very rapid expansion. Values are not clearly defined so that staff may lie anywhere on a continuum between extreme positions whilst claiming to share the same values. What, therefore, is of importance is not any supposed 'objective' situation but the psychological emphasis that the members put differentially on the elements in play at any given time. It is clearly important, then, to show empirically that there are systematic groupings of staff within the college, having different definitions of the situation, and amongst which processes of informal and formal negotiation take place.

To the tidy minded it might seem *a priori* that departmental affiliation would be the key factor in such groupings; though reflection on Cohen's point about members' differential participation in available activities would give ground for caution. Others might be tempted by the persistent mythology of colleges of education which would have it that the chief line up always takes the form of educationists versus the rest. This is a sociologically naive view if only because some disciplines (sociology, philosophy, psychology) are taught academically in education departments, whilst conversely, some members of subject departments are qualified only by the Teachers' Certificate, experienced largely with the primary age-group in schools, and concerned in the main with classroom method. If, in fact, there are significant groupings within the staff of a large institution, it is unlikely that they could be explained on any simple and obvious model of the foregoing kind. Colleges recruit staff who are already job-socialised, sometimes by over twenty years in school teaching. They come from a wide variety of previous teaching posts, all levels of qualification, and most types of school. What they bring in at recruitment in the way of attitudes, values and beliefs is likely to be at least as influential as factors which arise from their role in the college organisation.

III

To throw light on this situation I began by a pilot investigation in which I conducted interviews lasting about one hour with each of thirty members of staff who had been recruited during the preceding two years. Twelve were aged over thirty-five, two over fifty; they were well spread across the departments. Save for mean age and experience of work in the college, they were not, as a group, different in any fundamental way from those already staffing the college. Indeed, when I came to interview the established staff there was regular reference to the requirements that a new staff member should 'fit in', that his ideas and values should be in harmony with those prevailing in the department. I was thus able to construct on the basis of these interviews, a focused interview schedule for the main staff cohort, who numbered fifty-seven. (There were nine refusals or incomplete responses, which were ignored.)

Interviews with this group were then carried out. During the interview I invited colleagues to take away and complete for me an Osgood-type semantic differential instrument, which sampled eight major areas of college work and organisation, using ten scales for each area. A resulting matrix of 57×80 scores was factor analysed for principal components and varimax results, and the former further subjected to cluster analysis[1] to determine groupings amongst respondents based on component specifications. Four major factors were satisfactorily identified and these, alongside the completed interview schedules, enabled an understanding to be gained of the reasons why members of staff fell into particular clusters or groups. Full details of this are available else-where (Shaw, 1973).

The cluster analysis divided the respondents into two groups, as shown in figure 2.1, consisting of clusters 1 to 4 on the right and 5 to 7 on the left of the dendrogram, together with several unique cases. Those in the right-hand clusters on the whole tended to be staff with experience

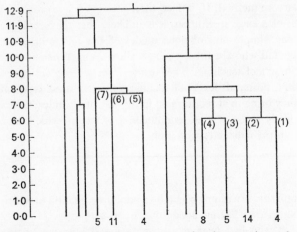

Figure 2.1   Simplified dendrogram showing numbers of staff in final clusters

of primary and non-selective secondary schools who were orientated to the professional formation of the students and whose work included teaching on classroom biased courses and the professional course. Of the thirty-four, ten were educationists. The most extreme scorers in this direction (cluster 1) consisted of three experienced educationists with respectively 11, 12 and 21 years of school teaching, and the staff member in charge of the college closed circuit television unit. The most extreme scorers in the other direction (cluster 7) were drawn from the English, music, science and mathematics departments. They were highly specialised in their work areas; only one was college trained and concerned with professional courses. They represented a 'hard-line' outlook, cherishing their academic discipline and personal expertise, and feeling severely the limitations imposed upon them by the need for a professional formation for the students. They held that true profes-sional formation came from love of the subject.

Sharp clustering is of course not to be expected from the nature of individual differences. But the clusters are defensible since they are discovered by empirical and mathematical techniques, not by armchair speculation; and they remained broadly stable when the data were run with a very contrasting programme. They make good sense as 'meaningful composites' consistent with observational data and interview responses. Respondents from several clusters can be found in each major department, and the educationists are spread over all clusters except cluster 7. This lends weight to the view that a considerable number of factors, including external ones such as prior socialisation to the profession, as well as those arising internally from specialisation in tasks and from response to particular sub-environments, are likely to promote diversity of perceptions, evaluations and meanings amongst a large staff. This presents a need for processes to maintain a common direction, to make strategic policy choices by agreement, to bring about requisite integration. It indicates how it is possible for common frames of reference to lead a group of staff to prefer one solution or statement of priorities, even though as individuals they belong to departments with different interests. No doubt departmental interests are uppermost in certain types of decision: the allocation of staff, services or money, for example. But frame-based interests may influence the sympathies of those not directly involved in the outcomes of specific disputes, and may well predominate when strategic policy is involved, or the code of priorities, new courses, or a new product-mix of students.

It is against this background that I now turn to the analysis of a major curriculum decision.

IV

The college had ample experience of large scale curriculum planning. In 1960, for example, when the first three-year students were admitted, a new course structure had to be worked out. Under the 1960 plan students took two main subjects, but did not begin to study their 'B' (second main) subject until the second year of the course. In the mid 1960s, however, the B.Ed. degree was introduced and required that both main subjects should begin immediately the students entered college. This innovation involved a second great internal reprogramming as well as negotiations to retime teaching practice with more than two hundred schools spread over the whole region of Devon and Cornwall. Both resequencing and alteration of proportions in the course were involved and the decisions intimately affected every member of the staff.

The machinery of decision on that occasion relied on sponsored plans advanced by heavily interested parties who had special knowledge of the complexity of the situation. Thus a revised plan put forward by the mathematics department, which traditionally put together the college time-table, was adopted. This plan had the backing of a 'steering committee' consisting of the heads of six large departments. It was virtually a Directoire which had been set up by the then principal after some experience of the large *ad hoc* committee which preceded the academic board. The plan suited the academic departments and reinforced the secondary aspects of the college work which had reappeared strongly during the Robbins period. It emphasised main subjects and reduced time spent on classroom orientated curriculum courses. But although a time-table which would work had been found – in itself no mean achievement – this plan was not in harmony with conditions in the environment and had maladaptive consequences. It led to excessive pressure on the limited number of secondary teaching practice places and was in conflict with the views of the Department of Education and Science on the balance of training. A major task of the eventual academic board five years later was to attempt, against considerable opposition from the academic departments, to reverse this decision when the DES took a stiffer line. It is the narrative of that attempt that will be told.

What, to begin with, was the machinery of decision? The legally constituted academic board was the successor to a series of irregular committees which met as required and lacked both constitutional standing and an electorally chosen membership. Before it was set up, decision lay with the principal and a 'magic circle' of senior staff. Competitive lobbying of the principal in private was the chief mechanism for securing changes in the balance of the curriculum and the reallocation of resources, including staff, on which the changes would rest. An executive committee was called into being by the principal to carry through the changes called for by the establishment of the B.Ed. degree. Its functions were later eroded by the small 'steering committee' and it was renamed the Ad Hoc Committee since it then only met as required to deal with issues as they arose. Meetings were one topic affairs without a formal agenda or opportunities for raising matters under Any Other Business. Initially the principal did not take the chair.

When the recommendations of the Weaver Committee were embodied in legislation in 1968 the college was still preoccupied with working through the new cycle of operations begun in 1966, a building programme, continuing growth in numbers, the further development of the postgraduate course, the admission of women students and the reconstitution of the governing body. The plans of a working party set up to plan the implementation of the Weaver recommendations in the college were rejected by the staff at a general meeting. Alternative plans were produced from the floor. One was a faculty based scheme. The other proposed an 'A' list of the 16 heads of departments to elect

6 members, all other staff, the 'B' list, to elect a further 6, and two ex-officio members, making a board of 14. This plan was adopted, though at the suggestion of the governing body the number was raised to 18 (8 + 8 + 2). This was ratified at a full meeting of the staff. The fact that the board was constituted in this very open way by the whole staff, probably against the preferences of the principal who favoured a smaller committee, and certainly against the proposals of the official working party, is important in the light of subsequent criticisms by 'hard-line' cluster 7 members.

Departments could not be guaranteed continuous representation. The board was not a heads of department oligarchy. Special interests could however be defended by the right of non-members to speak with the chairman's permission, a right which was much used. Heads who were not members, of course, could not vote; but then, votes were very rare. Heads of departments' meetings were very rarely held after the board began business. The board thus showed itself at once to be the public political forum of the college, though covert political activity and direct lobbying of the principal did not by any means cease. The board had hardly begun to operate when the curriculum decision I shall describe presented itself to the college.

One final point must be added for the sake of completeness. Since the teacher-training organisation for the area (ATO) is based on the University of Exeter which is the predominant partner in this system of association between colleges and universities, curriculum decisions substantial enough to require changes in the regulations under which the Teachers' Certificate is awarded must finally be approved by the delegacy of the University Institute of Education. Teachers' associations, local authorities, the DES, the university and others are represented on the delegacy, the body which co-ordinates all teacher-training activities in the area. Decisions taken by the academic board of the college must take account of this, particularly the limitation that the delegacy would not make special regulations for any one college in its area. As the certificate is awarded to successful students by the university, the views of university members on the delegacy carry great weight.

V

This was, then, one of a series of changes that had been going on through the 1960s. But whilst the previous changes had been welcomed and lubricated by the extra resources which accompanied rapid expansion, this 1969 change was unwelcome, forced upon the college and accompanied by a slight contraction in staffing. It was therefore more painful, and turned out to be a rehearsal for substantially greater and still more painful changes imposed on colleges of education by the James Report[2] and the White Paper.[3]

When the DES gave the principal indirect but unmistakable signs that St Luke's was out of line with its policy, meetings were taking place of the three institutions concerned with the training of teachers in the Devon and Cornwall area. They revealed a very serious situation. As a result of rapid growth in all three (two colleges and a university department of education) the pressure on secondary teaching practice places was too great. The figures for student preferences in St Luke's are shown in table 2.1.

TABLE 2.I   Students' choices for primary or secondary final teaching practice: January–May 1970, St Luke's College

	Secondary	Primary	Total
3-year students	222 (88%)	31 (12%)	253
2-year mature students	67 (50%)	66 (50%)	133
1-year postgrad. students	51 (70%)	22 (30%)	73
	340 (74%)	119 (26%)	459

Clearly the situation produced by the 1966 plan could not continue. This plan had held the balance in favour of the subject departments which, from small beginnings in a college of some 400 students, had built up powerful teams of staff during the expansion to teach to degree level. They were frequently very well qualified but increasingly recruited from staff who lacked experience in school methods, particularly for younger and less able children. Staff turnover was slow so that it was difficult to rebalance departments. The philosophy of the groups on the left-hand side of the dendrogram in figure 2.1 predominated, and it was acknowledged that the right-hand groups were fighting an uphill battle.

Largely because of changes in the teaching of mathematics, primary schools were unwilling to admit students to practice unless they had followed a special primary course. As the above figures show, only a small proportion (but a growing number) of students were prepared to commit themselves to this course. (It was still almost wholly a men's college. The proportion of mature students opting for a primary practice is also worth noting; they did not on the whole have to consider B.Ed.) A major change would force more students to do some version of the primary course, which was more orientated to the thinking of the groups on the right-hand side of the dendrogram and largely staffed by them.

The position of the large education department was somewhat special. Great tenacity had been required to accomplish its growth, against strong opposition. The primary course had originated in this department. Within it, a delicate balance had to be kept between secondary and primary age-group orientated educationists, and between well qualified academics and practitioners with distinguished service in schools (the categories were not mutually exclusive). With help from other departments, notably the mathematics department, whose staff had been rebalanced towards the practitioner side as a result of its more rapid staff turnover, it had been possible to provide an increasingly comprehensive primary course. It was not easy to combine with B.Ed. and consequently it attracted mature students, a few postgraduates, some of the still small group of women students, but rather few three-year students. As it was seen rather as an education department concern it had to rely on the precarious system of borrowing staff to teach options within the course.

The general lines of the subsequent discussions, wrangling, and on rare occasions open conflict, were consequently fairly forseeable. Many students would be reluctant to do the course, and interviewing tutors (invariably main subject staff except for postgraduate entrants) would hardly recommend it enthusiastically. Any movement towards the professional course would draw time and energy away from main subjects, and would appear to add to the power of the education department, thought by many to be too strong already. One of the senior staff of that department would certainly organise the new course and would be supported by the head of department who was one of the two indisputable political leaders of the college. A number of major departmental heads likely to resist the innovation fell into cluster 6; the most determined and vocal resisters fell into cluster 7. As might be supposed, the promoters fell into cluster 2. But for most participants the decision involved a delicate balance between the protection of departmental interests, and 'frame' based arguments for an adequate professional element in the total course.

Discussion began quietly at the third meeting of the new academic board in the autumn of 1969. The board was led through a very detailed paper on the difficulties created for teaching practice organisation by the overwhelmingly secondary preferences of the students. The main exposition was by the principal, the head of education and the tutor in charge of teaching practice; the last two had written the document. The major part of the proceedings, which lasted thirty-four minutes, was simply explanatory. Relatively few staff appreciated the problems of placing 460 students annually on teaching practice, since they tended to see teaching practice in a departmental context. It was not widely understood how a series of poorly co-ordinated decisions at various levels, which had been made in response to the rapidly changing conditions of the 1960s in an unsystematic way, had now led to a critical situation. An initial phase of exploration had in fact begun so that the participants could be educated in the known facts of the situation. Whatever else, the constraint of teaching practice places could not be argued away.

The role of the principal was crucial as he was the only source of DES information. Since there had been no formal circular, the principal necessarily interpreted the significance of the indirect pressures brought upon him, defined the situation, and set the key emphases. In this respect he had begun a process to 'unfreeze' the existing balance, introducing new critical information and raising anxieties. The other two major speakers pressed the need for change without specifying in detail its nature, beyond the obvious increase in primary emphasis. The two major representatives of large departments who fell in cluster 6 were absent from this meeting, fortuitously. Open opposition was not voiced apart from questions and observations. But an undercurrent was clear, from three suggestions:

(a) That headmasters should be persuaded to accept students without a special primary course (i.e., control rather than adapt to the market).

(b) That certain departments should have unchallenged rights over secondary teaching practice places (i.e., unilaterally opting out of the problem by some groups).

(c) That the timing of teaching practices should be changed to secure greater access to secondary places (effectively an unreal alternative which would neglect responsibilities to the other two teacher training bodies in the area).

The principal, referring once again to the indirect 'a nod and a wink' understanding with the DES, closed the discussion before opinions could harden prematurely.

At the end of this meeting the principal proposed an *ad hoc* heads of department meeting, that is, a return to an older and incidentally more manageable mechanism. The board, jealous of its new standing, resisted this suggestion which might have produced a *fait accompli*. Instead there was an open meeting, a fortnight later, of the board plus eighteen other staff members to pursue the problem. This meeting lasted one and a half hours. The facts were once again rehearsed with the additions that mature students could no longer be absorbed locally

– the schools needed more younger men and women – and that the attitude of schools to teaching practice was deteriorating.

Initial discussion was thus focused on the teaching practice aspect. Some attempt was made to dispute the facts, but the evidence was overwhelming. More seriously, criticism was directed at the timing of the professional elements in the existing course: they were not begun early enough to prepare students for a first-year practice in junior schools. It was argued, rather significantly, from the resisters, that professional studies interfered with the rhythm of main subject teaching 'which we agreed was paramount six years ago'. Since the discussion was not moving forward the principal intervened to restate the central matter in its full urgency. 'There is going to be a crackdown on the College of St Mark and St John [due to move into the region, and also very secondary in orientation]. There will be a showdown [i.e., from the DES] and we must not wait for it.' This led to the important question whether a more amplified professional course could be staffed; 'the expertise is not available'. Nothing less than a restructuring of the college, and hence a profound professional reorientation of many staff, would be involved.

The argument was thus led back to the practicalities of the scale of the operation. The intention was that 'not less than 75 per cent of the students must do a primary practice' and would in consequence have to be trained for it. The principal reaffirmed that for students on entry 'the assumption is primary, unless there is a very good cause for secondary'. Three aspects finally emerged:

(a) The timing of teaching practices within the three years of the course so as to give time for adequate preparation in primary English and mathematics.
(b) The reconstruction of the curriculum for three-year students.
(c) The entry-mix of students on the new assumptions and its impact on departments.

The principal concluded the meeting by remarking, 'We are not abiding by our agreement (i.e., with the DES on the balance of training). We will let it be known that we are correcting it.'

This meeting clearly exhibited to the staff how the dominant code of priorities in the college was out of line with contemporary needs. The delegation of staffing policy to departmental heads, the lack of a co-ordinated policy for balanced recruitment that had resulted, and the inattention to conditions in schools until the situation was critical, had led to a position calling for drastic corrective action. But as against the short term constraint of secondary teaching practice places, it could still be assumed that most students would strive to enter secondary teaching, regardless of their course of training. The means of changing the balance lay with the staff; but since staff are not substitutable a rather severe inflexibility existed in this area. A Ph.D. qualified pure scientist, with eighteen months teaching experience in a direct grant school, is hardly likely to be able to prepare students for primary school science and is even less likely to want to. And moving students, and thus resources, from the main subjects to the professional courses would be seen by many as a serious change in the power distribution in the college. There was inevitably basic opposition of principle between the cluster 2 practitioners, who included educationists, and the cluster 6 subject staff, who included powerful and vocal heads of large departments. (The extremist cluster 7 was not yet represented on the board.) The 'silent majority' were still trying to come to grips with the facts and their various implications for resequencing of courses and reallocation of time and staff effort. The main initial tensions were thus led to centre not on the issue but on the more familiar associated aspects of teaching practice and the procedures for supervision in primary schools. The length of time taken before even such a clear issue as this is accepted to be a problem, should not go unnoticed.

The technology of educational enterprises is unclear, in that it does not, of itself, impose specific procedures in the way that, for example, machines, once installed, limit the production possibilities of a manufacturing firm. In college an area of endeavour is specified from which there is an indeterminate number of outcomes (mixes of skills and knowledge states that students might possess) which cannot be assessed with precision and for any one of which the market finds a place. Therefore priorities and the curriculum which gives them expression are to a large extent influenced by cultural presuppositions and traditional values. Lecturers' own life experience, their prior socialisation to the profession and type of service, are at least as important determinants of their views of what ought to be done, what the college is for, as any notion of social purpose – much less market needs. Consequently priorities are problematic; profoundly so, not merely in some administrative sense of, for example, how to use staff and facilities efficiently. There is no simple way in which the problems can be resolved. All solutions will be temporary compromises. Power cannot be exercised except over resources; it cannot be used to impose priorities. It is only with difficulty, indeed, that it can be used to implement decisions. Most staff are aware, however, that when decisions about priorities are made they begin to affect the existing system of control over scarce resources (time, staff, facilities) since these follow the students. Hence the discussions necessarily have a political element; wrangling over details is to be expected. The board represented then, in my view, varying states of differential readiness to change, cross-cut by varying degrees of reluctance to accept the consequential changes that would take place in control over resources. It should not be forgotten, though, that discussion offers rather enjoyable opportunities for self-expression to some people.

The initial phase was one of exploration and education in the facts, definition of the problem and its degree of urgency, anxiety creation, and the taking up of positions by the chief participants in their roles, not so much as power wielders, as opinion leaders.

VI

Now began a period of manoeuvring. The next meeting in January 1970 was marked by a reduced sense of urgency. A well informed board member remarked to me when I mentioned this, 'The vested interests have now had time to have their say.' The method of lobbying the principal implied by that remark, was still cherished, if now more muted. It was being used to persuade the principal, who after a tenure of twenty-five years had great ascendancy, to use his powers as chairman to manage the meeting in a sense favourable to the lobbier. It may be confidently inferred that heads of departments who resisted the change because they would lose their second main students (those studying the subject as a subsidiary to some other, first main, academic subject, for a shorter time but, in some departments, large numbers) would have voiced their protests in no uncertain terms and argued for a slower pace.

Discussion lasted for fifty minutes. The resisters, mainly from the English, history and geography departments based themselves on returns from college leavers which indicated that 80 per cent of leavers for the past ten years had gone into secondary schools. The principal reduced his plea to 'a general feeling for more primary orientation. That's all we want, rather more.' The discussion settled on the idea of 40 per cent primary and 60 per cent primary/secondary students. The latter was ostensibly a training for the 8–13 years (middle school) age-group. It was a notorious euphemism for a non-primary course.

Tactically, the central part of the meeting was a rearguard action by the resisters who called for a leisurely pace to allow time for alternative schemes to be prepared, and for departmental discussions to be held. Three years would be needed to phase out the existing curriculum for which students were being accepted. There would be serious difficulty about interviewing students who had applied to the college as intending secondary teachers and who would have to be 'guided' towards a primary commitment. There was continuous pressure for the retention of the second main subject, held to be particularly valuable for physical education and science students. The seriousness of DES pressure was again questioned. In an unusually long intervention the principal further retreated. He now played down the DES pressure by saying that they were unlikely to interfere directly in the inner working of a college. Primarily the pressure came from teaching practice place shortage. Nevertheless 'it's absurd, being defiant . . . over the whole area of the course the absurdity of the existing primary-secondary balance will become evident.' The second main subject was overtaxing students and left no time for the basic teaching of professional courses in reading and mathematics. The DES would ask questions. Students would have to do a primary practice in greater numbers. There was an 'unintentional dishonesty' in the prospectus inasmuch as it did not stress the primary career likelihood.

The cluster 2 group added little to these points. The upshot was to concentrate on a curriculum to prepare students to teach the 8–13 age range. This step was cautious, non-committal, ambiguous in its implications, left room for individual interpretation, and for most departments implied no necessary change. Great attention was paid to semantics. The term 'primary' was to be avoided in favour of the phrase 'extended professional course' (EPC). By now the line up was clear. Having successfully provoked the situation, the principal had now moved to a more neutral stance, no doubt to avoid too close a commitment to the education department which would certainly demand extra resources to meet its extra load (the bigger EPC).

Associated problems arose at this time in two areas. Two mathematicians announced their intention to retire, which raised the possibility of staff reallocation to lubricate the change. A special meeting of the board was called, devoted entirely to staffing. This is without doubt the fundamental political issue; it is related to work loads, allowances for heads of departments and promotions. Loss or gain of staff by departments is public defeat or victory. The principal admitted he had advertised one mathematical post in advance of any board decision; but staff felt that in an already contracting situation (the college had been asked to run down by seven staff [6 per cent] over three years), no permanent appointments should be made until the situation cleared. This was fiercely contended in an animated meeting during which the rate of interventions by speakers was nearly double that of normal board meetings. The mathematics department stressed its increased participation in professional courses and the matter was, most unusually, pressed to a vote. They got one replacement.

One of the chief difficulties of decision-making in these circumstances is that any situation of change offers threats and opportunities differentially to the participants, who are as likely to see the situation in terms of gains and losses of advantage in an enduring contest, as they are to see it in terms of the overall objectives of the college. Departments are independent and rarely exchange services; scientists 'cannot and would not' teach mathematics. Since, then, staff are tightly tethered to their departments, any resource must go to a department. It cannot be an addition to 'the college as a whole'. This is most true of staff, and it constitutes a fundamental rigidity. It is an obstacle to change, though it has advantages for clarity and accountability. It is difficult to set up, and more difficult still to keep up, any form of 'pool' for new ventures.

The second associated problem was the standing of small departments. French, economics and environmental studies had only been offered as second main subjects. They would have no future if the latter were abandoned, particularly as they did not have a primary school application. The first two, being of very long standing, were at once accorded main subject status. But environmental studies was a special case, being a recent private venture innovation by a former biology lecturer. A subcommittee was empowered to discuss the situation, which entailed the personal position of the subject's originator, as well as the market for the subject. It might easily be kept as an elective within the EPC course; was it justifiable as a main subject? From which departments would it take students? History and geography, threatened already with the loss of their second main students, did not want another competitor. Very sharp opposition came from this quarter; nine of the thirteen members of these departments even went to the length of submitting a paper to the board opposing the grant of main subject status.

The report of the subcommittee was not received until the June meeting, at which further strenuous opposition was voiced. One subcommittee member had even resigned from it on the grounds that energetic lobbying had harried and bulldozed the group. However, environmental studies was granted main subject status by a 6:2 vote. There were ten abstentions. Even in a period of contraction few members, evidently, could bring themselves to vote in such a way as to cut off the career aspirations and rebuff the initiative of a colleague.

		N	%
Principal		67	16
Dep. Prin.		38	9
Acad. registrar		2	–
List A			
Hd Edn.		63	15
Hd Engl.		28	6·5
Hd Art		25	6
Hd P.E.		46	11
Hd Chem.		16	4
Hd Biol.		8	2
List B			
Rep. (rel. studies)		20	5
Rep. (PE)		10	2
Rep. (Music)		1	–
Rep. (Maths)		8	2
Rep. (Hist)		23	5·5
Rep. (Maths)		15	3·5
*Rep. (Edn)		8	2
Rep. (Geog)		13	3
Other speakers			
Envir. studies		7	2
TP planning		22	5·5
Physics		2	–
		422	100

Column headers (left to right): 6 mins. Admin. (minutes etc.); 16 " Introduction - background; 2 " Head of Education: Paper and discussion; 3 " Environmental studies; 10 " Electives - phase 1; 10 " Electives - phase 2; 3 " Religious studies; 62 " Electives - phase 3 / General discussion; 10 " Electives: staffing, org., etc.; 13 " Logistics and admin.; 5 " TP aspects, phase 1; 17 " TP aspects, phase 2

Figure 2.2   Academic board meeting 14 March, 1970: topics of discussion and distribution of interventions

List A, heads of departments
List B, other staff
• Author
TP = Teaching Practice

VII

In the meantime, however, a set piece confrontation on the main issue had taken place. This was a meeting of two hours, fifty-five minutes wholly devoted to the new course structure. The pattern of interventions is reproduced as figure 2.2 as an example of the method of recording.

By now the implications were more apparent; three and a half months had gone by. This slow time scale is important. The college is a large and complex system. Even to trace the administrative consequences (the first priority) of a major change calls for time, energy, a well developed information set and the will to attend to them. It is difficult for anyone at one vantage point in the system to see clearly how the shift will affect people at other points. Much explanatory discussion is needed to decide what is special pleading and what is hardship. If individual staff members are to know what they are consenting to, some tentative planning and a measure of translation of broad directional plans into day to day consequential arrangements has to be done. Agreement 'in principle' is not a decision and should not be mistaken for one. Only when it has been implemented can a large strategic decision be considered 'made', not before. Thus there had been a gradual build up of circulated papers which ended in a snowstorm of documents pressing individual and group viewpoints. The documents for this meeting are half an inch thick.

The principal opened the meeting by asking, 'Are all the competitors here?' His opening remarks traced the serious developments which were taking place in the context of higher education generally. A select committee of the House of Commons was taking evidence concerning teacher-training. Also, early in 1970, a letter to vice-chancellors from the Secretary of State for Education required the setting up in each area training organisation of a review body to examine the content and structure of college courses. (These two enquiries preceded and contributed to the James Report of 1972 and the 1973 White Paper.) The discussion was no longer merely a domestic matter and might be the prelude to more far reaching changes. The principal retreated even further from his initial stance wondering, 'Would it not be advisable to go on as we are, *pro tem.*, improving our present course?' The change could only be provisional until the new national policy became clear 'and nothing remains constant'. More attention would have to be paid to primary work, 'but we should improve the course with as little alteration as possible, I stress that – as little alteration as possible'. It was the business of the board to take decisions 'but we can't impose them without consulting people'. A few minor remarks interrupted this exposition, which concluded by directing the board's attention to a plan devised by the head of the education department which had been canvassed with all departments ahead of the meeting.

Since the group at the top of the education department administered teaching practice, the professional course, the large postgraduate and the B.Ed. courses, information available to the head of the department was extensive. Whilst other documents were concerned with generalities and special interests, the education plan was a detailed practical scheme for a rebalanced curriculum. He introduced it in a five-minute speech which recalled the swings in teacher-training policy in 1913, 1921, 1925, 1945 and 1957 as well as the Robbins period, between academic and professional emphases. The pendulum was once more swinging back after the academic emphasis of Robbins. But neither the governing body, nor the university delegacy envisaged a violent change, '. . . just a switch of balance, nothing too extreme; we're just too much biased'. Recruitment policy might have to change, but a list of safeguards ('accommodations for colleagues who find the change difficult') headed the plan.

In essence 'X' students, the majority, were to follow a revised curriculum consisting of one main subject, education and an extended professional course orientated to the 8–13 age-group. 'Y' students (mainly science and PE) were to do a 'double main', education, and a much reduced EPC and be regarded as secondary. Strenuous objections were again raised by those departments who disliked losing their second main students, but the general principle was accepted after fifteen minutes. At this stage the nature of the EPC was left vague.

A second phase of the meeting began with the attempt to foresee some consequences of this curriculum plan, and took the form of a long technical discussion of eventual staff and student workloads. The strategy of the resisters was to argue in favour of long or 'double' electives on the EPC (since music and French must have time to practise skills, a few long electives are necessary). In most cases long electives would be little but renamed second main courses. The promoters insisted on short, one-term electives focusing not on content of knowledge but on classroom methods.

A vague reluctant consensus on the plan was arrived at, leaving many loose ends to be tied up as need arose and as clearer information came in many months later, when the new intake was allocated amongst the various alternative elective elements. The keynote was the avoidance of a collision course with the most threatened groups. Stress was constantly laid on the long period of phasing in the EPC and phasing out the second main subjects. There was hope that further changes might slow down or even reverse the process. (The vagaries of national policy and its local effects were summed up in the wry remark *'Plans change hourly'* which became a catchphrase of the period in the college.) There was no voting. Complexity and special cases were stressed, leaving hope for accommodations at a later stage. The minutes of this meeting were thick with non-committal language: 'Consideration was given to the view that . . .', 'It was suggested that . . .', 'This might lead to the possibility that . . .', 'The hope was expressed that . . .'. There would clearly be a scramble by departments to get into the 'Y' category, and so opt out of change; to manipulate electives; and a real hope that the problem might go away in the two to three years before it was fully operational. Few staff would have to face up to the consequences until the next round of student admissions, still nine months away, when the interviewees had to be guided into their new courses. The pace was reassuringly slow and loopholes seemed abundant.

Not surprisingly, at the penultimate meeting of the board in June 1970 it was necessary for the academic registrar to present a paper explaining what the decision had in fact been; he also sought clarification of the machinery for developing the new electives and equalising students' choices amongst those offered. By now the revised timing of teaching practices, designed to spread the load and avoid the spring term peak, was a pressing matter. It necessarily involved far reaching rescheduling of courses and the timing of the professional courses designed to prepare students for the practices. It was relegated to a sub-committee, as being a technical matter, not one of principle. The end of the academic year was near at hand when most energy is devoted to examining, agreeing results, meeting external examiners and the like; departmental meetings are frequent. At such times meetings of the board tend to dispatch many small items, mostly five- or ten-minute affairs. However, feeling had built up in respect of the loose and untidy way in which 'decisions' had been arrived at, not embodied in formal motions and voted. It was felt by some that the position of environmental studies, the acceptance of the teaching practice plan and the treatment of the new curriculum structure had not been approached with proper procedural rigour. Recording was held to be often unclear and ambiguous. I think it is quite likely that more formal treatment and more votes would have reduced progress by hardening positions prematurely. Important progress had been made; reluctance had not degenerated into animosity quite possibly because the vagueness left hope for accommodations.

The former lecturer in charge of the primary course having been translated to the post of co-ordinator of the new extended professional course, it fell to him to report on progress at the final academic board. The new scheme would begin after an interval of fifteen months in September 1971. A booklet would be available for the guidance of interviewing tutors in the meantime and there would be teach-ins. This final meeting concluded with twenty-seven minutes of discussion of unforeseen administrative difficulties in the plan thrown up by departments as they began to come to terms with its implementation. It was claimed that there would be:

(a)   Likelihood of overload of students' time-tables.
(b)   Uneconomic use of staffing because of the multiplicity of electives.
(c)   Problems of co-ordinating electives with other work.
(d)   Need to repeat electives for different groups of students on different courses.
(e)   Problems of sequencing, i.e., whether mathematics and English should be done first or not.
(f)   Difficulties facing students who wished to change their minds.
(g)   Difficulties of assessment.

Finally, the whole plan still had to get university approval.

VIII

At the beginning of the next academic year, 1970–1, during which the first candidates under the new scheme would be interviewed and admitted, the area training organisation review of the colleges became more prominent. The submission made by the college to the review body would have to be ratified by the academic board. It would clearly be concerned with the college's intentions in respect of the mix of output, the curriculum and the like, and thus meshed very considerably with discussion of the new course structures. A committee was set up to examine the implications of the points listed above. But by now staff in general were forming a clearer picture of the implications for them of the new course structure. Feeling was now such that a general meeting attended by eighty of the staff, with the principal in the chair, was held.

He opened by reminding the company that 'the DES has become a little more restive each year' and that a change in the balance of training was inevitable. Uneasiness had been generated by the impact that the introduction of a more substantial element of method based courses was likely to have on the personal education of the students.

What became apparent to the assembly, though it must have been clear to some departments before this point, was that equalisation of misery was not possible. The change must affect departments differentially and hence increase tension. Some – PE, the sciences – were sitting pretty with 'Y' students by definition. Certain others – economics, heavy craft – could hardly adapt to a younger age-group and must perforce remain secondary. Others still, therefore, would have to accept a disproportionately greater reorientation, virtually to 100 per cent primary. This was a shattering prospect. 'You are literally doing away with some departments,' one of the threatened heads remarked. If they could not be allowed a few secondary orientated students the calibre of entrants would drop sharply – for example, in music. But once such a concession were granted the whole change would be undermined. There would be a fierce struggle for indulgences. The chairman thus insisted that only implementation could be discussed, not principles.

The extreme cluster 7 spokesmen who were most ideologically opposed to the change challenged the decision of the board, and indeed its very constitution. It was 'unrepresentative of the faculties'. (By the chances of election certain departments were unrepresented, including, that year, English.) Communication was held to be bad between the board and the staff; some staff were alleged to have preferential access to board communications. These criticisms were ruled out of order as fruitless and not suitable for prolonged discussion. (Board meetings were open to all. No one needed to feel insulated from communication, it was claimed, if he did his homework on the minutes and documents produced.) It was, as subsequent events showed, a vociferous minority who were discontented. Discussion then revolved around the following issues:

(a) That all departments should have some 'Y' students.
(b) That electives should be related to main courses, not free choice (to ensure that those subjects deprived of a second main would have a 'tied elective', i.e., English and drama).
(c) That the second main subject should be retained (a non-starter).

Great feeling was expressed in this meeting, though for all its alleged deficiencies, no one was able to point the way to a better solution than the existing plan. Alternative proposals were either arguments which had been considered by the board but had only just occurred to non-members, and thus had once again to be countered; or they were expressions of blatant vested interest; or they would leave the balance of training virtually unchanged in defiance of the DES. The plan was put to a general vote of the staff and passed by a huge majority (five only dissenting) though with obvious resignation before implacable facts.

The last part of this large open meeting was given over to a more general discussion of the place of colleges in the binary system in the face of competition from the polytechnics, then at an early stage of their development. According to my notes, it broke up 'not in disorder but in mounting confusion'. It did not assist morale. There was a discharge of feeling, but no constructive alternatives to the plan could be seen. The general feeling of the staff was one of powerlessness and baffled dissatisfaction. Vested interests had once more had an airing. There had been strident axe-grinding. There had been scapegoating of the board. But what this meeting in fact marked did not become clear until later. It was this. For twenty-five years the college had been in a sellers' market; for the last ten years it had been given its head. The DES had at length given a sharp tug on the reins, so that the staff were forced to become aware how vulnerable the college was to the outside controls of a determined government. It had come as a shock that the college had lost the initiative and had no countervailing powers once the teacher shortage had ended. A major evolution was to be forced on the college of which the changed balance of the curriculum was only the first, and perhaps not the most far reaching step. Tensions had been exhibited but not assuaged.

Further informal meetings of from five to thirty-five members were held to follow up the points raised. The role of the large and well organised education department became more conspicuous. Its strength in personnel and leadership made it prompt to act both in preparing proposals for the board and in responding to feedback by modifications, amplifications and lobbying for support. It had a well-developed machinery for gathering, evaluating and presenting information from outside college and its leader was close to the principal. Other departments were on one occasion described as 'encapsulated'. Departmental heads who did not systematically work through board decisions and argumentation with their staffs encouraged an information blockage that was hard to by-pass by the conventional machinery of circulating papers. But the integrationists, who were not opposed to the new plan in principle, spread well outside the education department. Even though departmental boundaries were well demarcated and defended, last ditchers were few, if vocal.

The degree of underlying acceptance of the basic direction was revealed in the January 1971 meeting of the board which ratified a document written by the head of the education department and the author, intended for submission to the ATO review body, as an official college statement. Discussion was very extensive and every member participated. No significant changes were made in the draft, or new ideas of substance proposed. The whole discussion could be summed up in a twenty line minute.

The issue was in the hands of an implementation committee and not reactivated until April. A notice was then exhibited expressing dissatisfaction with the working of the board, though in general terms. Its originators were the vocal dissident group, but it attracted thirty-three signatures from the staff. The prime mover was a cluster 7 hard-liner and member of the temporarily unrepresented English department. A full meeting of the staff was convened and presented with a paper by the latter, the essence of which is the following paragraph:

> If I am asked, 'What do you do at St Luke's', I say 'I teach English', or 'I work in the English department.' No other answer is possible for me. *Mutatis mutandis* no other answer is possible for *any* other member of the academic staff or for *any* student. A university is composed of faculties or schools. A college of education is the sum of its departments.

It followed that the academic board could not represent 'the interests of the college as a whole' unless it included a representative of all sixteen departments, exactly the number of elective seats. This was clearly a root and branch attack on the board and a serious matter. The principal, reading from the Instrument of Government, pointed out that only the governing body could reconstitute the academic board. In what was the board failing?

Another hard-liner read the notice and the paper. He pointed out that five small departments were not, that year, represented on the board. The board should consist of one representative of each department. There would be no elections, all interests would be represented, it would be more democratic. In support, a member of the staff who represented a small department consisting of himself, claimed that he was not represented on the board and felt disenfranchised. Two other left-hand side heads of large departments also pressed that representation be on a departmental basis. The essence of the complainants' case was expressed by another member of the English department who maintained forcefully that the first duty of a lecturer was to his subject.

Clearly the effect of these proposals would be to make the board a heads of departments meeting. Though departments varied from one member to twenty-two, each would have one seat. (The education department had twenty-two members.) The question was immediately put, 'Do we want a heads of department board?'; the answer was no! by acclamation. At this one of the two complainant heads said, 'But heads of departments represent the college', drawing a rejoinder from a by no means radical member of staff, 'Quite the reverse.' After some exchanges in this tenor the motion to continue the existing system was put to the vote and passed by a majority of fifty-one to twenty-eight. The result was strikingly similar to that taken at the meeting which constituted the board through a plan from the floor.

This was the last stand. The reader may well consider, taking account of what I think must be described as manifestly weak ground tactically, on which the complainants chose to take their stand, that the issue was as much symbolic as real. I think it an obvious, but fair, interpretation that the feeling aroused by the imposed change which could not be opposed frontally, discharged instead on the board. The most subject centred group, who saw their academic interests curtailed by the loss of second main students and diversion of effort into professional courses, protested most loudly. Clearly at the centre of discussion lay the question – Does the term 'the college' mean anything? Was it *just* an aggregate of departments? There is no unity in the product of the college since students belong to subsets of all departments. Nor is there any unity in the technology, since each department has its separate 'knowledge technology'. Any unity surely lies at the level of shared abstractions, that is, belief systems, common frames of reference, possibly even ideologies. Just as very different kinds of people can be 'patriotic' within a national community without it being very clear what this patriotism centres on, it could be argued I think, that the college, as a centre of loyalty and identity, transcends the departmental affiliations in some respects, and that these feelings predispose to a consensus. I think it might be held that the college embodies organised but partially discrepant belief-systems; that is what Cohen in his more dramatic phrase is getting at. They are organised round a negotiating system which operates formally through meetings, primarily those of the board, and informally through continually changing accommodations amongst staff. The discrepancies can be indicated empirically in the broadest sense, by the methods which produced the cluster diagram, and they show up during formal negotiations on important issues. Decisions are a compromise. If, however, any one of the belief-systems goes beyond these conventional procedures by propagandising, proselytising, exhibiting notices, setting up pressure groups, it is seriously threatening. Proceedings then have to be opened up to the full staff and the matter pressed to a final vote, despite the fact that votes are divisive. When this has to be done during a period of tension, it is likely to be a turning point.

By the end of the academic year 1970–1 it was possible to see how the new scheme would look in the round. About 30 per cent of students could be defined as 'Y' (secondary) in the PE science and economics departments. All others were defined as 'X' (primary). But some mathematics, biology, music and art/design (heavy crafts!) students were obviously secondary in orientation. In effect therefore about 25 per cent of students were in a vague marginal category. A number of departments wished to introduce at least some of their students into this category of 'modified X' students; so that in the wording of the minutes 'the original structure is becoming blurred and . . . the aim of the scheme is in danger of being lost'. It was only by pressing the matter to a vote that a slight modification to accommodate some craft and music students could be secured on that occasion and it was accorded most grudgingly.

IX

This was the last flicker of the formal decision stage. The final phase was resistance during implementation. Having reached a point in September 1971 at which a whole intake embarked on the new curriculum, the moment for frontal attacks had passed. The first implementation problem was that of assessment. It appeared possible for a student to fail, say, in professional course mathematics, and be heavily penalised for what was a relatively minor part of his total course in college. Nevertheless the course was not voluntary and had to be assessed, at least to determine a measure of practical competence; students could not all be passed as a formality. There was a debate of twenty-three minutes in the first meeting of the year between two cluster 6 academics and the promoters of the new course concerned with the possibility of able but reluctant students failing on a technicality. This was really about the rules of the game and who made them. There was further lamentation at the end of second main subjects, and demands for 'tied' electives.

A month later the scheme was embodied in a final booklet and presented to the board. There was an immediate altercation about the function of the professional course and the relation of curriculum electives to main subjects amongst the hard-liners and the professional course leaders. Since for conscientious reasons the religious studies element in the professional course could not be examined, an anomaly existed; and there was a degree of imbalance between the weight of demands made on 'X' and 'Y' students respectively. The argument had to be guillotined as 'an attempt to go right back to the beginning'. Whenever an administrative point arose the hard-liners used it to challenge the concept of the course.

Further there was the question of accountability. The professional course staff did not constitute a department, and there was anxiety that the education department should not control it. A committee (inevitably) was set up consisting of a member from each contributing department. Considerable trouble arose over the jurisdiction of the external examiner over professional course electives run by subject departments. The old squabbles between the long standing contestants were fought once more.

In January 1972 the discussion was reopened yet again, this time on the matter of students' work-loads. In essence the 'Y' course had only four elements whilst the 'X' course had seven. Once more the argument was for electives tied to main subjects (they were now renamed 'cognate' electives). Experience had shown to the resisters that 'students who are really "Y" but made to be "X" have a problem – some have withdrawn from the college over this'; 'volunteers to the "X" course are happy, but co-optees resent it'. Even more to the point, 'The main subject is being whittled away.' The 'X' pattern was described by the English department hard-liner as 'the disintegrated day approach', 'a travesty of higher education'. The minutes remark that 'discussion was both lengthy and tortuous, covering again most of the points discussed by the board over the last two years'. It had no outcome.

By the end of the year the matter had disappeared from the minutes, lost in the highly technical instructions for guiding students into an intricate network of elements with a wide range of choice. The James Report had appeared. It sounded the knell of the concurrent course. Beside its proposals adjustments stemming from the balance of training aspect seemed rather trivial. 'I complained because I had no shoes', the proverb runs, 'until I saw a man who had no feet!'

X

For institutions like colleges of education the key task for the introduction of curriculum innovations seems to be the management of working accommodations amongst the internal belief and priority systems, whilst promoting the enterprise's adaptation to the requirements of a changing environment, information about which is not easy to interpret. The task, in short, lies in the areas of tension management and strategic policy not in the area of operations.

It is, to adapt words from Lynton (1969), a matter of successfully overcoming the rigidities associated with successive revisions in the code of priorities current in the enterprise, as one set of environmental demands and the group and outlook it favours replaces a former one and the outlook which accompanied that. The environmental demands may be changing within the world of a particular discipline, the special sub-environment of a department; or the change may be in the general environment of the whole system of higher education. Whether the plurality of outlooks is called with Goffman 'definitions of the situation', or with Silverman 'meaning structure', or with Vickers 'shared systems of interpretation',[4] they certainly give meaning to communications originating both inside and outside college and differentially filter perception of what is happening. They are not simple, nor unitary, nor universal in the enterprise. Each new opportunity or requirement which stems from changed circumstances will be differentially appraised by different groups; what is a threat to some (whether the change in the balance of training or the recommendation of the James Committee for a consecutive instead of a concurrent course) is an opportunity to others; and to all it is an occasion fraught with the possibility that the present pattern of power distribution, and with it the sharing of resources, may be drawn towards or away from what they see as their vital interests.

Yet it is through the steady appraisal and revision of priorities, area by area, as the situation demands, and by embodying the results in decisions, particularly strategic ones, that the enterprise maintains its relationship to the environment, survives, overcomes entropy. To do this it needs consent. But this is not, however, the unitary consensus imagined by F.W. Taylor, and not necessarily a long-lasting agreement with established principles, a settled, institutionalised set of priorities. Rather, it is a requisite consent, for the here and now, holding in the area under consideration but not necessarily binding upon other areas of decision, and not necessarily enduring if the situation changes again. The broadest consensus, that which is the basis of publicly taken academic board decisions, needs continually to be kept up to date by the receipt and digestion of information, an activity which takes the form of digressive and often inclusive discussion, not obviously leading to a particular decision. This raises a point I shall return to, namely that in complex situations where information is difficult to get and to interpret, individuals and interest groups do not know what their objectives and preferences orders are, in detail, except when they are faced with a specific decision, a particular choice. They have to find out. And being unsure, they give a guarded, requisite consent on a particular issue, in the prevailing circumstances. They do not readily overcommit themselves to major policy statements. The achievement of this level of consent is the primary objective of management in this type of institution.

The new entrant to college is confronted in the process of socialisation to the enterprise with a plurality of sub-meaning-systems which mediate communications to him particularly about goals, values and priorities. He is usually guided by one member of staff, most often the head of department. From the beginning he is involved in departmental discussions and decision-making. He needs to find out what are the limits of his autonomy. As his informal contacts grow, centred on the staff club, he can voluntarily opt-in to an informal information network. His prior experience in the profession, mode of recruitment, exposure to prior courses orientated to college teaching, familiarity with colleges, and so on, will have the effect of filtering perceptions and influencing the emphases which he puts on the information that gets through. His departmental membership is of course related to these other variables; but it seems clear that it is not departmental membership which most influences the position on the dendrogram spectrum in which he falls. Staff with very varying positions in the clusters are in the same department. There is some accommodation of the actor to the structure: respondents do report changes, often of considerable magnitude, in their personal outlook as a result of working in college. Only for a small minority are these a source of frustration and unhappiness, and in nearly all these cases the scope of their work is a chief source of the difficulty. There is also some adaptation of the structure to the actor. Courses can be changed, options provided, to give new staff access to a preferred work area; personal enclaves and 'niches' can be achieved; the professional course is flexible and offers an important sphere of activity to generalists. New sub-units have been set up, a major structural change in the English main course was introduced to accommodate children's literature, and the first-year course of the education department was fundamentally reorganised to meet the more up to date views of a group of newcomers. Most significant of all (and however obvious, it ought to be stated) the academic board itself is a major structural change to accommodate staff – and eventually, as it turned out, students' – desires to share in, or at any rate witness, decision-making. Overall, and this is a key characteristic of educational enterprises, the degree of bureaucratic constraint on the individual is low. The price paid for this is the time spent in trying to co-ordinate activity and to discover policy by negotiations and discussions.

The enduring content of these discussions is:
(a) Control over conditions of work – staffing, nature of facilities and equipment, access to facilities, allocation of time, pattern of courses and teaching practices.
(b) Planned changes in personal and group relationships – control of staff and students, new sub-units, boundaries between main, professional and education courses, supervision of teaching practice.

(c) The rules of the game – administrative understandings about allocations, finance, division of responsibilities, access to information, who makes decisions.
(d) Clarification of meaning in new choice situations – whose interpretation is to be accepted? What frame of reference is to define the situation? Which code of priorities is to be adopted? Who is entitled to change the rules?

Zald (1962) has illustrated a similar process in the more dramatic situation of an American correctional establishment, stressing how a lack of clarity in the goals and incompatible policy outcomes combined with a degree of independence of groups on the staff led to problems of conflict management. In such situations the attempt to proceed by first defining the primary task is unproductive, partly because the task merely designates an area of activity without offering any guide to priorities or sequences of operations; but also because this approach would invite divisive ideological assertions about codes of priorities. It seems wiser to adopt an action frame of reference which seeks to analyse how people by observable processes maintain different definitions of reality and yet interact effectively. Enterprises, like persons, can harbour incompatibilities and yet persist.

The plan laid before the board in 1969–70, and discussed over a two year period, to substitute a professional course with elective elements for the compulsory 'B' or second main course, illustrates the protracted process of exploration, negotiation and learning. The view taken of the functions of the electives, the resistance to the principle of the change, the development of contracting out, seeking to lengthen elective elements until they resembled second main courses, argument about how the course is to be assessed, all offer opportunities for different definitions to find expression and influence the way the plan was implemented. Plans are changed, handbooks of courses are rewritten, the balance of components in joint courses is modified, new accommodations for small groups of students are accepted. What is conspicuously absent is a constraining written document passed by vote and used to impose a central policy on departments.

It would be misguided in the light of this to perceive the processes on the board as a power struggle in any naked sense, except on rare occasions. The power of the governing body can be invoked ('They won't stand for it') as occurred in the matter of the size of the original board or any threat to the position of religion in the college. The governors could veto proposals which might threaten the institutional basis of the college's existence. It is the main function of the governing body to protect and legitimise this (as is shown by the need to reconstitute the governing body from the moment that the college began to do degree work again). There may be pressure on the administrative bloc by teaching staff as in the matter of getting information about the estimates. But, as in the matter of buildings or contingency funds, the administration can seek to maintain that these are not directly academic matters. By not attending, the senior administrative officer can leave his interests in the safe and nearly unchallengeable hands of the principal. The students may press matters not espoused by any staff member, such as their desire for participation in the appointment of the new principal, the nature of their representation on the board, or the nature of the evidence to be presented to the ATO review body. They are, however, few and inexperienced in committee procedures.

The most plausible view seems to be one of circulating initiatives in leadership according to what task is before the board. No group is seeking to vanquish and direct; only to redefine boundaries in specific areas, promote a different code of priorities, assert principles (as of public accountability and discussion rather than private lobbying) or otherwise modify the rules of the game. The goals of the college do not fall into any obvious hierarchy; what is at stake may at times be legitimacy, effectiveness or adaptation. The criteria of achievement in any area are not clear, so that no group can show itself to be demonstrably achieving at a higher level than others, and so apt for leadership. The principal's style is one of facilitating accommodations, avoiding issues likely to lead to explosions, minimising occasions for divisive voting. He maintains harmony even at the cost of a slack rate of business and toleration of garrulity by his manner as a chairman, wit, manipulative dexterity, occasional prevarication, verbal skill and exploitation of very high personal prestige (not to mention occasional off the board negotiations and minor *faits accomplis*). He always remained behind for social discussions over drinks after the board meetings.

Below the chairman there is a hierarchy of power and influence related to size of departments and the spread of courses given by a department. These tend to go with experience of the consequences of decisions and awareness of the problems of co-ordination. But length of service in college, personality, standing with the staff and fertility of initiatives also count. The powerful opinion leaders tend to speak on almost every issue; in the first year of the board four of these contributed between a quarter and a third of all interventions, balancing the administrative bloc. Other members tend to act as watchdogs for special areas, speaking selectively on areas of their concern. The emphasis is upon avoiding conflict and challenges, and minimising occasions for voting. It might be argued that when the underlying technology depends upon personal relationships as it does in educational enterprises, rather than upon a machine technology, harmony is a major test of the effectiveness of management. Difficult and unpopular tasks are not always faced, such as the rational use of resources and money; thorny problems survive, such as the fair allocation of staff and work loads; not rational public objectives but negotiated settlements amongst segregated interests govern what is done. A negotiating stance is continuous, but it should be noticed that negotiations are amongst groups formally equal in status, not, as in the somewhat similar situation described by Strauss[5] amongst doctors, administrators, nurses and ancillary staff, where status differences add complications. Generally the students accept the situation, though they are well aware of some of its dysfunctional outcomes. The bureaucratic constraints upon them are also loose, and one suspects that they can and do, with experience, 'play the system' to their individual advantage like experienced hospital patients studied by Strauss. No student group I interviewed believed there was any organised counter-culture opposed to the system amongst the student body.

XI

A continuous negotiation process, institutionalised but not heavily formalised, and rooted deep in the culture of the enterprise, is at the heart of curriculum decision-making. Because its outcomes include both co-ordination of activities, and the discovery of implementable policy which gives these activities direction, the crucial managerial tasks consist in sustaining, facilitating and guiding this process and as far as possible increasing its effectiveness. I return here to my previous point. The decision-maker is as unreal as the economic man of the nineteenth century who could always instantaneously calculate and state his preferences. It is much more plausible that in situations such as that of the college, people only start to clarify their objectives, preferences and ends, in such a way as to enable them to make deliberate and systematic choices in conditions of uncertainty and low precision of information about consequences, when they are actually faced with the realities of a choice situation (Lindblom, 1958a and b). There is no well established theory to guide them. When generalised debate took place, as it did in *ad hoc* meetings on various occasions during the research period, gross differences among the major outlooks and interest groups showed clearly. But finer differences underlie week by week policy, choices and allocations. The importance of negotiation, whether at individual, departmental or board level, is that it reveals to participants as much their own preferences as other people's; and not in principle or hypothetically but on specific issues, in some detail and at the crunch. Additionally, the routine ways of implementing decisions and monitoring operations and performance, allow an increasing insight to be gained by a large group of staff into the integration of values and policies. The participants and observers learn more of both; retrospective evaluation becomes more realistic and responsible.

This helps to explain why the observable partisan groupings, coalitions, systematic opposition and so forth, which I had originally expected to develop, did not clearly appear. Even if the small extreme groups and unique cases are included, there is a degree of consensus on very general normative values, though, of themselves, these impose no priorities. Because of this, despite inevitable degrees of reluctance, there is usually a widespread agreement on the general character, direction and nature of foreseen change, such as, for example, enabled the college to submit evidence to the ATO review body without dissent. Particularly after the opinion leaders have pressed home the significant features of the general case under consideration (strength of DES pressure, financial position, availability of teaching places, the university's attitude, etc.), consent to strategic policy is not withheld. The long experience of smooth growth and its consequences has created a degree of confidence in managed change, so long as the change is not of a drastic order. Provided that it takes the form of small incremental changes made one sector at a time, it is not too difficult to foresee what will be the short term consequences. The possibility of reversing the movement without dislocating the organisation remains reassuringly in the background.

No formal policy manifesto seeking to command or impose assent is made, but rather a succession of bit by bit decisions that *some* change, more or less in *this* direction, emerges. The domain of decision under view can be kept small. Problems can be taken area by area as they appear, separated in time and without a pressing need to reconcile decisions in different areas until the discrepancy shows up as another limited problem some time in the future. Each member can hope to keep the number of considerations he has to be concerned with down to manageable proportions; those with wide concerns can use their large departmental meetings and interdepartmental negotiations to clarify their position. Although major decisions, such as fundamental changes in course structure, may be fragmented, and incompatible decisions are taken, in the meantime some progress is made; and the mutual adjustment of groups over serially presented choices is much simplified. The situation is too complex to allow for comprehensive policy statements except of a vague anodyne type, for they would close down the options and invite resistance and evasion at departmental level.

No one can say in any detail what would be a good future state of the college save in a purely Utopian or narrowly ideological way that would amount to no more than the assertion of one value system. Organisational learning comes from situations of marginal choice in which different value systems are exercised and competitively scrutinised in a situation of decision, not a merely verbal, speculative debate. In such circumstances it is likely that proposals will be evaluated for small resulting improvements not relative to some single, simple, major goal. More threatening, perhaps, in the situation in which the college finds itself, than ideological assertions about goals, is a refusal to think, an excess of devotion to previous procedures, an unwillingness to face up to a changing environment and new tasks.

I conclude that the decisions of the academic board are the results of low temperature partisan group activity. Interests ignored by one group are vigorously championed by another; or if not, as in the case of the interests of the extreme cluster 7, a new spokesman emerges on the board to defend them as they are recognised. To be successful any initiative must be reasonably acceptable to group interests upon which it will impinge. But the process of finding this out is largely public; reasonableness and reciprocity are fostered; and there is usually ample time. At best the result is an integrative solution where all get most of what they want, rather than a reluctant compromise. It can be a slow, untidy and energy consuming process. If in the future a situation arises where major decisions have to be taken quickly (until now a relatively rare thing for colleges) it seems likely that they will be taken not by the board but by the governors, the principal or a small inner steering committee. In the meantime the college can be content to cherish the benign and civilised aspects of a political process.

Notes

1 R.B. Ivemey-Cook, 'Programme for the analysis of taxonomic data', unpublished paper; A.M. Mather, *Cluster Analysis in the Natural and Social Sciences*, University of Nottingham, Department of Geography, 1969.

2 Department of Education and Science, *Teacher Education and Training* (James Report), London, HMSO, 1972.

3 Department of Education and Science, *Education: a Framework for Expansion*, London, HMSO, 1973.

4 E. Goffman, *The Presentation of the Self in Everyday Life*, Harmonds-worth, Penguin, 1969; D. Silverman, *The Theory of Organisations*, London, Heinemann, 1968; G. Vickers, *Freedom in a Rocking Boat*, London, Allen Lane, 1970.

5 A. Strauss, in E. Friedson (ed.), *The Hospital in Modern Society*, New York, Free Press, 1963.

3 Curriculum Development in an Art Project
Decker F. Walker

Editors' introduction

One typical response to the need to develop new curricula is to set up
a 'temporary system' independent of existing structures to design and
disseminate course plans and teaching materials. The inhabitants of
this system – generally known as a 'project' – can devote all their
energies to the task in hand, free from the call of other commitments,
can take a fresh look at the problems, unhampered by the authority
of existing solutions, and can utilize the insights of those who are
expert in the techniques of curriculum planning. This at least is the
theory. Walker sets out to test how far it is reflected in the reality of
one particular project by making a careful observational study of
how it reached decisions about what to teach, and what curriculum
plans and materials to develop.

Most curriculum theory follows a rational-scientific ideal which, in
Walker's words, 'holds out the promise of progress in practical
affairs through the combined application of a thorough-going means-
end analysis and scientific techniques of data collection and analysis',
confining the 'value-laden aspects of practical action to the initial
stage – the selection of final results to be achieved'. Therefore one of
the most interesting questions for him, in studying the Kettering
Project, was the extent to which the team did in fact follow a strategy
of this type and engage in the kinds of data collection which it would
imply. The answer was – hardly at all. But rather than concentrate
on the *negative* question of why the team did not behave in the way
that theorists might have approved of, he attempts the much more
difficult exercise of defining in a *positive* way the activities they
pursued and seeing how these might be conceptualized. Instead of

words like 'objective', 'analysis' or 'demonstration' he finds himself
having to employ terms such as 'platform', 'policy' and 'deliberation'
(this last providing an interesting parallel to Shaw's use of
'negotiation' in the previous paper). Working with very little to guide
him apart from his own observations of the events, he arrives at a
quite elaborate model of the process of curriculum planning which is
very different from that normally advanced in the textbooks. Nor is
his experience entirely unique. It is confirmed in its broad outlines
by his own observation of other projects, as well as by descriptive
literature produced by others as a record of the work of development
groups. But as well as seeming, empirically, to offer a reasonable
account of the activities of at least some project teams, the model also
has *explanatory* features which enable us to see why it is very likely
that curriculum groups should behave in the ways which it predicts.
If further studies support Walker's position, then we must take very
seriously his conclusion that we should stop trying to replace the
'natural' process of curriculum planning by artificial prescriptions,
accept 'deliberation' as one of its essential features, and apply our
resources of science and rationality to improving the quality of
deliberation and making it more effective.

I

In the late 1960s curriculum projects seemed to be everywhere. In my
four years as a teacher I had been involved in two projects, one in science
and one in art. Then I had come west to study education in hopes of
learning how curricula should be developed. I had seen what seemed to
me to be an inordinate amount of fumbling around, of false starts,
uncoordinated effort, misunderstandings of purpose, failures to sustain
an agreed-upon directness across long units of work and just plain
mistakes of conception and execution. I thought there must be a body
of lore somewhere that would enable curriculum makers to profit from
the insights and mistakes of their predecessors. Surely others with more
experience who had been able to give the problem more thought would
have written of these things ?

But when I began to read in curriculum I found advice that seemed
appropriate to another activity altogether.[1] 'First, state your objectives':
yet neither of the projects I had worked with ever stated objectives, nor
did it seem likely to me that doing so would solve any of their problems.
'Consult a variety of people representing as many points of view as
possible': but both of 'my' projects had had trouble explaining to a
few new staff members what they were attempting. Their problem

seemed to be how to fend off outsiders who would raise issues already settled among the staff at great cost in time and energy. When the advice in the literature seemed relevant and helpful, as in the general admonitions 'to screen proposals through a philosophy of education', and 'to base development on a thoroughly considered psychology of learning', all too often it also seemed too general to help much.

Therefore, when I learned that Professor Elliot W. Eisner, who, ironically, then taught the curriculum course in which I had read the unhelpful advice, was starting a curriculum project, I approached him with a proposal to observe and chronicle the project. I explained that I hoped either to make the connections that now seemed absent between the literature and actual practice or to expose the inconsistencies and look for ways to resolve them. That, in brief, was the origin of the series of studies of Professor Eisner's Kettering Project reported here.

The purpose of this research was to discover through an intensive study of one case how curriculum projects make decisions about what to teach and what curriculum plans and materials to develop. More specifically I wanted answers to the following three major questions:

1   *How did the Project team reach a common understanding of the purpose and direction of their work?* (Did they rely on objectives for this? If not, what sort of statements did they use for this purpose? How was agreement secured and maintained?)
2   *How did the Project team organize its work?* (What tasks did they undertake, in what order, in what manner?)
3   *How did the Project team use its understanding of the purpose and direction of the work to produce plans and materials?* (What procedures, formal or informal, were used to develop plans and materials? What information and assumptions or presuppositions did these procedures require? To what extent were these procedures and assumptions rationally defensible?)

To answer these questions I employed several investigative techniques, including participant observation, the administration to the Project staff of a rating instrument, an intensive content analysis of the Project director's publications, and an intensive formal analysis of transcripts of portions of the Project team's working meetings. These will be reported in detail, along with the conclusions drawn from them, in the subsequent pages of this chapter.

The immediate stimulus for the creation of the Kettering Project was an inquiry directed to Professor Eisner from an officer of the Kettering Foundation. The official had read something of Professor Eisner's work in which he had pointed out, among other things, how certain beliefs about the very personal role art played in the lives of young children had led to virtual abandonment of efforts to teach them art. Art had been seen as a purely natural outpouring of the child's developing psyche, not to be spoiled by the imposition of adult skills and ideas. Eisner decried this practice as educationally irresponsible and wasteful of artistic capacities that without proper instruction would probably remain undeveloped. The officer of the Kettering Foundation wanted to know if Professor Eisner had any plans to produce curriculum materials to implement these ideas. Whatever his intentions at the time of the inquiry, Eisner soon submitted to the Kettering Foundation an application for a grant of $70,000 to develop a curriculum in the visual arts for elementary school-age children. The application was approved, and in the fall of 1967 the Kettering Project began its scheduled two years of life.

In his previous writing and in the proposal submitted to the foundation, Eisner had already laid down many of the ideas that would form the basis of the Project's work. The first members of the Project staff he selected were from among doctoral students in art education studying with him. These students were already familiar with his ideas concerning the teaching of art. To round out his staff to the final number of seven graduate students, Eisner added in the subsequent weeks two other graduate students in general curriculum. These two students were selected from among a larger number who had expressed some interest in joining in the Project's work after hearing about it in one of a number of informal talks Eisner gave on various occasions in and around the school. In these talks Eisner emphasized those of his ideas that differed most from traditional wisdom. This usually disturbed some members of the audience who took very seriously such injunctions as the one that forbade adults to interfere with children's artistic growth, and questioning after these talks was frequently quite animated. Those who found Eisner's ideas unacceptable did not approach him about working on the project. A few who were intrigued by the ideas did make some sort of overture, and from these Eisner selected the other two members of his staff.

This staff then began meeting two or three times a week early in the fall of 1967. A typical meeting would begin sometime in the afternoon and last for one to three hours. The ten people who met – Eisner, five graduate students in art education, two graduate students in general curriculum, a product designer who was employed half-time by the Project, and this investigator – would sit around a table in a small back room of an old frame house on the Stanford University campus. From one to eight conversations flourished as we waited for stragglers. Within a few minutes of the appointed time Eisner would begin the meeting officially in any of a number of ways, such as by outlining what he hoped would be accomplished that day or by asking what problems were most pressing.

No matter how it began, the meeting invariably grew by seemingly natural processes beyond the control of any person or agenda, and it usually did so rather quickly. Arguments were common, but orderly and task-oriented. The group was, as far as I could tell, free of personal disputes, acrimony and bitterness. Even when feelings on substantive questions ran high, as they frequently did, people were open to reason. Not infrequently a group member would abruptly drop a passionate defense of some course of action when someone else pointed out a decisive flaw in it. Eventually someone would formulate the problems that seemed to be emerging from the discussion. After the issue at hand was disposed of, another would arise. Finally, someone would announce that he had to leave soon for another meeting or that he was getting hungry, and that would serve as the cue for closing the meeting.

The Kettering Project continued to meet over the next two years, more frequently in the early months than in the later ones, and more frequently when any sort of new ground was to be broken. Outside the meetings, members of the staff worked individually or in pairs on specific assigned tasks. The writing of lessons, for example, was done in this way, with meetings devoted to discussion of problems that individuals had encountered in writing them. After a few months, when the staff had constructed some lessons that they felt were adequate, teachers were sought out who could use the lessons with children while members of staff watched and reported back on successes and failures. The group of about twelve trial teachers who participated in this way were recruited in the spring of 1968. Trial teachers did not attend regular meetings; they met with the staff on Saturdays three times during the Project's two years. Otherwise, their contact with the Project staff came on visits made to their classrooms by individual members.

In their first few weeks of discussions the Project staff made several decisions that shaped their subsequent work. They decided to prepare some lessons immediately, rather than, say, prepare flow charts of the whole Project's work, or write a rationale or other planning document. Also they decided to do lesson writing outside staff meetings, working individually or in teams of two, reserving for general discussion only questions that arose in the outside work. This decision meant that the work would be divided into two ongoing parts – *production* of lessons and support materials and *discussions*, or as I later came to call it, *deliberation.* Another early decision which shaped their work in an important way was the decision to identify three *domains* of learning in art: the *critical* domain, concerned with learning how to look at art, how to deal with it conceptually, and how to consider judgments about aesthetic quality; the *productive* domain, concerned with how to *make* art; and the *historical* domain, concerned with the record of man's achievements in art and their relations to other spheres of life. The Project's intention to *instruct* children in each of these domains was seen as one of its important innovations in the teaching of art in the elementary school. Most current art teaching for young children focused entirely on the productive.

These and other early decisions played an important role in shaping the Project's work. For example, they began by writing lessons in the critical domain. First each person attempted simply to write a lesson which was then critiqued. In discussion of these lessons, it became apparent that it would be more economical to identify some of the most important learnings in the critical domain before attempting to write more lessons. So they searched for a few basic concepts and principles that would, if carefully taught, enhance young children's ability to deal with art critically. The activities of the staff and to an unknown, but surely large, extent the results they got, depended in important ways upon ideas they began with and decisions made early on the basis of these ideas.

Figure 3.1 shows the major activities of the Kettering Project from October 1967 – a few weeks after the project began – until its termination in May of 1969. The chart divides the Project's activities into two parts – discussion and production – in recognition of a corresponding division in the work itself. The Project's work can be divided into several rough stages. The first three months of the project were devoted mainly to discussion of matters related to the writing of the critical lessons. The lessons written during this period were later scrapped almost entirely, but the discussions surrounding them were instrumental in determining the shape of the second generation of lessons. The second phase of the Project's work extends from about February 1968 until May 1968. In this period the critical domain lessons were written again and tried out in several elementary classrooms in the area. In the third phase, extending approximately from June 1968 to September 1968, work was divided about equally between creating first lessons in the productive domain and filling in uncompleted parts of the already largely completed critical lessons. The fourth phase, from about September 1968 through January 1969, was concerned primarily with producing enough finished materials for use in the several trial class-

	Oct-Nov(67)	Dec-Jan	Feb-Mar(68)	Apr-May	Jun-Jul	Aug-Sept	Oct-Nov	Dec-Jan(69)	Feb-Mar	Apr-May
PRODUCTION	1st lessons written (critical); 1st list of basic principles written (critical); materials developed (critical)		critiques of 1st lessons (critical)	lessons rewritten (critical); observations of teachers in tryout of materials (critical); revised lessons criticized (critical)		production of materials for use in classes (critical and productive); lessons written (productive)	observations of teachers in tryout of materials (critical and productive); lessons criticized (productive); teacher report forms produced		observation forms produced; test items made; teacher report forms collected	
DISCUSSION	domains of art educ.; format for lessons; how to get feedback from tryouts; how do we articulate materials and lessons?; role of 'terms' in teaching	critical lessons debated, discussed; materials box debated, discussed; technical pedagogical problems are discussed (such as how to show some visual phenomenon); how are critical/productive related			productive lessons criticized, debated	procedures and instruments for evaluation; what remains to be done to get books and materials to teacher; merits of slides v reproductions; format for lessons; discussions of classroom observations and teachers comments				

Figure 3.1   An overview of the tasks undertaken by the Kettering Project staff from the fall of 1967 to its conclusion in the spring of 1969

rooms then in operation, and with discussions of how the lessons would be evaluated. The final phase of the work, from February 1969 to the end of the Project, was concerned mainly with the creation of evaluation devices and with evaluating the lessons using these devices.

Several features of the Project's method of operation are noteworthy. One is the way topics for discussion are concentrated toward the left or early side of the chart. More topics were discussed in the early months and, although it does not show on the chart, more time was spent in the early months on discussion than on production, while the reverse was true in the later months. Notice also that several different activities were carried on during any one time period. Only in the final months when evaluation was the only thing left to be done did any one activity occupy all of the group's time and energy. Notice, too, that discussion and production proceeded together, though discussion frequently turned to new topics before production was completed. To a certain extent this reflected the group's practice of jumping in first to try to do it, and then discussing problems as they arose. It is easy to imagine another group spending some time on discussion before attempting to write any lessons. It is not conceivable to me that a group might have begun producing materials more than a few days before having to discuss related matters. First attempts at writing lessons in an area always gave rise to scores of questions, large and small, on which agreement among members of the Project team was essential, and discussion of these matters seemed quite urgent. In fact, I would go so far as to say that no agenda could be covered that did not include discussion of problems encountered in working on a new set of lessons; the staff would simply interrupt and insist that they could not work any further without getting some things cleared up.

If we were to look more closely at what went on during the meetings, we would see that while at the highest level of generality the Project staff consciously shaped its work, deciding what to turn its attention to, in what order, with what purpose, the details of the work arose in a spontaneous and unpredictable way. 'Decisions' about what matters to discuss, for example, were typically made by someone trying to change the subject, to introduce a new topic. If others protested and asked for more time to discuss the matter currently under discussion, then the current topic would be discussed further. If others took up the new issue, the topic was changed.

A closer look at the discussions would also show an intricate interplay between abstract ideas or notions and concrete practical considerations. Sometimes a 'difficulty' posed itself as a seeming contradiction between different leading ideas. Sometimes it arose as a purely practical difficulty – cost, a lesson that took too long or seemed too difficult, and the like. But much more frequently the difficulties that arose concerned the articulation between abstract ideas and practical action. Was a certain sort of lesson consistent with a particular idea to which the Project was committed? Did a decision to scrap a particular lesson mean that an idea heretofore accepted was now being rejected or simply that this particular lesson was defective? In short, the gross features of the Project's work were generally consciously designed on the basis of leading ideas and practical demands. Art was divided into domains, decisions were made to produce lessons and materials for use by typical classroom teachers with no special training in art, and time was allotted accordingly. But the finer features of the Project's work were determined largely on the spur of the moment on the basis of an intuitive sense of what was most pressing and important.

This brief overview of the Kettering Project's work is thoroughly consistent with what I know of other projects' work from my previous and subsequent experience and from written accounts. Recent curriculum projects typically did *not* set aside time at the beginning of their work to state objectives. If objectives were stated at all, they came in the course of the development work, not before it. Furthermore, the projects did not usually employ formal evaluation procedures during the development of their materials. Evaluation came after they had produced materials they considered to be reasonably satisfactory. The development was done by a small, homogeneous group of subject specialists with past teaching experience, but not by practising teachers, and with no significant involvement of students, school administrators, or laymen. In all these respects the operations of curriculum projects were inconsistent with practices advocated in the curriculum literature.

When a project staff first sit down to talk together, they are already agreed on many principles that help them define their task. For example, in most cases the project involves the teaching of an established academic subject. The planners know what other students have studied about this subject, and what scholars have written about it, and this common knowledge helps them work together as a team. But initial agreement goes only so far. There are sure to be disagreements about important matters even among people who have received a similar training in the same tradition. Furthermore, a project that did nothing more than repeat past practice would hardly be worth doing. A project must begin with some innovative ideas as well. How do members of the project team get together on their ideas for curriculum reform? And once they have reached agreement, how do they maintain it over months of work together?

In the case of the Kettering Project, the main outlines of an answer to these questions are already apparent from what has just been described about the Project's work. Initial agreement came in part from selection and self-selection of persons to be members of the team. Those who were not enthusiastic about the approach described to them might pursue the matter no further, nor, if they did, were they likely to find a warm reception from the director or the rest of the staff. Eisner's talks and writings no doubt persuaded many who had not already formed strong opinions on the matters he spoke and wrote about. And in some minor matters individuals swallowed their reservations in order to get on with the work.

To a large extent the Project began with the ideas of one man. As they worked, these ideas were supplemented, modified and, in rare and relatively unimportant cases, abandoned. All members of the team played a part in this fine tuning of ideas, but the starting point was established by the Project director.

This concentration of initial ideas in the mind of one person is not unusual in curriculum projects of recent vintage and it is most convenient for one who would study in some detail the nature and form of expression of a project's initial purpose and direction. Fortunately Eisner had expressed his ideas in several published articles.[2] A preliminary investigation seemed to indicate that the ideas accepted and used in the Project's early work coincided in large measure with the ideas expressed in these articles. So a logical beginning seemed to be to launch a search through these articles for statements which would indicate in any way the kind of curriculum the author preferred.

Accordingly, every statement in them which seemed in any way capable of helping the reader form a more accurate image of the kind of art curriculum material or activity the author would prefer was transcribed on to an index card. When more than one statement was found which expressed the same idea, all but one were discarded. Statements expressing separable ideas in separate clauses were rewritten as separate simple statements. This procedure yielded ninety-nine statements. Table 3.1 shows a selection of almost one quarter of these,

TABLE 3.1   Major planks in the Kettering Project platform

Art

1 An understanding of the culture of which a work of art is a part can enhance its import both substantively, in terms of its historical meaning, and formally, in terms of its qualitative meaning.

2 Theories of art call to our attention what is significant about art.

3 Artistic activity is among the most sophisticated and highly complex modes of cognitive functioning of which men are capable.

TABLE 3.1—*contd.*

Art education

4 A variety of skills and understandings beyond those found in the studio are important, indeed necessary, for providing an adequate education in art.

5 Linguistic labels, vocabulary if you will, can serve as handles or tools for thinking about important phenomena in art.

6 What art education has in common with other fields is less important than what it can provide that is unique.

7 Art education has no franchise upon creativity.

Teachers

8 The teacher of art has a responsibility for instruction in art and is not to be merely a stimulator, motivator, and dispenser of media.

9 The teacher should have curriculum options.

10 The teacher should not only understand the concepts, principles, objectives, and attitudes he is to use, but also the reasons why the concepts or principles are important.

Children

11 Even very young children can be helped to obtain both competence and satisfaction in the visual arts.

12 Students need to learn how to look at art, and they need to have tools with which to look.

13 When students have overlearned the basic technical skills in handling a medium, they can feel free to concentrate upon expressive and aesthetic issues.

Curriculum

14 A curriculum in art should select and arrange activities so that they require the use of more complex and sophisticated forms of behavior as students progress.

15 *Any* subject, well taught, can develop the creative thinking abilities of students.

16 Theories of child development and learning in art are at best general and do not provide as much direction for formulating curriculum activities as the experience of good teachers and doctoral students in the field.

Materials and activities

17 Media are vehicles for the development of perceptual and productive skills and concepts as well as material out of which something is to be made.

18 Every unit that is formulated should contain an array of instructional materials designed specifically to enhance and facilitate a specific type of learning.

TABLE 3.1—*contd.*

---

19 Materials must meet at least three criteria for classroom use:
   (*a*) They must be clear enough to be used by a teacher relatively untrained in art.
   (*b*) They must teach nontrivial content.
   (*c*) They must be interesting and appropriate for the range of children for whom they are intended.

Evaluation
   20 Accompanying each unit or lesson within a unit there should be one or more suggested evaluation procedures.
   21 There should be instruments designed to assess productive skills, critical skills, and knowledge and understanding of art history.
   22 Evaluation materials should provide the teacher with feedback regarding the effectiveness of the activities and materials that have been employed.
   23 The quality of the product of an art activity is a major data source for making inferences about what children have or have not learned.

---

arranged by several important themes. The reader can judge how rich and detailed a picture of the Project's purpose and direction they provide. Some evidence will be provided later on the extent to which these statements actually represented the Project's shared sense of their purpose.

I was especially curious to discover whether these statements took the form of objectives, i.e., specifications of end results to be achieved. If all these statements were in the form of objectives or could be translated routinely into that form, then current practice and received wisdom about curriculum making would be consonant. On the other hand, if many of these statements seemed to be substantially and irretrievably different from objectives, then some sort of adjustment would be in order.

Simple inspection of the statements seemed to indicate that few of them actually specified results to be achieved by an art curriculum for young children. For example, in table 3.1 only statements 4, 12, and 21 specify what children should learn in an art curriculum. Several other statements, 1, 5, 13, and 15, for example, strongly imply certain objectives. But many statements remain that can be squeezed into the form of an objective only with great difficulty if at all. Consider statement 2 in table 3.1. 'Theories of art call to our attention what is significant about art.' It tells us that the author considers theories of art to have a legitimate function. But it does not tell us whether the author would favor teaching young children about theories of art. Consider statement 8: 'The teacher of art has a responsibility for instruction in art and is not to be merely a stimulator, motivator, and dispenser of media.' It certainly does not specify what children are to be able to do after instruction. Equally certainly, however, it does give the reader some information about what sort of curriculum its author would prefer. Most of the remaining statements have a similar character. They convey something of the author's curricular intentions, yet they do not say what final result is to be achieved with students.

Having reached this conclusion, I then decided to study *how* each statement informed its reader, what sort of information it gave, and what function this information might play in the early stages of curriculum development. After much study it seemed to me that the statements could be divided into five distinctive types based on the sort of information they provided and the form in which they provided it.

Aims state what the project intends to do or produce. Educational objectives – statements of desired student learnings – belong in this category. *Aims* guide one in visualizing the final curriculum plan by specifying directly what that plan or its components are intended to be or do. 'The child needs to develop the ability to conceive, to visualize, and to imagine' is an *aim*.

Explanations are generalizations which relate two or more elements of importance in curriculum making – such as characteristics of teachers, learners, or art – to one another. Since *explanations* specify relationships which are supposed to exist between elements of the final curriculum plan, they provide important information about that plan. 'There has been some work in psychology and linguistics that suggests that linguistic labels facilitate some types of perceptual acts . . .' is an *explanation*.

Conceptions, like *explanations*, relate elements of the curriculum plan to one another and they, too, inform by specifying relationships that are supposed to hold between elements of the plan. *Explanations*, however, specify a kind of relationship which is in principle empirically testable. In contrast, the relationships specified by *conceptions* are not empirically testable *even in principle* because they define, characterize, or classify or because they involve a value judgment. Roughly speaking, *conceptions* show how the world is being divided up while *explanations* show how the parts are to be put back together. 'What art education has in common with other fields is less important than what it can provide that is unique' is a *conception*.

Exemplary products describe learning devices, classroom activities, or other curriculum products which are considered to be models worth imitating. An *exemplary product* can be thought of as a kind of concrete *aim* specified by pointing at a curriculum material or instructional plan or policy. 'Devices can be constructed which will illustrate important visual concepts by allowing students to change selected features of a work of art using plastic overlays' is an *exemplary product*.

Procedures describe a particular way of going about some part of the task of curriculum planning. They describe how the group should proceed in various situations. 'Each activity should be accompanied by a series of evaluation exercises to help the student and the teacher to assess the effectiveness of the activity' is a *procedure*.

Each of these five types of goal statements – *aims*, *explanations*, *conceptions*, *exemplary products*, and *procedures* – has a distinctive form. To make sure of this I trained six other persons to distinguish among them and found that they were able to distinguish them almost as well after only a few hours of training and practice. To be specific, after training their categorizations agreed with mine 70 per cent of the time. I believe they also function in distinct ways. That is, each helps to specify purpose and direction in its own way. But for the present this must remain a matter of speculation.

However this may be, it appears certain that when members of a curriculum project try to explain to others what they are about, they resort to a variety of different types of statements. In the case of the Kettering Project, 30 per cent of the goal statements I was able to identify were *aims*; the remaining 70 per cent were split among the other four types as follows: 34 per cent *conceptions*, 16 per cent *explanations*, 6 per cent *exemplary products*, and 14 per cent *procedures*. An analysis of similar articles by members of three other projects, at least one of which relied heavily on objectives in their work, showed similar patterns.[3] In none of these articles did the number of *aims* exceed 30 per cent of the total number of goal statements.

So far, the identification of goal statements taken from Eisner's articles with the shared initial ideas of the Kettering Project is an assumption, plausible but unsupported by direct evidence. To see if Project members really did accept these ideas as their working basis, I constructed an instrument in which I asked them to rate a large number of statements of their probable usefulness in orienting a new member of the Project. The instructions read in part:

Imagine that you were assigned the task of composing from these statements and these statements alone, a message that would be given to a Stanford graduate student in art education entering the Kettering Project this fall. In this message you should try to give him the kind of guidance that would be maximally effective in helping him to write lessons, devise suitable support materials, and in all other ways to function as a full-fledged member of the Project . . .

Staff members were told to rate each of more than a hundred randomly ordered statements presented to them according to the following scheme:

A   A rating of A given to a statement indicates that the statement would be a *very useful* guide to a person working on the Kettering Project. Such a statement should certainly appear in the message to the new member.

B   A rating of B indicates that a statement would ordinarily be a *somewhat useful* guide, but for some reason it is not as useful as statements rated A. Such statements might appear in the message with some *reservations* or *qualifications* attached to them.

C   A rating of C indicates that a statement is of little or no value in guiding a new member's work. Such a statement would be *omitted* from the message.

D   A rating of D means that a statement reflects, by and large, an opinion or position that the Kettering Project would be *opposed* to. If such a statement were included in the message it would be used as a *negative example*, that is, it would appear with some negative phrase attached such as 'This statement expresses an opinion to which we are generally opposed.'

E   A rating of E indicates that a statement is a *very useful negative* guide in that it expresses an opinion which the Kettering Project *rejects*. Such a statement would be *openly repudiated* in the message to the new member.

The members were not aware when they were rating the statements that forty-eight of them (eight groups of six statements each) were direct quotations from Eisner's articles. The forty-eight statements consisted simply of six goal statements of each of the five different types I had distinguished, the number six being chosen because I had only found six *exemplary products* in my analysis of Eisner's articles. I chose from the larger number of statements of other types according to my judgment of which statements seemed most important in Eisner's articles and in the Project's work, because I wanted to include the best specimens I could find of each type.

The ratings given by the eight members of the Project staff to these thirty statements are shown in figure 3.2. This figure makes apparent the fact that *all* statements were generally endorsed as useful in a positive sense. (This was not true of all the statements included in the instrument. In fact, considering all statements taken together just as many statements were given ratings of C, D, or E as were given ratings

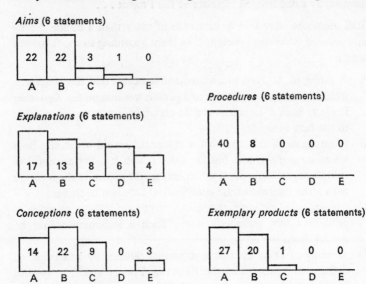

Aims (6 statements)

22	22	3	1	0
A	B	C	D	E

Explanations (6 statements)

17	13	8	6	4
A	B	C	D	E

Procedures (6 statements)

40	8	0	0	0
A	B	C	D	E

Conceptions (6 statements)

14	22	9	0	3
A	B	C	D	E

Exemplary products (6 statements)

27	20	1	0	0
A	B	C	D	E

Figure 3.2   Histograms of ratings given to each type of goal statement by the Project staff

(N = 8 persons × 6 statements/type = 48 ratings per type of statement)

of A or B, whereas among this group of thirty statements taken from Eisner's articles, positive rankings outnumbered neutral and negative rankings combined by more than eight to one.) Furthermore, *aims* were not rated as more useful than the other types of goal statements. On the contrary, *procedures* and *exemplary products*, the more concrete forms of goal statements, were rated as being more useful than *aims*. On the other hand, *explanations* and *conceptions* were rated slightly less useful than *aims*.

Members of the Project staff, it appears, agreed that the goal statements taken from Eisner's articles would be useful things to say to a potential new staff member, and they did not find statements cast in the form of *aims* to be more useful than statements cast in the other forms. These findings pose problems for those who argue that objectives are essential starting points for curriculum development. It remains to be seen whether the Kettering Project might have done better work if its members had relied more on objectives. Still, they did develop a curriculum package, and when they began this work they expressed their sense of purpose and direction in a number of different forms, objectives being one of these, but by their testimony not an especially useful one. Furthermore, it appears that other projects, even some who relied rather heavily on initial statements of objectives, also relied on a variety of types of goal statements in attempting to convey their purposes to outsiders. This result sharpens further the contrast between actual practice and received doctrine.

II

The body of initial ideas shared by members of a project team on which they base their work I have called the project's *platform*, by analogy with the platform of political parties. The central role in which the platform was cast throughout the previous section may have left the reader with the impression that the rest of the curriculum making task could be little more than logical deduction from platform beliefs. Such an impression would be misleading. The platform is necessary and it facilitates the work but its application to the practical problems of curriculum making is by no means automatic, for several reasons. First, the platform is incomplete. One cannot anticipate all the working principles he will need. As the work progresses the need for principles of some unexpected kind will become acute and they will be devised and incorporated into the platform. Second, platform statements are too vague and imprecise. One must have some guidelines to interpret general principles and make them bear sharply on concrete situations. Any concrete situation falls under several principles. When viewed in the light of one principle one situation may be desirable. Under another equally applicable principle the same situation may be undesirable. Interpretation is required to disentangle the overlapping jurisdictions and to establish hierarchies among the elements of the platform.

In short, the platform must be elaborated and interpreted before it can be applied to concrete problems. Consider the following example of elaboration of the platform taken from the transcript of the February 27 meeting:

EISNER: These technical skills are specific kinds of skills that can be taught in a series of productive lessons which will develop competencies that can be used in working aesthetically and expressively and, hopefully, creatively in the visual arts with the visual materials.

MARTHA: Now, when they are concentrating on those technical skills though – are you looking for any particular aesthetic outcome or are you just trying to, at that point, get the children to know how to use the skills?

EISNER: I think that it is quite possible to have exercises which are not concerned at all with developing anything that is aesthetic or anything that is hang-upable or displayable, simply – let me give you an example – Just putting a line across the paper just to see how straight those lines can be – you know – that is nothing that we are concerned about with respect to – it is simply to develop some kind of competency. Doing motor exercises – where you repeat the same form. You know – to develop *that* kind of skill [gestures], which it has to give a certain kinaesthetic motor control. Now, once they are able to do this – then this can be employed in things that you want to work with which *do* have aesthetic and expressive characteristics. So to answer your question now simply – in the development of productive activities there can be identified activities which are of an exercise nature – which are strictly technically oriented activities.

MARTHA: Now how do you classify the type of thing – like children are taught, for instance, a variety of ways of using crayons say to get different effects? Like, you know, on the side, or with the point or rubbing hard or –

EISNER: Those are technical skills.

MARTHA: But they don't end up – sort of like – they don't end up with much, they are just practice exercises.

EISNER: That's right – just practice exercises and the thing is now – once having 'discovered' that the crayons can be used in these various ways, now if you are doing a drawing with crayons you have expanded, so to speak, the repertoire that the kid can employ in dealing with the production of a visual field.

A project with a sound, comprehensive, but as yet unused platform is in somewhat the same position as our legal system when a new law has been passed. The formulation and passage of the law is only the beginning of an often extensive set of precedents that must be established as that law is applied to particular cases. Similarly, agreement on a platform principle in the Kettering Project was only the starting point of a process of particularizing, clarifying and extending shared knowledge and perceptions of the group's goals and standards.

The platform – a shared system of beliefs and working principles – must be transformed into policy: 'definite courses or methods of action selected ... from among alternatives and in the light of given conditions to guide and usually determine present and future decisions' (*Webster's New International Dictionary*). The process by which this transformation takes place is the subject of this section.

It was plainly evident to me when I was observing the Kettering

Project, and I hope it is clear to the reader by now as well, that in the simplest terms the answer to how platform became operating policy is simply this: they argued about it. For instance, the Kettering Project was committed to a particular sort of role for the teacher. Yet they argued about how to get feedback from the teachers on the strengths and weaknesses of their trial lessons. The Project was committed to having children work with reproductions of recognized works of art. But they argued about whether this was better done with slides and a projector or with paper reproductions mounted on cardboard. Should the lessons be written so as to allow for more circling back to previous topics? Should productive lessons be mixed with critical lessons so as to show how the ideas can be applied, or should the two be confined to separate portions of the school year? Is this or that idea too sophisticated for young children? Most of the Project team's hours together were spent discussing some such question.

The same appears to have been true for other projects as well. For example, consider the following descriptions of how the School Mathematics Study Group operated:[4]

Those selected to write first drafts had to be prepared for criticism of their efforts of an almost unprecedented intensity. It is not too much to assert that the critical reading of SMSG material prior to its publication exceeded that devoted to any similar textbooks ever produced, with respect to both quantity and quality. . . . The criticism of a writer's first draft was usually devastating, and it took persons of great character and dedicated purpose to accept it cheerfully and carry on with the preparation of a second draft. In many cases, a writer had to be prepared to see his work completely rewritten by another person, who, in turn, might have his effort rewritten by a third. One writer, upon seeing some material he had originally written come across his desk in fourth draft form, remarked that all he could find remaining from his treatment were the punctuation marks!

This continuous writing and rewriting, discussion and criticism, suggesting and commenting was the very essence of SMSG production.

In most groups it was soon found that when differences of opinion arose, it was better to keep talking and bringing out pertinent ideas until there was general agreement instead of voting on the issue prematurely.[5]

Not all of the talk that occurred in a project was of this sort, however. There was the usual amount of agenda-making and -reviewing, making of announcements, reviewing progress to date, and the like. So it is well to distinguish at the outset that I was and am concerned with the intellectual processes of inquiry, judgment, decision, and action that preceded, surrounded, and underlay the design of a curriculum. Talk that is directed toward such substantive problems is most aptly called *deliberation*. This term is most familiar as a characterization of what a jury does after the evidence and arguments have been heard and prior to the announcement of a verdict. Aristotle taught that deliberation was the process by which one determines what he should do when he has a choice and when there is no exact knowledge by means of which the choice can be resolved. He contrasted deliberation with demonstration or proof which served the same function in areas like mathematics and logic where exact knowledge was thought to be possible. Deliberation, by contrast, provided only justification for actions in those practical endeavors (morals, politics, medicine, navigation, and the like) wherein exact knowledge did not seem possible.

A number of recent writers have turned their attention to deliberation as a process of reasoning, most notably in education, Joseph Schwab; in philosophy, David P. Gauthier and Stephen Toulmin; and in political science, Charles Lindblom. In my treatment of the Kettering Project's deliberations I have made free and heavy use of their ideas.

In the Kettering Project's deliberations a wide range of topics was discussed in a variety of ways for many different purposes. The group reached decisions by consensus. When this consensus could not be attained on a question the decision was postponed or, as the Kettering staff said, 'put on the back burner'. No crucial decisions were deadlocked in this way. Occasionally one member of the group, usually Eisner, would give an impromptu talk or lecture designed to convey information or to organize information for the group. No deliberation or decision-making of immediate significance to the Project's work went on outside meetings. Therefore what was said and done in the meetings was the final word on any subject.

These features – decision by consensus, a variety of topics, a variety of treatments, talks, the back-burner – have been identified by casual observation. Other seemingly more important and certainly more evanescent regularities can be identified in the same way. For example, the Kettering Project's deliberations exhibited ebb and flow of intensity. At certain periods events pressed in upon the staff; they would devote up to an hour of intense debate to one question which seemed somehow crucial. Usually this general area of concern had been a subject of less intense scrutiny for several meetings. After the question was resolved, that area of concern dropped out of subsequent deliberations almost entirely. Thus progress in the deliberations seemed to occur in spurts in relatively circumscribed areas of the Project's concern. Like an amoeba the Project lurched forward by extending the very stuff of its life – its deliberations – in localized forays into the territory ahead.

But my goal was to devise objective methods for discovering and exhibiting the regularities I thought I was able to detect in deliberation. In pursuit of this goal I first tried to see what a simple record of who made each statement would reveal. It showed some of the ebb and flow of deliberation quite plainly, for there were some periods in which the floor changed hands rapidly and others in which one person talked for a long time. I next tried to categorize the subject of each statement. This proved a difficult job, because a single statement could be about many different things; as a result I did not have such confidence in my own categorizations. Still, the ebb and flow of deliberation stood out quite clearly in peaks representing a concentration at one time of statements about the same subject and valleys representing periods when that subject was not mentioned at all. I was also heartened by the fact that the peaks and valleys on the two charts frequently coincided. I was also surprised to find that so many statements seemed to be about the Project's own affairs – ideas, problems, methods of operation, goals, and the like – and relatively few were about the sorts of things that are traditionally supposed to be considered in making curriculum decisions – learners and their characteristics, the society, the subject, teachers and their characteristics, and the like.

This informal investigation made me more curious than ever about the form and content of curricular deliberation. Would the ebbs and flows be sufficiently distinct to be used as separable episodes whose significance in deliberation could be assessed individually? Could ways be found to articulate smaller units which could in turn shed light on the structure and function of these episodes? Could ways be found to deal with the content and meaning of these units as well as their form? In short, could I find a way to analyze the details of curriculum deliberation that would reveal the order and rationality I thought I saw there?

For this formal investigation I chose a small sample of the Kettering Project's deliberations, about three consecutive hours of deliberation which had taken place in three meetings spread over a week and a half near the middle of the Project's life, and sought out similar samples of deliberations from other curriculum projects. I was eventually successful in obtaining permission to work with tape recordings of the meetings of two other curriculum projects, both, as it turned out, in elementary science. These recordings were transcribed and the transcripts numbered line by line for reference and reproduced for use by the judges I had in mind to train to use the system of analysis I was then developing.

As I studied other samples of deliberation and authors such as Schwab, Gauthier, Toulmin, Lindblom, and Aristotle on deliberation, a three-tiered scheme of analysis began to evolve. The grossest and most general level of analysis would attempt to locate *episodes* in the deliberations. I understood an episode to be a consecutive portion of transcript having a degree of unity and coherence and being separable from the surrounding discourse by subject and style of discussion. One type of episode I knew existed was the *issue*. An *issue* consisted of argumentation concerning what course of action the project or some part of it should undertake or follow. Discussion of *issues* took the form of rapid and brief contributions from a number of people arguing different positions on a single problem or family of related problems.

As I thought about the meetings I had witnessed and listened to tape recordings of many of them, ideas for other sorts of episodes occurred to me. Eventually I settled on four types. In addition to *issues*, I proposed *explications* – little lectures by one more knowledgeable member of the Project explaining some situation to his colleagues; *reports* – a recounting of the activities of some member or subgroup for the information and enlightenment of the others; and *brainstorms* – rapid fire generation of suggestions for solving some problem or coping with some situation. It seemed to me that somewhere in my past experience with curriculum projects I had seen a number of examples of each of these episodes. The problem now was to determine whether these episodes were sufficiently distinct from other discourse to be differentiated from it and, if so, whether I could describe these four well enough to enable others to spot them.

A second, more detailed and microscopic level of analysis would search for smaller units that I called *deliberative moves*. These were single remarks or a contiguous series of remarks performing one of a specified number of functions in deliberation. *Statements of problems* (*problems*) served the function of identifying for everyone involved what was the problem they were dealing with or should be dealing with. *Proposals of courses of action* (*proposals*) served to suggest things the group might do, usually but not always in response to a given problem. *Arguments for* and *arguments against* gave reasons why something, usually proposals or problems, was or was not useful or important.

These three deliberative moves were suggested by various treatments of deliberation, especially those of Schwab and Gauthier. But as I experimented with these categories on portions of recorded deliberation other than those to be analyzed by other judges, I thought I saw a need for two other moves – *instances* and *clarifications*. *Instances* were neutral references to specific objects, events, or situations offered as illustrations of some abstraction. *Clarifications* were remarks serving to elaborate or rectify another deliberative move. *Clarifications* were unique in that they served to modify one of the other types of moves. For this reason, a *clarification* of a *problem* was recorded as a part of the *problem, clarification* of a *proposal*, and so on. These moves seemed necessary because I frequently found in my preliminary trials of the categories (on portions of deliberation other than those to be analyzed by the judges) that a long speech would consist of material all of which contributed to one main point which was a deliberative move of some sort, but that this one point was stated in only one brief remark, or sometimes not directly stated at all. In the heat of debate a person might offer an example instead of an abstract characterization of his point. Similarly many people had a tendency to begin with a crude but dramatic and simple statement of their position, perhaps to get attention, and then clarify it in their later remarks. By adding these two deliberative moves, I felt the system would be more inclusive and would more faithfully represent what I understood to be going on in these discussions.

The third tier of the three-tiered scheme of analysis consisted of categories for analyzing the content of various deliberative moves – what topics or subjects they were about, and what information or data they made use of. Since the number of significant questions one might ask about these matters is impossibly large, I decided to focus my energies on the analysis of *arguments*. These were likely to be the most frequently occurring type of deliberative move, and my hunch was that they were closer to the most interesting intellectual activities involved in deliberation, for it was in *arguments* that the developers came to grips with conflicting or opposing considerations.

After constructing and trying out several classification systems for studying the data in *arguments*, I finally settled on two systems, one designed to characterize where and how the data originated, and the other to characterize what subjects the data were about.

The first system consisted of the following four two-valued categories:

1 *Observational* or *judgmental* – Is the item of data cited an actual observation; or, is it a judgment based on experience, conventional wisdom, or speculation?
2 *External* or *internal* – If this item of data is observational, does it come from within the project, its members, or its meetings; or, do the data come from the world outside the project?
3 *First-hand* or *reported* – Was this item of observational data gathered by a member of the project: or, was it reported by someone outside the project or in a book or other outside source?

4   *Purposefully* or *incidentally obtained* – Was this item of observational data actively sought by one or more project members; or, was it obtained fortuitously?

Given an item of data in an *argument*, the judge, using the system, was to classify that item in one of each pair of categories.

The other category system included in this third tier of the analysis characterized the things that were the objects of the group's attention in their *arguments*. This category system is in reality two sets of categories. The judge must first decide whether data cited in a particular *argument* concern internal matters or external matters, or both. If he decides that this item is entirely about internal matters, then he must decide whether or not it is about each of the following six internal subjects:

> staff members
> curriculum materials
> curriculum strategies (activities or approaches to teaching art)
> objectives
> curriculum framework (specialized terms or concepts)
> resources (the project's time, money, space, etc.)

If the item is not about any of these subjects but is nevertheless about some internal matter, it should be placed in an 'other internal matters' category.

If the judge decides that this item is about an external matter, then he must decide whether or not it is about each of the following six external subjects:

> students
> teachers
> schools
> society
> subject matter
> resources (somebody else's time, money, etc.)

An 'other external matter' category was provided in case the item fit none of the foregoing ones.

If a judge decided that an item was about both an external matter and an internal matter, he was instructed to classify that item in both sets of categories.

With this three-tiered '*System for Analyzing Curriculum Deliberations*,' as I christened it, I hoped to exhibit some of the regularities I sensed in deliberation and to discover something more of the structure and dynamics of curriculum deliberation.

Tier I: THE MACROSCOPIC ANALYSIS
    – consists of the identification in transcript of the following
     deliberative episodes:
      Issues
      Explications
      Reports
      Brainstorms

Tier II: THE MICROSCOPIC ANALYSIS
    – consists of the identification in transcript of the following
     deliberative moves:
      Proposals
      Arguments for
      Arguments against
      Clarifications
      Instances
      Other deliberative moves

Tier III: THE CATEGORY SYSTEMS
    – consists of the application of two systems of categories to
     some of the deliberative moves identified in Tier II.

    Category system A: data sources: are the data:
     Observational or judgmental?
     First-hand or reported?
     External or internal?
     Purposeful or incidental?

    Category system B: subjects of data: what are the data about?

Internal matters	*External matters*
staff members	students
curriculum strategies	teachers
curriculum materials	schools
objectives	society
conceptual framework	subject matter
resources	resources
other internal matters	other external matters

Figure 3.3   Outline of the categories employed in the System for Analyzing Curriculum Deliberations

Identifying episodes in deliberation proved to be difficult and not too rewarding. My own analysis revealed that while four-fifths of the lines in all three transcript samples fell within an episode of one type or another, thirteen of the seventeen episodes I identified in the three transcripts were *issues*. For this reason these samples were not good tests of the objectivity of the other three types of episodes. Furthermore, the agreement between the two judges I trained to perform this analysis and my own ratings was only slightly greater than ·50, much greater than chance and therefore great enough to indicate a modest degree of objectivity in the analysis, but not great enough to make the analysis practically useful. One bright spot in this otherwise disheartening situation was that the portions of transcript not showing any episodes seemed to contribute little to the curriculum making task, consisting mostly of discussions too brief to qualify as episodes or purely organizational talk. Probably the most important shortcoming of the first tier of the system was its low benefit/cost ratio. The identification of episodes required fine judgments to be made throughout the reading of a long transcript; training took several hours. And in the end all that was to show for this effort was a slicing of the discourse into a few 'natural' units.

I came away from this part of the study with my faith in the orderliness of deliberation unshaken, bolstered, in fact, by the degree of agreement obtained, but pessimistic about the practical value of such a difficult and unrewarding enterprise.

Luckily the even more complicated second tier of the system proved to be easier to learn and gave more interesting results. The coefficient of agreement between the other two judges' ratings and my own was 0·71, quite a satisfactory figure for a system as complicated as this one. Apparently deliberative moves are easier to spot than episodes.

Here is a portion of the Kettering Project's deliberations analyzed in the study. See if you can find examples of *problems, proposals, arguments,* and *clarifications*:

EISNER: Any other observations about Saturday's meeting?

GIL: Well, I talked to you about this yesterday but one of the things that impressed me was this call for repeatability of some of the concepts that these teachers were talking about – the need for repetition in the primary grades and I was talking to Dr Eisner about the fact that perhaps in terms of turning out new lessons – rather than applying them to new principles, we should be writing new lessons for the principles we already have written lessons for with different activities, so that the teacher would have the repertoire of four different activities to reinforce the same principle – which she might pull out – one this week, one the next and one the next, and she could be reinforcing the principle without teaching the same lesson over again, which I think is probably something that the teacher would like to have actually.

BILL: I don't see the need of this, because just by the nature of the material and the way it flows there's continual opportunity for reference to refer back to review. And these lessons I'm developing now, I'm stating this as part of the lesson and trying to use the same reproduction throughout so that the teacher can continually review back to what has gone before.

GIL: I think it depends, too, on what we're talking about. Now your for instance – your lessons on primary and secondary colors, I doubt if you'd need to repeat this without changing it pretty drastically. But I think when you're getting into concept-learning of the kind that would be in say composition or even some of the coloring lessons that would be later on, when you're talking about emotional values and so forth. Then I think you want some built-in repeating.

BILL: Well, this is why I'm doing this. These lessons I am dealing with now deal with emotion and feeling. But to sit down and re-write another, you know, ten or fifteen lessons just for additional activities, say or. . . .

GIL: Well, it isn't only this. It's also the fact that what we've done is, we've written one lesson for one principle and we're getting it tested, but how do we know that another lesson for that principle might not be a lot better, and might get better learning, too, for the class, be accepted better by the teacher? If we only have one lesson for each principle, we haven't tested any possibilities but one.

JACK: It takes, though, a couple of class sessions to get across that lesson and then there's a certain amount of repetition kind of built into it. It would seem also that a teacher who was worth his or her salt could very easily construct supplementary activities.

Figure 3.4 shows in graphical form the deliberative moves present in this bit of deliberation. The entire portion is a discussion of one *problem* – the need for repetition in the lessons. The *problem* is stated, a solution proposed – have new lessons devoted to principles previously covered instead of to new principles – and *arguments* offered for and against the *proposal*. In the course of these *arguments* another *proposal* is made – using devices within the lessons, such as a fixed and recurring set of reproductions, to insure repetition rather than writing new lessons on the old ideas – and *arguments* offered for and against this one. Formally, this is a perfect example of discussion of an *issue*. Most people are surprised, as I was initially, to discover, as this form of analysis permits one to do, the intensity and thoroughness with which such matters are discussed. At first listening, these discussions seem like cocktail party arguments. But the closer look provided by this part of the System for Analyzing Curriculum Deliberation shows clearly that it is highly compact and task-relevant argumentation. In the space

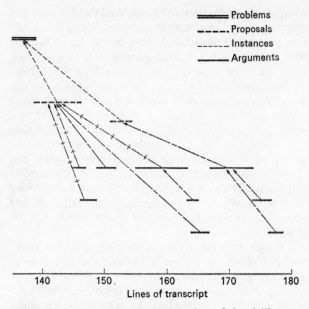

Figure 3.4   A graphical representation of the deliberate moves found in an excerpt of the art transcript quoted in the text

of less than three minutes this project team has formulated a problem for discussion and considered at least nine arguments in an effort to respond appropriately to the problem. (More arguments may have been considered but left unspoken because they were judged to be defective or not sufficiently powerful or important.)

This analysis of deliberative moves seemed to represent about 70 per cent of the transcripts very well – every line was part of a move and the moves fell rather clearly into one of the five established types. This 70 per cent included essentially all of the lines I had judged to be part of *issues* or *brainstorms* in the earlier analysis of episodes and some of the lines that were not included in any episode. The 30 per cent of transcript not well represented by deliberative moves included the single *report* identified and the single *explication*, as well as the remaining non-episodic material. Hindsight makes this finding not surprising since *reports* and *explications* are not basically argumentative, but rather informative and pedagogical in function. Perhaps eventually categories will be devised which illuminate the structure of these two types of episodes.

The basic pattern represented in figure 3.4 – a *problem* followed by several *proposals* (four on the average), each accompanied by a number of *arguments* (six on the average) and an occasional *instance* (one and one-half on the average) – covered about half of the well-represented portion of the transcripts. The other half exhibited many of the same moves but not in this pattern. *Issues* and *brainstorms* consisted almost exclusively of moves arrayed in this basic pattern, *brainstorms* differing from *issues* in having more *proposals* and fewer *arguments*. The one *explication* and the one *report* identified in the transcripts showed a small number of deliberative moves approximately equally distributed among the five types, except that the *explication* showed practically no *arguments*.

The boundaries of *issues* and *brainstorms* coincided with the discussions of *problems*, so that each of these episodes can be thought of as consisting of the discussion of a small whole number of *problems*. This result lends credence to the earlier analysis of episodes, but it also tends to make this analysis superfluous: if an analysis of deliberative moves would also identify the boundaries of episodes, why search for episodes separately?

While some *problems* were discussed for up to almost an hour, half of them were discussed for less than fifteen minutes, and one-third of the *problems* stated received no discussion at all. This could indicate that the staff was not spending time discussing just any *problems*, but were exercising a fairly severe critical judgment concerning what *problems* deserved discussion.

In all these respects the differences among the Kettering Project and the science projects were small. They suggested differences in style rather than fundamental differences in method or approach to curriculum making. The major differences found were: One of the science projects tended to spend less time discussing each *problem*; the other science project showed more *arguments against* than *arguments for*, in contrast to the other projects where this situation was reversed; and the Kettering Project showed fewer *arguments* in proportion to other moves. Otherwise, there were no substantial differences among the three transcripts.

The samples of curriculum deliberation I had chosen for analysis were not exemplary, but typical. I could not help wondering if good deliberation might not have a form quite different from that disclosed by this investigation. To find out, I read through all three transcripts again looking for impressive examples of deliberation. I did not try to define good deliberation in abstract terms; I simply responded to what I read holistically and impressionistically. If a portion of transcript struck me as better than the rest after I had thought about it for a time, I marked it as an 'exemplary' portion. Eventually, I identified seven exemplary portions, three in one science transcript and two in each of the other transcripts. I then performed on these exemplary portions all the analysis I had already performed on the entire sample. The results showed no substantial differences. Figure 3.5, for example, shows the proportions of different types of deliberative moves in the exemplary sections as compared with the proportions found in transcripts as a whole. The only difference between good deliberation and the ordinary run from a purely formal point of view seemed to be that good deliberations are slightly richer in all deliberative moves than ordinary deliberations.

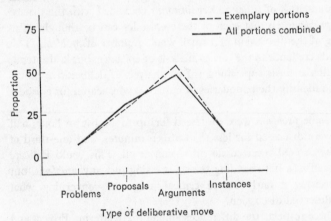

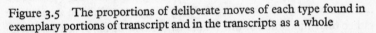

Figure 3.5 The proportions of deliberate moves of each type found in exemplary portions of transcript and in the transcripts as a whole

All things considered, this tier of the system seems to me to be successful. Although the analysis is difficult and time-consuming, the distinctions that must be made seem to be objective and capable of being carried out with almost any desired degree of reliability. The analysis really does seem to grasp some essential features of deliberation as I know it. Having used it for a while, I find it easy and natural to think of deliberation in these terms, to the extent that I sometimes find myself mentally constructing diagrams like figure 3.4 while listening to a discussion. I also find it helps me remember essential points made in fast-paced, wide-ranging discussions. It should be of help to someone who wants to keep a condensed, running record of extended deliberations. And I thought the moves identified in this way could be subjected to separate and even more intensive analysis of their substantive import. This was the purpose of the third and final tier of the system.

In devising the categories for content analysis I was guided mainly by a desire to compare actual practice with received wisdom. It seemed to me that one of the strongest traditions in the curriculum literature was the rational-scientific ideal of curriculum determination, stretching from Franklin Bobbitt, generally regarded as the first professional writer on curriculum, through Ralph Tyler and his many followers to modern day behavioral scientists and educational technologists. The rational-scientific ideal holds out the promise of progress in practical affairs through the combined application of a thorough-going means-ends analysis and scientific techniques of data collection and analysis. The basic strategy here is to confine the value-laden aspects of practical action to the initial stage – the selection of final results to be achieved and to conduct all subsequent activities in strict accordance with the demands of scientific rationality. One of the characteristics of this ideal is the value it places upon the use of objective data secured in a scientifically defensible fashion from direct observations or experiments with students attempting to learn from the materials. Neither the Kettering Project nor either of the other two projects carried out formal studies of student learning during development. But it still might be reasonable to ask whether the facts they did appeal to in their deliberation had few or many of the characteristics of good data according to rational-scientific ideals.

The first part of the content analysis, therefore, called for each argument to be read and for four judgments to be made about the factual basis, explicit or implicit, upon which it rested:

Is the item of data cited an actual *observation*; or, is it a *judgment* based on experience, conventional wisdom, or speculation?

If this item of data is observational, does it come from within the project, its members or its meetings; or, do the data come from the world outside the project?

If this item of data is observational, were the observations made by a member of the project; or, was it reported by someone outside the project or in a book or other source?

If this item of data is observational, does it appear that the item was actively sought by one or more members: or, was it obtained fortuitously?

Figure 3.6 shows the results for the transcripts from all three projects. It shows that slightly more than half of the *arguments* were based on judgments rather than data; that about equal numbers of *arguments* judged observational were later judged to have arisen inside the project and outside it; that of the *arguments* based on actual observations, an overwhelming majority were observations made by members of the project; and that most of the observations were made incidentally rather

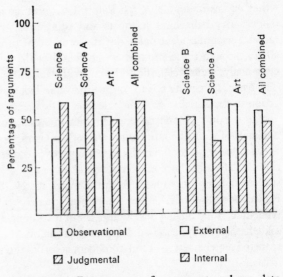

Figure 3.6 Percentages of arguments whose data originated in different ways

than purposefully. A straightforward application of the rational-scientific ideal would indicate that *arguments should* be based on *observations* rather than judgments; that the observations should be of students in schools and thus *external*; that they should be made *first-hand*, although reported data should be acceptable if it reports scientifically defensible observations; and that the observations should have been made *purposefully* rather than obtained fortuitously. Judged by this ideal, the data on which these projects based their deliberations were far from satisfactory.

The important question, of course, is whether the ideal is at fault or the practice. Reliance on good judgment by experienced persons can certainly be more economical than exclusive reliance on actual observations – scientifically adequate observations are expensive. But the economics are false if the judgment differs from what good observations *would* show. So the question hinges on how much faith one has in the judgment of project members. This, in turn, depends upon the question being considered. For example, I would place great faith in the collective judgment of Kettering Project members concerning the value or

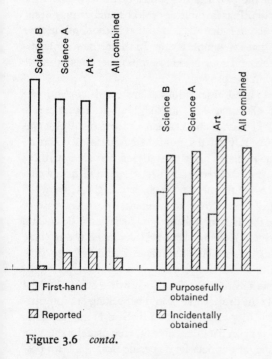

Figure 3.6   *contd.*

importance of an item of content from one of the domains of artistic learning. On the other hand, I would be more dubious of their judgments about students' reactions to such an item. Moreover, I can appreciate that persons of good will could differ very much in the amount of skepticism or credulity they were able to tolerate in curriculum development. For this reason, I doubt that a resolution of this difference is possible. We must simply live with the fact that people differ in the degree to which they are comfortable in relying on judgments instead of direct observations.

The relatively large number of arguments based on internal observations reflect the heavy reliance placed on observations of early prototype versions of materials. From the point of view of the project staff, the production of curriculum materials and strategies – lessons, apparatus, plans for activities, ways of handling important types of situations – is the immediate pressing job. They spend most of their time working on these or talking about them. And most of this working and talking is based upon what they find out in their personal experimenting, tinkering, and manipulating. *Arguments* based on internal observations also arise in consideration of the practical difficulties of carrying out some action under consideration. For example, a project member may argue that a certain course of action is out of the question because of the time it took to construct just that one sample lesson. In short, there are legitimate reasons for citing observations made in project meetings or in the work of individuals within the project.

Heavy reliance on first-hand observations seems consistent with the rational-scientific ideal of curriculum making, but it, too, raises a problem. Any one group of eight people can make only so many observations. Normally scientists rely on the published reports of others to supplement their observations. This almost never occurred in these projects. If relevant and useful observations have been published, which I doubt, they were not used by these projects, nor, I think, were the projects aware of the existence of any such reports. A special case of this general pattern is the lack of reliance on social and behavioral science data or conclusions. None of these projects made use of these in this sample of their deliberations, though each did refer to such works in their platforms.

It is difficult to imagine a justification for so many data being obtained incidentally. Presumably the project staff would be seeking out information bearing on problems they encountered. Yet the evidence seems to show that they happened upon data that later became useful more than twice as often as they sought out data for a specific purpose. Two possible explanations suggest themselves. Perhaps the group sought out all the data they could seek, given their limitations of time, energy, money, and the like, but still found themselves forced to rely frequently on fortuitously obtained information. Alternatively, the project staff may have consciously adopted a strategy of scanning a wide variety of situations, remaining alert for anything of significance that occurred. Even so, one would expect them to check such data by deliberate observations if this was possible. So I am left with one of two conclusions. Either the expense of seeking out data in response to specific needs was too great, or the staff was content to use data obtained incidentally. The former procedure seems defensible in a curriculum development project, the latter not.

The second part of the content analysis classified *arguments* according to what subjects the data they appealed to were about. Figure 3.7 shows the results for the three projects of this part of the analysis. There are only two potential surprises on this chart. First there is the almost complete absence of talk about society, about the world outside the school. Traditionally this source of information has been regarded, along with the student and the subject matter, as one of three factors that should always be considered in developing a curriculum. Some writers have gone so far as to subsume the others under this one, since many characteristics of students and presumably all characteristics of subject matter are socially determined. Yet virtually none of the *arguments* in this sample of the deliberations of three projects appealed to data about the society.

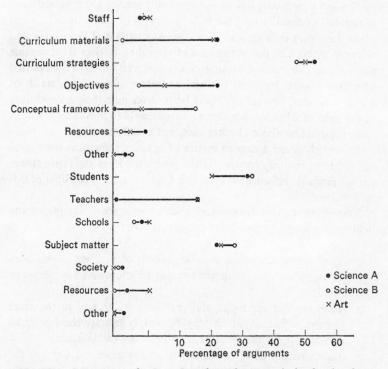

Figure 3.7   Percentage of arguments whose data were judged to be about various topics

Since the Kettering Project's platform was equally silent on matters social, and since the post-Sputnik curriculum reform movement was also little concerned with social problems in its drive for improved academic performance, perhaps the lack of data about society is natural and even intentional, in a way. It is difficult to see how, beginning with the ideas and commitments these projects subscribed to, social considerations could be integrated in a working way into their discussions. The Project staff did not share a conception of the ideal society or of needed changes in society or even a commitment in any concrete way to active maintenance of the society as they found it. In short, silence on matters social by these projects, even if unexpected, is not surprising.

The other possibly unexpected finding apparent in figure 3.7 is the high percentage of data about matters internal to the Project. More of the *arguments* appealed to data about matters internal to the Project than to data about the external matters which are supposed to be the curriculum's 'determinants'. Like reliance on data obtained from inside the Project's precincts, this pattern probably reflects the practical need of the staff to consider very carefully the properties of the materials and plans they were creating and their own capacities and limitations as a working team. The major function of appealing to data from outside sources is to determine if a course of action is well suited to the external situations it is designed for. The major function of appeal to data about internal matters, by analogy, could be to determine their acceptability in the light of what has been learned from earlier efforts. The passage from information about children, art, and society to curriculum plans and materials is not a routine matter of drawing inferences from data, but rather a genuinely creative task of generating ideas and testing them against available information by arguing their merits in the light of this information.

Simply stated, this survey and analysis of a small sample of the deliberation of three curriculum projects reveals:

1 That this deliberation consists largely of a string of episodes during which the group gives sustained attention to one topic or problem.
2 That most of the topics and problems are treated in the same fashion, a fashion which may be simply characterized as task-relevant argumentation. (Such episodes are called *issues*.)
3 That virtually all of the discourse within *issues* and some of the rest of the discourse resembles very closely what is commonly called practical discourse or practical reasoning[6] or deliberation.[7] That is, problems are identified, formulated, and stated; proposals for the resolution of these problems are conceived and articulated; and arguments are offered for and against the proposals and the formulations of the problems.
4 That the information on which project staffs base their arguments seems to come at least as frequently from the general experience of the staff as from distinctive observations; when information comes from distinctive observations it seems to originate in situations and locations which are part of the project staffs' common work more frequently than in such external situations

and locations as schools, art studios, or scientific laboratories; it seems almost always to be an observation made by one of the staff rather than an observation reported to a staff member by someone outside the staff, and it is twice as likely to be judged as having been made incidentally rather than purposefully.

5 That the data on which arguments are based are principally about three subjects: curriculum strategies, students, and subject matter, although during brief periods other subjects may also be important; rarely is an argument based upon data about the school as a whole or about the larger society of which the school is a part.

6 That the differences among projects in these respects are minor.

III

In this study two aspects of curriculum development have been singled out for special attention: platform and deliberation. Clearly other aspects exist. Two that come immediately to mind are creation of plans and materials and tryouts of them. Since my eventual goal is a unified, systematic account of curriculum development that shows how each part leads into the next and grows out of its predecessor, some attention must be given to the relationship between the two parts treated in this study.

We know from this study that project staffs identify and formulate problems, generate and evaluate proposals, devise and weigh arguments, and find appropriate instances. By asking what is presupposed by a group's being able to accomplish these tasks we can perhaps determine how earlier phases of the process contribute to deliberation. By asking what remains to be done after these deliberative episodes have concluded, we can perhaps discover something about subsequent phases of the process of curriculum development. Proceeding in this way, we can infer something of the character of the whole process from our knowledge of one part.

The feats of deliberation, whose accomplishment presupposes earlier achievements and paves the way for future ones, consist essentially of those actions required to deploy the deliberative moves. These are:

Stating and evaluating problems;
stating and evaluating proposals;
stating and evaluating arguments;
weighing and comparing conflicting arguments; and
stating and evaluating instances.

We know that the staffs of the three projects studied were able to perform these tasks repeatedly during their deliberations. What antecedent conditions are necessary in order for a group to perform these tasks effectively and with reasonable dispatch?

A straightforward analysis of the presupposition of effective performance of these tasks leads me to hypothesize that before curriculum planners can successfully decide on the form of their plans and materials, they must:

1 Concur in a conception of what would be good and bad in the conduct and results of both the curriculum they are creating and the process of curriculum development in which they are engaged.
2 Agree on a body of principles, explicit or implicit, relating educational practices to their effects.
3 Possess reasonably accurate and complete factual knowledge of important external and internal factors affecting the viability of educational practices and the likelihood that they will have the desired effects.
4 Agree on a body of principles, explicit or implicit, relating important external and internal factors to educational practices and their effects.
5 Be familiar with a variety of types of educational practices and be able to adapt these to their own circumstances.
6 Be committed to certain basic principles of rational action.
7 Have an (implicit) list of topics or commonplaces to be considered whenever a decision is being made.
8 Be able to understand and use at least a minimal set of abstract terms and ideas about educational practices and their effects and about other important factors internal and external to the project that are likely to affect these practices and their effects.

These prerequisites of effective curriculum deliberation bear a remarkable resemblance to the components of a project's platform. Earlier, five types of goal statements were identified, which revealed significant information about the Kettering Project's purposes and the directions its work would take (see pp. 103-4).

There is a considerable similarity between this list of what platform goal statements provide and what the foregoing analysis of the presuppositions of deliberation shows deliberation requires. It is not likely that this similarity is purely coincidental. More likely, platforms provide what deliberation requires.

Just as the knowledge that certain feats of deliberation are accomplished in projects enables us to infer that certain earlier tasks have been completed, so the knowledge that projects eventually use the results of deliberation in the construction of plans and materials for use in classrooms enables us to make inferences about later stages in the process of curriculum development. We know from informal accounts that the actual construction of plans and materials consists mostly of the creation by individuals and small subgroups of prototypes and tentative first versions. No studies have been made of the actual creation of plans and materials, so there is no way to check any speculations about this part of the process. Nevertheless, we know that plans and materials are made, and we are somewhat familiar with the important processes that precede and accompany the actual construction of plans and materials, so we should be able to propose some hypotheses about the process of construction itself.

It is a mistake to think of deliberation as invariably preceding construction. Rather, deliberation and construction proceed concurrently, with deliberation sometimes initiating or modifying construction, and construction sometimes generating problems for deliberation. Consequently, we should probably think of construction and deliberation as two interacting processes, if not two different aspects of one process. The constructor of plans and materials, like the deliberator must generate alternatives and weigh their merits according to various criteria. In some cases, at least, the thoughts of the constructor must be very like the deliberations of the full staff. In fact, in many respects the construction of plans and materials is simply an extension of the techniques of deliberation to the concrete particulars in all their three-dimensional reality.

The staffs' deliberations are necessarily confined to topics potentially important in more than one situation or, if not, at least to topics really crucial to an important particular situation. But the constructor of plans and materials must consider matters that are of little or no general interest or significance but which are vital in the creation of his particular product. For example, if he is creating a device of some kind, he must consider the cost of the item, its weight, its color, its durability, its size, and so on. If he ignores any of these factors his product may be too expensive, too heavy or bulky for children to handle, too easily broken, or not attractive enough to evoke children's interest. But, while these are important problems in curriculum development, their resolution in this case is not likely to contribute to the resolution of similar problems in other cases, and, consequently, these problems are well left to an individual or small group specifically concerned with this product.

To a large extent, then, curriculum construction is simply an extension of the process of deliberation to the more particular and concrete problems of design and construction of plans and materials. But construction also involves at least two other nondeliberative processes: *creation* and *trial*. I can say little about creation except that it is undoubtedly guided by the principles and the examples found in platform and deliberation. This is evidenced by the fact that every project's materials contain activities and devices which are obvious extensions or variations of activities and devices from other sources or adaptations of things created by a staff member for another purpose. Trial refers to the testing of plans and materials for feasibility, effectiveness, efficiency, and the like. Trial may include imaginative rehearsals, personal trials by the creator, informal trials with project staff and students, and formal trials with students using experimental controls and objective measures.

Finally, all these components of the process of construction of curriculum plans and materials – deliberation on concrete particulars, creation, and trial – presuppose the internalization by the individual or subgroup concerned of the platform components and the products of deliberation. If an individual or subgroup were to construct plans or materials on any other basis – using terms, procedures, examples, conceptions, aims or principles other than those that appear in the platform and deliberations – the methods or results would eventually come to the attention of the rest of the staff and, if they were not tacitly approved, become the subject of deliberation which would either endorse or reject them. In such cases deliberation disciplines construction. Deliberation also inspires construction through the examples and principles it generates.

The complete chain of effects from platform to deliberation to development is well and briefly illustrated by the following description of one of the first of the projects, the Physical Science Study Committee course in physics. The description was written by one of the project's directors and a pioneer in the new curriculum movement.[8]

One might wish to provide the student with an intimate knowledge of modern technology, or with an acquaintance with the manner in which physics has grown. During the early days of the Physical Science Study Committee, both of these were entered as possibilities and were warmly debated; if either had carried the day, the Committee physics course would be quite different from the course as it now exists. In fact, it was decided instead that the course would be directed toward familiarizing the student with two central notions of modern physics: the wave-particle duality and the modern concept of the atom. Behind this decision was the view that these two notions lay at the heart of the modern physicist's outlook upon his universe, and that it was this outlook that the course should convey.

This answer set boundaries upon the answer to the question of selecting and ordering. If a one-year course was to deal intelligibly with the wave-particle duality and nature of the atom, much that has been conventionally taught as physics would have to be ignored or skimped. Physics is too rich to be taught in its entirety in a single year; the criteria of selection would have to identify those portions of physics which contributed to the elucidation of the wave-particle duality and the nature of the atom.

As a consequence, the Physical Science Study Committee course contains little about sound, or electric circuitry, or relativity. They are omitted, not because they are devoid of interest, but because they are not central to the theme. Instead, the course proceeds through optics and the behavior of light to the kinematics of waves, then to Newtonian dynamics, electric forces and, finally, the atom. All this is told as a continued story, in which each chapter is firmly bound to its predecessor and leads to its successor.

This account of curriculum development as it happened in one project is now as complete as I can make it.[9] The time has come to compare it with the standard accounts of how curriculum development *should* be done.

Some points of difference found in this study are:

1 The Kettering Project did *not* state objectives at an early stage in their work and use these objectives as guides to the rest of their work as generally recommended.

2 The Kettering Project did *not* use formal evaluation of student outcomes during the development process (except observations of classes using their trial materials). They did use formal evaluation later to guide them in pinpointing needed revisions in the already completed materials.

3 Development was accomplished by a small, exclusive, homogeneous group of former teachers and specialists in the teaching of art, not by committees representing all parties normally having a say in curriculum determination. Students, teachers, and laymen played a negligible part in development.

4 From their earliest days of working together, the Kettering staff shared a commitment to certain beliefs and ideas which guided them in their development work. They did not begin with an open mind and ask – with the aid of a 'needs assessment' as is frequently recommended, or in any other way – what beliefs were required by the situation they faced.

5 The intellectual heart of the Project's work consisted of practical reasoning or deliberation during which problems were identified,

formulated, and stated; proposals for the resolution of these problems were conceived and articulated; and arguments were offered for and against the proposals and the formulations of the problems. The deliberative process is *not* essentially that of *deducing* the form of the curriculum from given information about students, subject matter, and society as is frequently stated or implied in works about curriculum making.

6   The information on which the Project based its work was not the sort required by the scientific-empirical ideal. In the Kettering Project, data came frequently from the general experience of the staff; when data came from specific observations these seemed to be mainly observations made incidentally in the course of the staff's work rather than purposefully sought observations of students, schools, or other external objects and locations.

7   Data about the society were not used in the Project's deliberations, even though tradition demands that the students, the subject matter, and the society all be considered in developing any curriculum.

8   Most of the arguments appearing in the samples of deliberation studied did not appeal to any of these three traditional determinants; rather, they appealed to practical matters related to the Project's own operations or to events arising from, or circumstances encountered in, its work.

For me, the most important finding of the study has been that the logical essence of curriculum development is practical reasoning. This finding is important, first, because it shows that curriculum development has, or can have, a type of rationality, that development is not just an expression of irrational prejudices or preferences. On the other hand, this rationality does not consist simply of deducing or calculating the form of the curriculum from given facts about 'determinants.' On this view curriculum development is a genuinely creative endeavor, but one governed by rational consideration of the merits of the things created.

If this view of curriculum development were generally accepted by educators, foundations, governmental officials, behavioral scientists and others influential in educational planning, the chief consequence would probably be to stop trying to replace this process with another, more formalized method of curriculum development that seems more rational or scientific. This does not mean rejection of rationality or science. Rather, it means recognition that these play important but partial roles in a larger enterprise characterized by open-ended, no-holds-barred, multi-valued, integrative deliberation. Curriculum development procedures which call for one group to choose objectives or set policy and another to convert these into curriculum plans and materials overlook the practical difficulty people experience in stating what they want educationally. If members of a project team find it necessary to resort to other types of statements in addition to objectives simply in order to tell another prospective member of their team what they are up to, how much more would a local school or school district need to resort to them to convey their purposes to a distant group of developers?

Of course, it is not the function of theories to deal with every facet of a situation. Theories gain their power by abstracting out some facets for separate treatment. But in the case of curriculum development, the matters neglected by the theories seem to be so fundamental to actual practice as to make theories that leave them out practically useless.

The upshot of this, it seems to me, is that there are situations for which the traditional accounts and ideals seem more appropriate than the deliberative account and ideal presented here. Likewise there are other situations for which the latter seem more appropriate. Each ideal can boast of strengths the other does not have, and each can be criticized for weaknesses absent in the other. Depending upon the relative importance they ascribe to various of these strengths and weaknesses, different persons could come to prefer one or the other for a given situation. Furthermore, I consider it highly likely that a hybrid which grafts some of the formalized, systematized procedures deriving from the traditional ideal onto the basic stock of the deliberative ideal would prove more desirable than either of its parents. Also, I do not think that the possibility of still other persuasive ideals emerging can be ruled out.

In short, I think the search for a single best way to make a curriculum is a hopeless quest. We need many ways to match the many circumstances in which curriculum development takes place and the many different patterns of educational value different people embrace. At the present moment in history I think it most important to try to explode the widely believed myth that all curriculum development should begin with objectives and work in a formal and systematic way toward the creation and evaluation of plans and materials. Adherence to this ideal has already led to some bizarre excesses in the US. I have in mind the Kafkaesque image of thousands of teachers in schools and colleges throughout the country at this very moment writing behavioral objectives or selecting them for purchase (that's right, they are for sale) in response to demands from officials operating under the assumption that the use of behaviorally stated objectives is absolutely the only way to secure program evaluation. It is not true. There are other ways. While they may not have some of the desirable characteristics of this way, they have other compensating advantages it does not have. I hope the work reported here contributes to official recognition of this fact.

Finally, I hope this work stimulates others to seek answers to the deeper and more significant questions which remain unanswered in both accounts, questions such as:

> What is the nature of the principles curriculum developers rely on to connect facts or assumptions about the world to platform commitments (or, if you prefer, objectives)?

> Or the nature of those principles that connect facts or assumptions about curricular effects to plans and materials?

> What relation, if any, do these principles bear to psychological theories and findings?

> What aspects of curriculum plans and materials in use by students and teachers operate as cues to the developer that something is going well or poorly?

> What is the implicit system of reasoning by means of which developers judge particular observations to have a bearing on some aspect of their work?

> How dependent are all these processes on the supposedly foundational concepts, methods, and ideas about which editorial scholars write and do research?

Notes

1 See, for example, Tyler, 1949; Taba, 1962; Smith, Stanley and Shores, 1957; Wheeler, 1967.

2 These include: E.W. Eisner, 'Curriculum ideas in a time of crisis,' *Art Education*, 18, 1965, pp. 7–10; 'Arts curricula for the gifted,' *Elementary School Journal*, 66, 1965, pp. 3–7; 'The challenge of change in art education,' *Art Education*, 20, 1967, pp. 27–9; 'Changing conceptions of artistic learning,' *Elementary School Journal*, 68, 1967, pp. 18–25; 'Curriculum making for the wee folk: Stanford University's Kettering Project,' *Studies in Art Education*, 9, 1968, pp. 45–56.

3 The three articles analyzed were: B. Glass, 'Renascent biology: a report on the AIBS biological sciences curriculum study,' *School Review*, 70, 1962, pp. 16–44; R. Gagné, 'Elementary science: a new scheme of instruction,' *Science*, 151, 1966, pp. 49–53; L.E. Strong, 'Chemistry as a science in the high school,' *School Review*, 70, 1962, pp. 44–50.

4 W. Wooton, *SMSG: the Making of a Curriculum*, New Haven, Conn., Yale University Press, 1965, pp. 76–7.

5 Ibid., p. 43.

6 David P. Gauthier, *Practical Reasoning: the Structure and Foundations of Prudential and Moral Arguments and their Exemplification in Discourse*, Oxford University Press, 1963.

7 Schwab, 1969.

8 Zacharias and White, 1964.

9 See also Walker, 1971.

4

The Head Teacher as Innovator: a Study of an English School District

N. B. Dickinson

Editors' introduction

All design teams must accept the possibility that their schemes may undergo modification when they reach the point of implementation, but in no fields is this consideration more likely to lead to disappointment and frustration than in those such as curriculum planning, where implementation implies changes in the structure of institutions and the orientations of individuals. Dickinson's paper leads us back to the realities of the school and the part played by head teachers or principals in mediating the entry into the curriculum of new materials, methods or programmes. These may arise from national or local curriculum projects, from the experience of other schools, or simply from 'ideas in good currency', but all must be accepted by the administrators of the school, and be absorbed into its existing network of activities.

In making an intensive study of the secondary schools in one city in the north of England, Dickinson found that the incidence of curriculum change was much less than one might expect, but that, where innovations had been introduced, they were almost invariably regarded as successful. Practically without exception heads reported that, if they had to carry them through again, they would plan and execute them exactly as before. Not only does the study provide interesting data on which to build speculation about the ways in which ideas for change are mediated through the communications network of the school, but it also offers a refreshingly candid view of how individual head teachers handle suggestions for innovation, and manage the adaptive processes which both precede and follow a decision for adoption. Parallels can be drawn with analyses developed in preceding papers of the conditions under which institutions tend towards maintenance or change, and of the strategies individuals employ for accommodating innovatory initiatives to the need for preserving consensus and consent among those affected by them.

I

It was not the purpose of this study to examine the pressures for curriculum change, nor to investigate the forms of resistance that evolve in response to these demands, but to look at the ways and means that were employed by head teachers to bring intended change about, and to look at some of their motives.

The head teacher has been described as an organiser of multifarious relationships and attachments to a diversity of groups, allocating to their various positions of importance the numerous big parts which he is called upon to play successively (and indeed sometimes simultaneously) – listener, encourager, dissuader, reporter, watcher, judge, critic, decision taker and, on occasions, commander. His role is that of one who occupies a boundary position between the school and its wider social environment and he is therefore in consequence particularly receptive and sensitive to the expectations of the many counter positions that constitute the complement of his effective role set. These counter positions are occupied by parents, teachers, administrators and the many other individuals from these groups that are in contact with head teachers. As the chief executive of a professionally staffed organisation, his style of leadership is both governed and influenced by his relationship with subordinate members of his staff, a relationship based upon a common professional socialisation and collegiality.

This relationship may or may not be helped by the head teacher's ability to influence and control staff; although he rarely has the power to hire and fire, his influence in the corridors of power is sufficient to give him effective control of appointment and dismissal and, as a referee, he can be an effective force in the promotion, or otherwise, of his staff. By controlling the disbursement of allowances, and departmental grades, the head teacher can encourage the sycophant and conformist and the persistence of his historical pre-eminence is evidenced by his being the sole representative of the staff on the governing body in the majority of schools.

These various aspects of the head teacher's role display the reaction of the social order to the former despotism of the head teachers. Constraints and balances have been created to limit the authority of his position and, whilst he may appear to have power, it is nowadays more that of the umpire with the ability to always give the 'right decision' because this is part of his role. Decisions, however, are public and open to discussion and criticism and, whilst he has authority, it is less certain that he has power.

II

The schools chosen for this study were located in one educational district in the north of England. It had a population of just over a quarter of a million, a long period of Labour controlled council and a social structure heavily weighted in the semi-skilled and unskilled labour classes. Its main industries were fishing, timber, docks and transport, and paternalism existed in an acceptable way at all levels of industry. This structure was reflected in its educational system, where time-served teachers eventually emerged as its headmasters, and 'progressive' education was generally seen as a threat to the system as a whole.

The schools chosen were those that had been least subjected to imposed change. Two types of school were studied, the Senior and the Junior High Schools, and for the Senior High Schools stability was limited to two measures, continuity of direction and absence of change in the school building and site. For the Junior High School a third factor was the school's history prior to secondary reorganization.

A school was regarded as fulfilling the measure of continuity of direction if the head teacher in charge of the school at the time of the study had been in continuous charge of the school, as the head teacher, for the last six years. Additionally all the schools studied were those that had been housed in their present premises, without addition, or structural alteration, for this same six years. This condition applied also to the school site.

The period of this study extended from 1965 through to and including 1970, and included, therefore, those years in which the Local Education Authority commenced and completed its reorganisation of secondary education.

This reorganisation from a selective 11+ transfer system of Primary, Secondary Modern and Grammar to a three-tier comprehensive system of schools housing 5–9 year olds, 9–13 year olds and 13+ pupils took three years to complete and commenced in 1967. Of course all schools were affected by this reorganisation, and indeed pressures for change are brought to bear upon schools from many sources – local and central government, ministry standards of building and staffing, socially imposed changes to name a few – but the prime objective of this study was to attempt to eliminate those changes, introduced by headmasters, that could be seen to be a direct response to outside pressures and use only those curriculum innovations that head teachers saw as school based, staff or head teacher initiated.

Due to the decision to concentrate on schools that had had the least changes imposed upon them (measured in terms of the tenure of the head teacher, and lack of alteration in the physical school building) only those Junior High Schools that formerly had been secondary moderns were used, as those formed from primary schools had had extensive building programmes to bring them up to a satisfactory standard as Junior Highs.

Of the 18 Senior High Schools available for this study in 1970, 5 had been built since 1966, and 6 had had a change of head teacher in these years. One was a Special Agreement School with imposed restraint upon its curriculum, and one had been created by amalgamating two secondary moderns. These schools failed to comply with the criteria of selection and left 5 schools that did. All these schools were studied.

Of the 49 Junior High Schools, 18 were formerly primary schools and had had substantial building additions, 12 had been built after 1966 and 9 had had a change of head teacher. These schools therefore failed to fulfil the requirements of selection but the remaining 10 that did comply were all studied.

III

The major part of the investigation was based on a series of semi-structured interview schedules that provided both a set of case studies and some tables of formal responses to previously formulated questions. Two constant factors affected each of the semi-structured interview situations, and were used to increase the area and depth of the discussions that took place on each aspect of the innovation. One was the experience of the interviewer, as a head teacher with the Local Education Authority in which all the schools were situated, and the other was the relationship that existed between the head teachers and the interviewer. This relationship was that of colleague and friend, and this encouraged a response to be expressed in terms of the real situation, as understood, even perhaps endured, by a professional co-worker. The sample was small, selected and interrelated and cannot therefore be regarded in any way as a random sample of any population, nor are the data arising from it susceptible to sophisticated forms of statistical analysis.

The choice of methodology, that of the semi-structural interview, together with the selection of particular schools based on stability criteria, determined the first step in the experimental procedure; an approach to the head teachers of the selected schools to see if they would be willing to answer questions about changes that had been brought about in their curriculum. They all agreed, without any hesitation, and they were, then, asked to complete a questionnaire, referred to in this study as 'Schedule A'. This questionnaire asked the head teachers to list, as far as possible, the curriculum changes that had been made in their schools since September 1965. They were instructed to limit the list to ten, and if they could recall more than ten, to confine themselves to the ten they felt made the most significant contribution to an achievement of the aims and goals of the schools. The questionnaire also asked the head teacher to describe the changes as 'major', 'intermediate' or 'minor'. These assessments were a measure of the number of pupils involved in the change, a 'major' change being one that involved most of the pupils in the school; an 'intermediate' change one that involved a group of classes, a year group or a house group or groups of classes; and a 'minor' change was one that was confined to one class or one group only. Schedule A also asked the head to date the commencement of the innovation, together with the date of its completion. For example, a school that had decided to introduce a second language for all its pupils, may have done so by introducing it initially to its first year pupils, and increasing the area of teaching year by year, so that, for a five year course, this would, for our purposes, define an innovation as one that took five years to complete. On the other hand, a head teacher may have decided to unstream his school, and 'go the whole hog' at once when school opened in September. Such an innovation is described as 'immediate' or not requiring any period of time for the completion of the operation.

Schedule A was handed over to the head teacher in a face to face meeting, and this meeting was used to clarify the nature of the word 'change' as used on the schedule, as a term relating to change that the head himself considered he had brought about or had allowed to be introduced into his school. Change imposed by forces outside his control were not the subject of this study. Schedule A was left with the head teachers for ten days and, as soon as possible after this period, a second interview with the head teachers was arranged to discuss all the changes on Schedule A and to discover the nature and basis of change and for how long the innovation had lasted. This time-measure is not to be confused with the time taken to complete the introduction of the innovation. At this interview also a decision was taken about the choice of one innovation for a full discussion, based on an interview schedule which sought to determine the fundamental process of change procedures and the impetus behind the change. The choice of a particular curriculum innovation was based, firstly, on the willingness of the head teacher to discuss fully the process of change and, secondly, preference was given to the one that appeared to have involved the head, staff and other interested members in detailed planning, consultation and involvement. The innovation chosen for the study in depth by semi-structured interview was left entirely to the head teacher of the school. No indication of preference was given by the interviewer.

IV

The total changes recorded by the Senior High Schools are given in table 4.1, together with the date of the commencement of the innovation, and its classification of major, intermediate and minor, i.e., whether the change involved more than half the school, less than half but several classes, or a small group equal in size to a class or less. The total changes recorded on Schedule A for the Junior Highs are given in table 4.2.

TABLE 4.1   Curriculum changes by years for the Senior Highs
$N = 30$

Year innovation commenced	1965	1966	1967	1968	1969	1970	Totals
Major	0	0	0	1	1	2	4
Intermediate	1	1	2	4	7	1	16
Minor	0	1	0	5	1	3	10
Totals	1	2	2	10	9	6	30

TABLE 4.2   Curriculum changes by years for the Junior Highs
$N = 63$

Year innovation commenced	1965	1966	1967	1968	1969	1970	Totals
Major	3	2	3	1	18	6	33
Intermediate	2	0	0	1	6	6	15
Minor	2	3	1	0	3	6	15
Totals	7	5	4	2	27	18	63

In an earlier section (p. 138) we briefly recorded the way in which reorganisation of education in the district took place in the years 1967, 1968 and 1969 and this change in the schools' intake of pupils is recorded graphically, in figure 4.1, for both types of school, together with the total changes listed in tables 4.1 and 4.2. The rate of change of intake

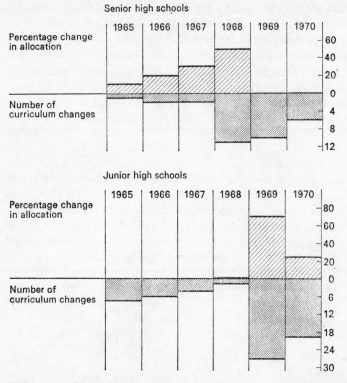

Figure 4.1   Innovation rates and percentage change in allocated intake

to the Senior High Schools is based on the assumption that, had the 11+ selection procedure been maintained at the figure of 25 per cent of the total year group (as in previous years) then this number of selective pupils would have had to be shared amongst an increasing number of schools. Allowance has been made for the size of entry to the schools.

The rate of change of intake to the Junior High Schools is based on the assumption that the new age intakes provided the largest item in change. The rate of change graphs, therefore, accurately display the time and trend, together with the total annual innovations of the two groups of schools.

Figure 4.1 shows the percentage change in intake and compares it with the number of innovations reported in each year. The percentage change in intake must not be taken to indicate the percentage change in the school population. It applies to the intake year only, and its significance will remain until that year has completed its schooling at middle or senior level.

The graphs clearly demonstrate a relationship between change in pupil intake and curriculum innovation. The graph suggests that, without a change in intake, the rate of innovation would have been much less and that the rate of innovation closely follows the rate of change of intake. Such a conclusion supports the hypothesis that, within these schools, the rate of internally initiated innovation varies directly with the rate of change imposed on the school from outside.

TABLE 4.3   Innovations listed by head teachers

	Type of innovation	Number	
	Modern maths	12	
	Nuffield French	10	
	Nuffield technology	2	
	Nuffield science	7	
Group 1	Total, nationally promoted		31
Group 2	Addition of a traditional subject		14
	Team teaching	3	
	Closed circuit TV	5	
	Mixed ability grouping	11	
	Setting	4	
	Classes for the less able	8	
	Interdisciplinary studies	11	
Group 3	Total, nationally discussed method		42
	Italic handwriting	1	
	Esperanto for the less able	1	
	Gardening for the less able	3	
	Latin dropped	1	
Group 4	Total, others		6
		Sum total	93

All the innovations listed on Schedule A, by the head teachers, are summarised in table 4.3. Only six of the ninety-three fail to fall into any of the recognised areas of recent educational argument, or promotion. Of these six, deliberate dropping of Latin is a trend that has been freely talked about and implemented throughout a large section of secondary education; and gardening, too, has commonly been offered as a solution to the problem of teaching science in a streamed situation to the less able child. Italic handwriting and Esperanto seem to be the only innovations that did not have wide and much discussed experience to refer to and, on the basis of this table, the only innovations that head teachers encourage are those that offer the promise of success on the grounds of satisfactory experience in other schools.

The length of time taken to complete an innovation could be one measure of the importance attached to it in achieving the aims and goals of the school – a measure of the effort that the innovator would make to provide satisfactory learning situations within the school.

The length of time taken to complete the innovation, according to the information on Schedule A, was as shown in table 4.4.

TABLE 4.4   Time taken to complete innovations
$N = 93$

	Immediate	*1 year*	*2 years*	*3 or more years*	*Total*
Senior Highs	29	0	1	0	30
Junior Highs	56	3	4	0	63
Totals	85	3	5	0	93

These time estimates are remarkably low. The introduction of a 'modern maths' syllabus, for instance, to replace the traditional one, would, one would expect, take four or five years depending on whether it was a four- or a five-year course. Yet in actual fact most of the curriculum innovations on the modern maths side were 'immediate'. The innovation for this subject never involved the defining of new goals, nor the formulation of a new syllabus, but rather, topics were taken from the modern maths syllabuses and added to the traditional one. Such an innovation was described as 'the broadening out of the maths scheme', or 'some modern maths introduced', and was more a measure of educational climate than of innovation. Table 4.4 shows that the commonest type of innovation was that that was introduced 'immediately' and figure 4.1 (p. 142) shows quite clearly that the rate of innovation followed very closely on the rate of change in the basis of the school population. It is reasonable to suggest that some innovation is a response to a need that has expressed itself within the school due to a change in intake. This response follows the need and its implementation is usually of the type we have described as immediate.

The face to face interviews with the head teachers showed the need to redefine the terms, 'major', 'intermediate' and 'minor'. As measures of the number of pupils involved – for which they had been designed – they were adequate, in that they defined the pupil area of innovation, but it became apparent that large pupil involvement was not necessarily large school involvement. If we refer to the example of 'modern maths', discussed in the previous paragraph, we see that such an innovation can involve all the pupils in the school without affecting the stated goals of either the school or the subject syllabus, and without affecting the timetable arrangements of staff or pupils. The change was one of content only, and frequently this change was only generally defined. A more meaningful measure of the size of the innovation could be the interaction between pupil involvement and staff disturbance. By staff disturbance is meant changes in the nature of the work the member of staff would be expected to do. Unstreaming, for instance, would mean for many teachers a reappraisal of method and involve a major change in the way in which they would present their subject. A new discipline introduced into the school syllabus may throw a great burden on the teacher expected to teach it, if it is only distantly related to the subjects in which he has been trained. Subjects such as geology, as an alternative to geography, or statistics, as an alternative to one of the mathematical options, may mean the creation of fresh syllabuses, fresh groups of

TABLE 4.5 Categorisation of curriculum innovations

Staff disturbance	Pupil involvement			
	Minor	*Intermediate*	*Major*	*Totals*
Small				
Junior High Schools	8	11	25	44
Senior High Schools	1	7	3	11
Total	9	18	28	55
Medium				
Junior High Schools	0	2	1	3
Senior High Schools	0	3	0	3
Total	0	5	1	6
Large				
Junior High Schools	7	2	7	16
Senior High Schools	9	6	1	16
Total	16	8	8	32
Sum totals				
Junior High Schools	15	15	33	63
Senior High Schools	10	16	4	30

pupils, and fresh timetabling for staff and pupils. Table 4.5 attempts to show how the changes based on pupil involvement relate to staff disturbance. The classification for pupil involvement is the one that has been used throughout this article, and staff disturbance is given three categories. Where the innovation has not involved the member of staff in changes of classes, or changes in timetabling, but has been a change in the content of his subject, then we have categorised such a disturbance as 'small'. Where, however, the member of staff has had to introduce a new subject, or to make a major alteration in method, then we have described this as a 'large' staff disturbance. An example of a 'medium' staff disturbance would be of the kind that involved the teacher in an extension in the amount of time that he would have to spend with a particular group for his particular subject.

There was a tendency for innovation that involved a majority of pupils to occur within the existing teacher/pupil framework, with little or no change in the timetabling arrangements. This suggests that when innovation is introduced to major pupil areas of the school it is usually a modification of the existing subject matter content. The majority of innovations involving minor groups of pupils, however, involved large staff disturbance and were, in fact, a response to a new type of pupil. The large staff disturbance/minor pupil area was most frequently encountered when arrangements had been made for the less able child, with members of staff being prominent in bringing this particular need to the attention of the head teacher, and offering to work with these groups. In the Senior High Schools there were nine minor pupil/large staff disturbance innovations of which six related specifically to the needs of the less able child, a need that was new to many of the Senior High Schools, which had previously been selective schools. The picture for this type of innovation was rather different for the Junior High Schools, which as former secondary modern schools had had extensive experience of the needs of the less able child. Here, the most frequent of the innovations of this type – four out of seven – related to the heavy craft subjects where, although there was a lack of children suitable for this work, the specialist teacher was still in the school. This gave rise to small experimental innovations in method and materials. The innovations included the use of new materials such as fibre glass and plaster and adjustments in the length of time spent in the craft rooms. In both the Senior High and the Junior High Schools these minor pupil/large staff disturbance innovations were concerned with the kind of pupil who was new to the teacher, subject and school.

An important observation about these innovations, based on discussion with the head teachers about their Schedule A list, concerns the permanence of the change once it had been initiated. It is likely that the majority of secondary moderns before their conversion to Junior High Schools had had special courses for their fourth and fifth years, and such courses would naturally cease on the transformation of the school. Only one of the schools in this survey had actually introduced such courses during the period covered by this study. Of the total ninety-three innovations, only two came into this category and with the exception of these two, all the innovations listed on Schedule A over a period of six years were still functioning and it was the intention of the head teachers to continue with them indefinitely. The permanence of the change, once it had been introduced, is fully discussed later (p. 174).

All head teachers spoke of all the innovations as highly successful, indeed, in one sense, successful introduction of the innovation was frequently seen as a measure of success of the innovation itself, and success in these terms appeared to be a major goal of the school; though this goal was not necessarily a conscious one and never a written one; but success, whether in a football league, or GCE results, or in reversing a decision made by the 'office', or in curriculum innovation, was generally viewed as a tangible measure of positive evaluation. It was evidence that the right course had been taken. The success, say, of modern maths in the early heady days of innovation was assured if it was successfully introduced. Real measures of evaluation in terms of learning outcomes, or understanding, appeared to be irrelevant provided the innovation was successfully brought about. The case studies reveal in some detail the measures of evaluation that head teachers tend to use to justify the introduction of their curriculum innovations. It is clear that they are almost never related to specified educational goals of the school.

V

Schedule A served as an introduction to the school and its processes of initiating curriculum change. A further purpose was to effect a compilation of changes in the curriculum over the previous six years. From this list, the head teachers selected a single innovation as a base for a detailed examination of their innovative role. The choice was made as one that was acceptable to the head teacher, and which also displayed the process and technique of innovation. Some innovations were departmental in origin and fulfilment, with the head playing the part of the contented bystander. This study concentrated on a detailed examination of change that the head considered he himself had initiated.

In opening the discussion on the chosen innovation with each head teacher, the first few minutes were spent in trying to measure the attitude of the head to change itself. In fact, the opening question was, 'What would you say was your general attitude to change?' A five point scale was used to place the attitude:

1 Very much against change.
2 A dislike for change.
3 Neutral.
4 Happy about it.
5 Very much in favour.

Some of the head teachers' replies (together with their scores in brackets) were: 'I would like to see radical reform in the whole gamut of school

TABLE 4.6   The head teachers' expressed attitude to change

Scale score	Number
1	2
2	4
3	3
4	5
5	1

life' (5); 'You cannot stand still, some change is necessary' (4); 'Well, of course, unfortunately, there are times when you must change, circumstances demand it' (2); 'It's quite unnecessary' (1). Where it was difficult to decide between 2 and 3, or 3 and 4, then the response was put into category (3). The results are shown in table 4.6.

It would be unrealistic to suggest that any significance could be attached to these results. It is the sort of distribution that one might expect from a small randomly selected sample but, on the other hand, this was not a randomly selected sample and the distribution is not the one one would expect in the light of the discussion that followed.

Towards the end of the interview, the final question to determine attitudes to change was, 'In the light of your experience with this change, what would your immediate reaction be if faced with having to do it again?'

The response was always immediate and positive – 'I'd do it again, exactly', 'Do it immediately', or 'No hesitation in doing it again', were typical replies. Only one head teacher expressed the possibility of re-examining the change with a view to modification, in the event of having to repeat it. The answers are summarised in table 4.7.

It has already been said that innovations tended to become a per-

TABLE 4.7   Head teachers' reaction to repetition of innovations

Category	Number
Would do it again, exactly	14
Would do it again, but would like to reconsider it	1

manent feature of the teaching of the school. The average rate of innovation was 1·2 per year per school, and this rate would certainly have been much lower were it not for massive reorganisation of the schools in the city in three of the six years of this study. Supporting evidence of the permanence of any introduced change is the attitude of head teachers to repeating it if the conditions were repeated. There is a striking lack of evidence of any innovation that failed, or of any innovation designed to meet a unique set of circumstances. The lack of innovation designed to meet a unique set of circumstances is understandable. When they occur they may well be such as to *impose* change on the school and therefore fall outside the area of this study. Innovation that failed, however, is a rather different matter. It would be expected that in a survey of a group of fifteen schools over a period of six years some innovations would have been tried and found wanting, and that the answer to such an innovation would be modification or rejection. The failure to find modification or rejection could be due, we suggest, to either:

1 Inadequate measures of evaluation.
2 Only innovations which are certain of success are allowed to develop.
3 That innovation is not recognised unless it is a success.

It is difficult to comment on the schools' measures of evaluation of the success of the innovation as this was not a part of the enquiry, but comments on answers to other questions in this study suggest that the success of an innovation is measured by the reaction of the pupils to it. Expressions such as '[the children] were very excited about it', or 'you couldn't keep them away from the subject', were the kind of comment that was often made, and this sort of subjective evaluation tends to make a success of almost any innovation. It is easier however to come to some sort of an assessment of the suggestion that innovation succeeds because the innovation is not recognised unless it has succeeded or that only those innovations which are certain of success are allowed to develop.

Some measure of confirmation for the hypothesis that failure to recognise innovation unless it would be successful was obtained from answers to the question, 'How do you view the many changes which seem to be in the air at the moment?' No head roundly condemned them, but the support was lukewarm, if there at all. 'They're not realistic', 'They are too many and untested', 'I find them interesting', 'I question a lot of them, they don't seem to be going anywhere', 'I don't take much notice of them', 'Empire building', were typical of the comments. Table 4.8 attempts to classify them into three broad groups.

TABLE 4.8   Head teachers' reactions to widely canvassed innovations

Category	Number
Positively approve	2
Neutral	12
Against	1
Total	15

The two heads who positively approved of the innovation both qualified their approval by suggesting that many schools, but not their own, were in need of change. One head teacher found change quite unnecessary, but the other twelve were studiously neutral and faintly condemnatory. Remarkably, all of the thirteen heads who had not positively approved of the many innovations in the air at the moment, had introduced one or more innovations based on nationally promoted schemes. This reinforced the view that the head teachers prefer proven successful innovation, which is then favourably recognised as the kind of innovation they would like to see introduced into their own schools. Metaphors such as 'the climate was favourable', or 'the time was ripe', were frequently used to explain why innovations were initiated at the time they were, and this again suggests that the conditions for success are important. It could well appear that the first question asked about any suggested innovation is 'Will it succeed?'

Table 4.9 shows the answers to the question, 'Would you be happy to have change imposed upon you by some professional body like the

TABLE 4.9   Attitude to imposed change in their own school

Positively approve	0
Neutral	0
Definitely against	15

Schools Council, or Nuffield?' There was never any hesitation, nor any doubt about the views of the heads on imposed change. 'Certainly not', 'Would fight it all the way', and often added was the expressed view that 'no one knows better than me the needs of these children and it would be stupid for an outsider to suggest otherwise'. Only one head teacher showed any favourable response and that was not on behalf of his own school. 'I certainly wouldn't want it in my school but I know what goes on in other schools in this area and I think there could well be a case for it there.'

The attitude to curriculum change was precise. If it could be seen as answering a need within the school and could be successfully introduced then the attitude was favourable; but if, however, the inference was that change was necessary in the opinion and on the basis of work done by people remote from the school itself, then defensive attitudes were adopted to suggestions that the change was essential. There was, however, an acceptance over time of innovation that could be seen to be working successfully in other schools, and it was this kind of innovation to which these schools were most susceptible.

Three other questions are dealt with in this section. First, 'Have you any changes in the pipeline?' This question was looking for details of change that was about to be brought about. To qualify, it was expected that some definite move had been made, such as the fixing of a date for its introduction, or its planning had been fully discussed in a staff meeting. The results are shown in table 4.10.

TABLE 4.10 Number of changes in pipeline

Number of changes	0	1	2	3
Junior High Schools	8	1	0	1
Senior High Schools	4	0	1	0
Total, all schools	12	1	1	1

Although head teachers may not have had any change about to be fed into the system, it could well be that changes could still be made in the near future and thoughts had been expressed and informal conversations held, and the question was asked, 'What changes do you expect to make in the next two years?' Eight of the heads took this opportunity to express what they considered to be the most urgent area of reform, measured in terms of present weaknesses in the schools. Weaknesses in organisation, or the teaching of a particular subject, were the kind of things the head teachers spoke about, and one felt that they were waiting for the opportune moment for change in this area of need. The results are given in table 4.11.

TABLE 4.11 Changes expected to be made in the next two years

Number of changes	0	1	2	3 or more
Junior Highs	5	5	0	0
Senior Highs	2	1	2	0
Total, all schools	7	6	2	0

The third of these questions asked, 'If you could have it, would you prefer to have as little change as possible?' and the answers are recorded in table 4.12.

The implications of tables 4.10 and 4.11 suggest that change is not welcomed. Only three of the heads had any change in the pipeline, and twelve had no plans for change for September 1971. Seven had no proposals or suggestions to make about innovation or change they would

TABLE 4.12   Head teachers' preferred degrees of change

	Junior High Schools	Senior High Schools	Total
As little as possible	5	3	8
Neutral	4	0	4
Happy with change	1	2	3

like to see introduced into their curricula during the next two years, and only three of the heads displayed a positive approach to change by expressing some welcome or need for it. The experience over the last six years in these schools was an innovation rate of 1·03 per school per year at least, because schools recorded those innovations they 'remembered', and one would expect therefore to find about fifteen planned changes for next year and a total of about thirty planned changes over the next two years, if innovation were not a response to pressures and restraints that arise from outside the school. I would suggest that the results tabled support the evidence already quoted that shows innovation in these schools to owe less to parentage based on forward thinking and planning, than to birth based on the replication of seen successful innovation in other schools, or on the need to respond to a pressing and obvious problem. The replication of seen successful innovation in other schools could be described as a 'fashion', and the fashionable innovation might well be a nationally promoted scheme that is supported by the local authority, and proves acceptable to the school because the head teacher sees it as an answer to need, or as the harbinger of prestige, or as the path to favourable notice by the LEA.

It was shown earlier that the rate of innovation closely followed the rate of change in the status or organisation of the schools, and that therefore some innovation was a response to change which produced new needs within the school. It has also been suggested that some changes are the result of wanting to be fashionable. Frequently modern maths was imposed on a traditional maths scheme for no other apparent reason than the delights of change. The introduction of additional areas to the formal syllabus was justified on grounds such as pupil interest, teacher interest or training, but was always confined to those subjects that were heading the list of professional discussion. These innovations could well be defined in terms of fashion. Some innovation was based on prestige, and this was particularly true of subject areas which were supported by the Local Education Authority. To take part in the pilot French scheme, or Nuffield science, was not only prestigious, but profitable in staff and equipment. It combined elements of need and fashion with the aura of having arrived.

VI

The semi-structured interview provided two types of material – the immediate answer to the question, which was recorded as it was given, and information inferred in the discussion that followed the answer. The length of the discussion depended upon the head teacher's desire to enlarge upon the answer, and the degree of questioning provided by the interviewer. At all times, however, the aim was to encourage the head teacher to talk freely. The nine case studies that follow are a record of these discussions, grouped to show particular aspects of change. The first three studies show an apparently common impetus for the innovation, but also show the innovation as a means employed by the head teacher to further less obvious change.

Case study 1*

Abbey Junior High School, built in 1933, is typical of its period. The long, two-storied brick building facing on to an asphalt playground is neatly divided into two wings by the main entrance that has the head teacher's study on one side of it and his office on the other. At either end of the building and as far apart as possible are the cloaks and lavatories for the boys and girls, and this formal distance between the sexes epitomises a basic aspect of the school's climate.

In common with many schools, it served the neighbourhood, which forty years ago had consisted of neat streets of owner-occupied and privately rented 'semis'. Now age has removed much of this tidiness and proud ownership though the area was still attractive and full of character and reflects the needs and hopes of its semi-skilled workers, clerks and young married couples.

In 1969, the junior and infant school which shared the grounds was, together with the secondary modern, formed into a single unit – Abbey Junior High School – and in September of that year opened with a school population of some 510 boys and girls.

The head teacher acted the part of an important man; he was busy, critical of office-bound administrators, students and university academics, very especially the latter, who 'knew absolutely nothing about the problems of running a school'. His secretary supported him in his head teacher's role, oversaw his schedules and was quick to provide him with answers on organisation. She, too, adopted the role of a very important person and much consultation took place between her and Mr Williams, the head teacher.

* The names used in these accounts are fictitious.

In 1968, prior to secondary reorganisation on comprehensive lines in 1969, the local inspectorate, in response to suggestions by Mr Johnson, one of Her Majesty's Inspectors at the Department of Education and Science, had asked six head teachers to hold a series of meetings, with a balanced, co-opted staff, to mull over and clarify ideas on the curricular structure and organisation of the emergent middle schools. Mr Williams, the head teacher of Abbey Secondary Modern, was asked to lead one of these teams and a major part of their consideration on 'the dummy run' was teaching strategy. 'If Integrated Subject Teaching is to be attempted, how is it likely to be implemented?' asks the report that was compiled on this dummy run, and Her Majesty's Inspector, Mr Johnson, was keen to have an answer. He attended many of these meetings and exhibited particular interest in an inter-disciplinary approach. The consideration of ways and means of basing some, or all, of the class teaching on this method was the meat of the report. A secondary theme was the staff, and the position of the head teacher. 'It was clearly apparent', runs the report, '*at this early stage* that the head teacher could not in isolation dictate and define his philosophy and policies for a completely new kind of school'.

The 'completely new kind of school' that opened in September, for Mr Williams, following the dummy run, was housed in the 1933 buildings, and staffed by the teachers who had formed the junior and secondary schools. Many of them had spent much of the previous year considering the curriculum of this Junior High School, and, in the terms of the report, and in the words of the head teacher, had, in theory, 'all agreed on the need to break down the barriers of subject disciplines'. In practice, however, all the staff resented this approach – the former secondary staff because of their specialist training, and the primary staff because of their desire to be responsible for one class throughout the whole of the week.

Nevertheless interdisciplinary studies were introduced in 1969 in a very big way. The first, second and third years had 'environmental studies' for two afternoons each week, a subject based on elements of RE, history, geography, science and English. The first years had additionally 'social studies', a subject that involved RE, history, geography and science, and the second, third and fourth years had 'English with drama' that was linked with history, geography, art and music. These interdisciplinary studies were block timetabled so that whole year groups could hive off into units based upon the needs of the child, and the head expected (perhaps naively, in view of his twenty years' experience as a head teacher) that these units would vary from week to week. For both environmental studies and social studies, topics of relevance such as 'weather' or 'Canada' (the royal visit to Canada took place about the time of the interview) were to form the unifying core.

These innovations were complicated and far ranging and were introduced at that moment in time when staff were having to adjust to a novel situation. 'A new school requires a new approach,' said Mr Williams, in defence of his innovation, 'and in any case, the HMI was breathing down my neck. There was no use in staff consultations as they were all against it. You just have to force it through. Even the deputy head was against it – he still is.'

The innovation was not working well. No one member of staff had any responsibility for overseeing this area of the timetable and no formal syllabus existed. 'I thought teachers would love to get away from things like that and be free,' said Mr Williams; but the staff were able to manipulate the system to satisfy their own wishes. The groups never varied from week to week, and this enabled the teachers to promote their own subject, within the normal class structure.

Mr Williams felt that one of the unintended consequences of the innovation was a deterioration in the relationships of the staff with himself. 'There is some distance now between us,' he said, 'but their attitudes are very correct.'

Case study 2

Mr Davis, the headmaster of Church Junior High School, had in 1969 introduced interdisciplinary studies for his first years, calling it 'project work' on the timetable. All the first years met together on Wednesday and Friday afternoons to contribute a collective piece of work, that would involve them in the use of English, history, geography, woodwork, domestic science and art and craft. Their last project, which had taken a whole term to complete, was called 'Elizabethan England' and, apart from essays, poetry and music based on that period, they had eventually produced a large model street scene, with stocks, timbered houses, costumed dolls and shops to grace the main entrance of the school where in such a place of prominence it attracted comment and approval.

The head teacher was well pleased with the favourable comment, and it satisfied him to think that yet another success had been accorded the school by parents, teachers and press. The innovation was something of a departure from the more formal order of previous years when, as a new school, in an estate that had both modern owner occupied houses, and superior high rise council flats, it had concentrated on examination success in a network of rigid streaming, and compulsory homework. The change from modern to middle schooling had created the need to think about the organisation of the nine and ten year olds and ideas came from many sources. An important influence for Mr Davis was the part he played in the dummy run project the year before with his colleague, Mr Williams, where interdisciplinary studies had been much discussed. The ideas gained on this course suggested the possibility of such a subject for his own school and it was accordingly made a matter of discussion at the monthly staff meetings. Mr Davis was excited with the idea as he had been with many others and persisted in the formal dialogue with staff. 'You can't bulldoze your way through, but with time and persuasion you can usually get what you want.'

Compromises and adjustments in the staff arrangements were important items in ensuring the acceptance of the innovation. Posts of responsibility that had lost their relevance in reorganisation were reallocated on the basis of the new school structure, and the head of metalwork, now a defunct subject, took charge of the practical side of the project work. By taking all the first years together, for two lessons a week, the head teacher himself created a period of time in which all the participating staff could meet to discuss the week's work and programming, and class teachers were happy to find some direction in their English and allied subjects.

Mr Davis, like his colleague, Mr Williams, had been a head teacher for over twenty years but his present school was modern and in attractive surroundings. It lent itself to display and there was a tradition of innovatory experiments that were frequently of an opportunist nature. All members of the staff were encouraged to exploit their special gifts and the exploitation was pushed and publicised in a way that pleased them, and brought glory to the school.

Case study 3

Church Junior High School was similar to Kings. Kings Junior High School opened in 1963 as a secondary modern school for 480 boys and girls, and the well kept gardens and lawns to the front reflected the orderliness inside. The headmaster, Mr Jones, however, was comparatively young, in his mid-forties and first headship. Before his appointment, he had been the deputy head of the school and also head of English, and as head of English he had experimented with project work with the less able children and found it successful, in the sense that they had enjoyed this approach to English and had worked with more enthusiasm at the subject. He had not informed his headmaster of his experimentation as the head had carefully defined the boundaries of work and the lines of communication. This action could be seen as an expression of the hierarchical nature of the government of this Catholic school which had, by nature of its religious base, more constraints built into its administration than other secondary moderns. The tradition of regulation from above, together with the expressed belief in the value of service to the community, formed the accepted milieu of the school. Mr Jones regarded himself as 'the boss' but he was receptive to suggestions from staff and his authoritarian attitude was not rigidly held in the face of reasonableness. He found conversation with his colleagues and teachers a main source of influence and inspiration, and when Her Majesty's Inspector, Mr Johnson, talked about the value of interdisciplinary studies, he remembered the success of his project work in English and decided to explore the possibilities of reintroducing such a scheme. The HMI arranged for Mr Jones to look in on the dummy run exercise, and later to receive its report. Mr Jones discussed the report with members of the staff and was pleased to find support in these informal conversations from all except his head of English, with whom he lacked rapport. 'He's set in his ways', and 'He doesn't do anything with the library that lends itself to project work' were two of his comments on this member of staff, and the thought of the opportunity to make him change his ways was as much an encouragement to Mr Jones as the support he knew he would get from the remainder of the staff to proceed with the innovation.

Although Mr Jones expresses his distaste of staff consultations, staff meetings are held, and 'I told them what I was going to do and that was that'. Discussion with staff, however, modified the expressions of intent, and they were able to adjust the length of time to be spent on project work and also to decide on the nature of the project. History, geography, art and science were combined with the full support of the staff concerned, and the head of English was required to organise the library so that a section was devoted to the topic concerned and the number of sessions when borrowing and browsing could take place were increased.

What was uppermost in the minds of these head teachers when they had introduced their innovation? This question was asked and the headmaster in Mr Williams said, 'New schools need a new approach', and that in Mr Davis, 'It's good for the school as a whole and gives early training in expected behaviour patterns in the practical rooms.' Mr Jones, headmaster, aphorised, 'Education is not compartmentalised', but for each of these head teachers the innovation had brought other

much sought after objectives; the approval of an HMI, public esteem and
the successful reorganisation of method in a major department on the
lines that the head had wanted.

In the case studies 4 and 5 that follow, the head teacher had a clearly
stated ideology that determined his attitude to school and departmental
organisation, and defined the school's aims and goals. The studies show,
however, that unforeseen factors control and restrict the head teacher in
his innovation.

Case study 4

Mr Lee is direct and friendly ('Now what's your christian name?
Mine's William, though some people call me Bill. I don't mind which')
and fully aware of his position as head of a prestigious school, Newtown
Senior High, the largest in the authority and one of the newest. His
commitment to the comprehensive ideology is total: 'I have an unshake-
able conviction that mixed ability teaching is basic to the comprehensive
philosophy, and maths and language teaching are the only groups that
persist in seeing their subjects as elitist and examination based. My
school is not going to modify its attitude to accommodate this antique
view.' By school he meant himself, and mixed ability teaching was now
the method in all departments of the school. The last department to
adopt this method was the French department and the innovation took
place last year after 'four years of continuous dialogue'. 'There were
only two departments that used selective procedures – maths and
French – but maths fell fairly early on and, of course, I have this bee
in my bonnet about language teaching. English is my subject and I can
see no basis of need for a difference in method between English and
French.'

The French department had resisted, however, and had maintained
this resistance to change for four years. In that period of time Mr Lee
had attempted to bring about the change to mixed ability classes by a
variety of schemes and pressures. 'Staff meetings are impossible in a
school of this size, and no head would survive without delegating power.
The heads of departments are left to organise their own subjects and I
maintain a continuous dialogue with them until I get what I want.'
Continuous dialogue failed to get Mr Lee what he wanted so he resorted
to a more powerful stratagem: 'I called a meeting of the heads of
departments and made the head of French justify his method to them.'
It was, said Mr Lee, a traumatic experience for him, but he persisted
in a system of setting for his subject. The head teacher then imposed a
solution. Children would be free to choose an aspect of French that

appealed to them, and courses based on 'language', 'holiday French', 'French culture and society', etc., were produced, but this selection procedure based solely on the desires of the pupil produced a replica of the streamed situation, and an impasse was now reached in that the imposed situation enabled the departmental head, by suggestion and encouragement, to produce a setted* arrangement. Another line of attack was open to the headmaster. Staff replacement was based on the desire of the new recruit to teach in the mixed ability situation, and when the head of the department left to take up a post in a college of education, his position was filled by a person who committed himself to mixed ability teaching at the interview. However, problems of mixed ability teaching of French have arisen with the new departmental head because of arrangements that have to be made to accommodate those pupils who envisage taking the subject to 'O' and 'A' level. A consenting head of department, together with the pupil-based selection procedures based on alternative courses of 'language', 'holiday French', etc., is producing a pattern of classes in which ability emerges as a predominant factor. 'At least, we don't do the selecting,' said Mr Lee, 'but in order to achieve what I want in the teaching of French the universities will have to change the elitist attitudes that they inculcate into their post-graduate teachers.'

Case study 5

The local authority had striven to achieve an ideal for almost thirty years – comprehensive education. Houses were more important than schools in the immediate post-war years and the early years of the Conservative administration that arrived in 1951 had allowed the authority to build campus schools but not comprehensives; it was, therefore, with a great sense of real achievement that they viewed their first purpose-built comprehensive school in 1963, and the occasion demanded the Secretary of State for Education and Science for its opening and the appointment of a man with a national reputation for its head teacher. There was a concerted determination on the part of the authority, the governors and the head teacher to make a success of comprehensive education and no expense or effort was spared. For all concerned, comprehensive education was epitomised by the rejection of any form of selection, and the concomitant was mixed ability teaching. Success had, however, to be seen and one of the areas in which Bridge Senior High School chose to display it was in that of its 'O' and 'A' level results.

The maths department organised itself on a traditional syllabus and

* *Setting* is a system whereby basic classes are regrouped for the teaching of particular subjects.

setted classes, and in 1964 the head teacher, Mr Kemp, decided that this selection procedure would have to go. This expressed desire on the part of the head teacher was resisted. 'You cannot have mixed ability groups with this syllabus,' said the head of the department. 'In that case we must change the syllabus,' said the head teacher. 'Not if you want to take our "O" and "A" level examinations,' replied the departmental head.

Mr Kemp was determined on change, however, and his first efforts were the process of 'continuous dialogue': 'If I am right, then conversion must take place, because resistance is due to inadequacy, or age, or training on the part of the staff. To not oppose such a situation would damage the children's chances.'

Continuous dialogue was slow and unsuccessful in effecting the much wished for change and additional pressures were brought to bear. Two 'nationally known figures' on the 'new maths' were invited to lecture to the school in general and the maths department staff in particular. 'They persuaded me that no serious obstacle was present to successful "O" and "A" level teaching based on the modern maths syllabus and mixed ability classes for teaching, but the departmental head wouldn't budge. But you know, you can't insist on a man doing something he hasn't any faith in, so I was back to square one and persuasion.' The persuasion of continuous dialogue was, as a matter of policy by the head, spiced with regular criticism of all those aspects of the department that contributed to and maintained the 'setted class', and the outcome, though not necessarily a direct one, of four years' persuasion laced with criticism was the departure of the head of the department to another school. He was replaced by a teacher who committed himself at the interview to end the system of 'setting'; indeed he was enthusiastic for a mixed ability arrangement on taking up his appointment within the school.

There was now complete agreement on organisation of the department between the head teacher and the head of the department, but after three years a pattern is emerging which appears to be very little different from the former one. The 'A' level group is recruited from the 'O' level class, the 'O' level syllabus differs considerably from that of the CSE, and many of the fourth year leavers have a syllabus based on need, vocation and interest. The final result of the innovation imposed in ideological terms was a pupil organisation almost identical to that of the system the ideology condemned.

Both Mr Lee and Mr Kemp have promoted their ideologies in the belief that they could be achieved. The problem of institutional frustration of the ideological innovation was not recognised until it was met, and perhaps not even then. Both of these headmasters had authority for change and the full support of all sections of the organisation for change; but change did not come easily and in the end energy was expended in justifying the ideology in the context of the innovation and not, as was originally planned, justifying the change on the basis of the ideology.

Case study 6 shows an innovation designed to satisfy an ambition of the head teacher within the context of the school. It is a study in serendipitous innovation.

Case study 6

Mr South, the head teacher of Preston Junior High School, spoke freely. 'We could have done German, Latin or Spanish as our second language. I suppose that, strictly speaking, we should call it our third language if we call English a language.'

'Why the choice of German, Latin or Spanish?'

'We are equidistant from three senior high schools and approximately one third of our leavers go to each of them – Roper Boys' does German, Hailey Girls' does Latin and Broad Senior does Spanish.'

'And why a second or, as you call it, a third language?'

'Oh, I don't know really. I wanted a second language and I got it. You see, when we were a secondary modern, there was no need for it, but now we're supplying children to three grammar schools.'

'You mean senior comprehensives?'

'Well, yes, I suppose that's what they are now, but they were pukka grammar schools and I don't think that that tradition will die, will it?'

'I can't think of any other Junior High School in the city doing a second language – especially as the authority is so keen on its Nuffield French, and I don't really see the Senior High Schools providing courses in two languages for all their pupils.'

'We certainly get no help from the authority. In fact, the chief inspector told me to stop it – refused to help with teachers, etc. – and the HMI raised an eyebrow, but I'm the head and I know what I want. In any case, we only do Latin with the "A" stream in the top two years for three lessons per week.' Mr South clearly had no regrets about the innovation and no doubts about its place on the timetable in spite of authority's frown. 'We have to accommodate to the new situation. We have a grammar school intake so we have to provide a grammar school education – and Latin *is* a grammar school education.'

'What was your objection to German or Spanish? Would you consider them at least as equally relevant, and probably find the staffing situation a little easier?'

'Staff was no problem whatsoever. In fact I have four members of staff who can take Latin and, strangely enough, all of them have expressed a desire to teach it and in fact it was first suggested by a member of staff and it has been a topic of conversation at staff meetings for three or four years. So when I raised the matter officially at a staff meeting they were very keen. You know, I've always regretted the passing of Latin. I enjoyed it immensely at school; it was my favourite subject and I was top in it for years. I remember, all of ten years ago, being a platform guest at Hailey Girls' Grammar Speech Day, when it was a grammar school you know, and the whole of the service was done in Latin. That's my great ambition – to hold my Speech Day in Latin. . . .'

If Mr South had not had such tranquil recollections of success as an excellent Latin scholar forty years ago, and if the staff had not suggested on occasions their willingness to teach it, and if the reorganisation of the school had not created a rationale for its introduction, would Mr South have instigated such a selective change within his school?

Case study 7: a study in opportunist innovation

The transfer from tripartite to comprehensive schools in the education authority of this study was smooth, efficient and, almost without exception, welcomed by its head teachers. In the process, secondary modern schools either closed or became Junior High Schools and the grammar schools became Senior Highs. Many secondary schools had equipment that had no relevance to their new role as Junior Highs and this was particularly true of typewriters that formed the main item of equipment in their commercial courses. The authority trusted its head teachers to dispose of unwanted equipment within their schools to those schools that expressed a need for them.

Mr Dukes had spent the whole of his teaching career, spanning some forty years, with this authority and for the last twenty was one of their more esteemed heads. His first headship had been at an old and now demolished all-age school; then a city centre secondary modern and now a Senior High School. He came to his present headship while it was a grammar school of some eminence within the city, and some two years before it was to begin to receive its first batch of non-selective pupils. This was a period, however, when many old secondary moderns were being closed and replaced by purpose built comprehensives, and equipment was available for disposal. Mr Dukes, with a long association in the city and many friends, had no difficulty in obtaining the complete commerce course equipment – 'I didn't need to buy a thing – even the textbooks and paper were there – I drove round in my car and carted it away.' Mr Dukes now had the complete equipment for a commerce course, in a school that had no vocational courses and no proposals for introducing them.

Mr Dukes had a feeling for typing. He was trained and qualified in both typewriting and shorthand and in his early married life had augmented his income as a teacher by evening work in these subjects. He therefore had no difficulties in finding a use for his newly acquired equipment, and his pupils were the upper VIth. 'It is very useful to be able to type your essays, and shorthand is a *sine qua non* for lectures. They had lots of spare time on their timetable so it didn't interfere with their main studies. Staff were against it at first, but their misgivings have gone by now.'

Typing proved very popular with the VIth form, who saw it as an insurance against the contingency of not getting into university. The subject proved so popular that the following year it was introduced to the lower VIth and also to those in the Vth who were returning, but only after completion of the 'O' levels. 'Always difficult to know what to do with your fifth year students after completion of "O" levels. This of course was ideal – though I limited it to those who were good at English; after all, if you can't write it, how can you type it? You know, it has great therapeutic value to the child on stiff academic courses.'

The meeting with Mr Dukes was to discuss his innovation in curriculum studies, described on Schedule A as 'commercial studies'. As the headmaster of a comprehensive school for the older child, he sees it as an essential part of the curriculum for the less able. To accommodate the course, he has recently appointed a full-time teacher of 'commerce' and a part-time teacher deals with typing. The academic staff now welcome it. 'They are delighted to see these people doing this sort of thing. They know that their own specialities are irrelevant to this type of child.' Mr Dukes had a fitting word to describe the position now. 'Of course, when we went comprehensive, I realised what a blessing the equipment was going to be – I was the first head in the city to introduce "commerce courses" in the secondary modern schools, and now we have a lot of children of this sort coming into the school.'

Continuous modification of content and method to meet changing demands is an essential element of school organisation and the ability to use material within the school to further these modifications is a measure of the executive's ingenuity. This case study shows opportunism as a factor in promoting the head teacher's aims, which do not always coincide with the aims of the school.

Case study 8: the gift based innovation

Ramsey Junior High School, two years ago the Ramsey Secondary Modern School, was housed in an old, gaunt Victorian building separated from the condemned terraces of houses by a band of asphalt. The secondary modern had had, however, a well established record of success in GCE and CSE examinations, together with a reputation for precisely streamed classes, strict discipline and a belief in the authority of the head teacher. The head of science was well known for his work on the CSE science panel and the Secondary Modern Leavers' Certificate and also as a frequent lecturer to study groups at the Teachers' Centre on the teaching of science. He was 'well thought of' by the Local Education Authority science adviser.

In 1969 the LEA decided to back the Nuffield Combined Science Curriculum Project by offering to meet the full support costs of such courses in two schools: one a Senior High and the other a Junior High, if such schools could be found. The LEA science adviser was told to find two such schools. Ramsey Junior High was one of them and his first approach was to the head of science with the suggestion that such a course could be most profitable to the school in terms of prestige and equipment and, should the head of science support such a scheme, then the science adviser would approach the head teacher, Mr Kelly, suggesting that the authority would like to see his school adopt the Nuffield Combined Science Scheme and would welcome his permission. The head of science readily agreed and the science adviser then approached the head. The head teacher sought the views of his head of science and, not unnaturally, readily gave his permission.

The head delegated the whole of the responsibility of arranging, organising, introducing and maintaining the Nuffield Combined Science Scheme to his head of science, who, with this authority, chose the classes, devised the syllabus and worked out organisational procedures. Against the general organisation of the school and the Nuffield scheme the head of science was allowed to 'set' his science classes in the top two years.

In 1969 and in 1970 the head of science attended Nuffield Combined Science Courses and the head teacher introduced him to both sessions that were held in the school as part of the present study. 'I don't know anything about it, but the head of science, Mr Jacques, can answer all your questions.'

Mr Jacques was very firm on the need to change the arrangements he had first introduced. 'Streaming is absolutely essential if the bright child is to be effectively helped to success and I want a return to directed teaching of physics and chemistry. In fact, I want them timetabled as physics and chemistry so that classes will know which lab to go to. I want to get back to the system we had as a secondary modern – that was successful and I enjoyed it. I knew exactly where I stood and precisely what had to be done.' The head teacher agreed: 'Mr Jacques can have whatever he wants – I've complete reliance in him; he's been here for fifteen years and the authority thinks highly of him.'

'And what will happen to the £1,500 of equipment?'

'Well, we've won that, haven't we? Of course, it will be most useful for us in the real teaching situation that will be commencing in September.'

Mr Kelly, the head teacher, was certain the innovation had been a success, and further that its success would continue and improve with the modifications that had been made by Mr Jacques. 'I wanted some change in the science teaching when we went Junior High, to cater for the new set up, and I'm satisfied I've got it,' said the head teacher. When Mr Jacques completes his next batch of modifications, the only difference between his former scheme and his present one will be £1,500 worth of science equipment.

Case study 9: another gift based innovation

A major curriculum innovation for Mr Smith, headmaster of Hall Junior High School, and one that gave him immense satisfaction, was the introduction of modern maths to replace his more traditional syllabus. 'I have a marvellous head of maths – a woman actually – and she's dead keen on this new maths. You treasure staff like her, and naturally I give her her head in the organisation of her department. She produced a completely new syllabus. Of course, she is well in with the local inspector – goes on all his courses, and it pays dividends you know. She gets invited to help with the in-service courses and one of the spin-offs has been three calculators. They didn't cost us a penny and I suppose they're worth all of £150.'

'What modifications did you make to this course once you saw it working?'

'Absolutely none. I left it entirely to the head of department. It was her change and she didn't bother me with suggestions. The kids like her and they thoroughly enjoy the new maths, and I think that that is as good a test as any, don't you? When we were a secondary modern we concentrated on GCE and CSE and, as you know, we no longer have this to bother us and we now aim to pass children on to the Senior High School who will do equally well when their time comes.'

'How do you think modern maths will help them?'

'Well that's the fly in the ointment, of course. With traditional maths you knew exactly where you stood, but who knows with this modern stuff? I've real doubts but, as I said earlier, it's the head of maths's idea and the local inspector seems very happy about it. It's working well as far as I can see, no problems of discipline or anything like that, and I see absolutely no reason for me to interfere.'

VII

Many suggestions for change are stillborn, and we have not concerned ourselves with them. This study is based on change and is an attempt to show how head teachers play a part in bringing it about. It is only concerned with those initial suggestions that ended in change and this point is important in this section that deals with the path of the idea from that of a *possibility* to that of *probability*. All the ideas referred to in this section resulted in change and those ideas that did not do not figure in the statistics. The first step in the progress of change is the idea of the possibility and it is now necessary to examine the way in which the head teacher who has accepted the idea presents it to the school with a view to its implementation.

The question was asked if, before the change was effected, consultations were held with certain categories of people. A distinction was made between meaningful consultation and that kind of talk which merely passes on information and listens to comment but refuses any discussion leading to modification of the intended change. By consultation, it was made quite clear that what was meant was discussion that could lead to modification. The replies are listed in table 4.13.

TABLE 4.13   Categories of people consulted about the intended innovation

Category of person	Times consulted
Deputy head	1
Staff	12
LEA advisers	1
HMI	2
Pupils	0
Parents	0
Governors	0
No consultation whatsoever	2

In one case the visit of an HMI to the school enabled the school to hear his comments on the proposed change (adverse as it so happened), but, as the head teacher did not seek his advice, it is not recorded as a

consultation. Two head teachers implemented change without any consultation whatsoever. 'If you ask staff for an opinion,' said one head,
'you will get as many answers as there are members of staff. So I don't
ask them', and the other head believed in the controlled leak. 'I don't
believe in consultation, but I do go to selected members of staff, whom
I know are influential, and who think the way I do, and tell them of what
I intend to do.' One head consulted with his deputy, but the other twelve
all consulted with staff. On six recorded occasions the head consulted
with the head of the appropriate department, as well as members of
staff, about the intended change. Consultation with people other than
staff was rare; on one occasion there was discussion with one of the LEA
advisers, and on two occasions with the HMI, and these were in addition
to the staff consultations. On no occasion were pupils, parents or
governors invited to give their views, though technically governors are
responsible for the curriculum, and pupils, and through them their
parents, are affected in varying degrees. Consultation was always with
the professional and never with the amateur, or interested onlooker. An
interesting point that arose in discussion about the answers to this
question by the heads was that consultation was always about the
method of implementation and administrative arrangements for its
introduction and continuance. Discussion never took place on its
justification or relevance. This could well be due to the concern that
teachers have for the present needs of their children, and this ever
present concern removes from the teachers' consideration more distant
factors like the goals of the school. Needs create major demands that
look for speedy relief and the constant informal dialogue that takes
place in the school between the head teacher and his staff prepares in a
way the kinds of innovation that will be acceptable to staff, and seen by
that staff and the head as those areas that require attention. This view is
supported by the replies that were received in answer to the question,
'What modifications did the teachers suggest in these consultations
prior to the introduction of the innovation?' The answers are placed in
four categories, two of which are supportive, one non-supportive, and
one category confined to those schools where no indication was given of
staff attitudes because the head teacher did not indulge in consultation
(table 4.14).

No modifications were possible in two of the schools, and in five
others modifications were of that kind that suggested restrictions on the
proposals put forward by the head teacher. Schools are humane institutions, unrestricted by any codes of secrecy, and small enough for staff
in their social organisation to discuss needs and express views. Head
teachers frequently search out and appoint staff who are sympathetic to

TABLE 4.14 Modifications to innovations suggested in consultations

Type of modification suggested	Junior High Schools	Senior High Schools
Fully supportive, with no suggested modifications	2	2
No modifications suggested, but the innovation welcomed	4	0
A request for a partial or total reduction in the change	2	3
No consultation permitted	2	0

contemplated innovation (case studies 4 and 5); argument, compromise and adjustments take place outside the formal staff meetings and the process of continuous dialogue, informally based, creates the opportunities for staff to air their views, voice their opinions and modify their attitudes. It is unreal, therefore, to expect staff meetings to concern themselves with anything but administrative procedures. The fact that the innovation, and the head teacher's views on it, have been known about before the formal meeting takes place may well account for the fact that ten schools recorded in table 4.14 did not offer any suggestions for modifying the proposed innovation and that, of these ten, four fully supported the innovation, and said so.

There was a tendency in all these schools to place more emphasis on informal discussion than on staff meetings. Indeed, the staff meeting had almost an aura of caricature in many of these schools. Certainly the large Senior High Schools saw the staff meeting as an ineffective forum for discussion as their staff numbers in all cases were over fifty, some as high as seventy-five, and size, together with the problem of finding occasions when all could meet, militated against this form of consultation. In the Junior High Schools, staff meetings were looked upon as the occasion when the head teacher held court and handed out duty lists and class arrangements. Informal discussion, however, was an accepted method of consultation in all schools, as the following table shows. Information was gathered as to ways in which staff were prepared for change and the amount of discussion and preparation that took place. The questions and their answers are recorded in table 4.15.

In only four cases do we find that much discussion took place in staff meetings, though obviously some of the innovations might be seen as inappropriate for discussion at such a meeting, since they concerned a single department, or even perhaps a single teacher. Outside staff meetings, however, it was felt that discussion at length with the head of department was important, and equally important was discussion with

TABLE 4.15   Types of discussion demanded by innovations

	Junior High Schools	*Senior High Schools*
Did you find that the change needed much discussion		
in staff meetings?	4	0
with the head of the appropriate department?	6	4
with the deputy head?	4	1
with individual members of staff?	8	2

individual members of staff. In fact, discussion with individual members of staff took place in eight of the ten Junior High Schools and two of the five Senior High Schools. Table 4.15 also shows that the head teacher did not confine himself to a single category within the classification of the table. Allowing for the fact that in two of the Junior High Schools the head teacher did not believe in consultation, in those schools that did have it, the consultation appears to have been comprehensive and to have involved different arrangements or combinations of staff. In the Senior High School consultation with the appropriate head of department was an important avenue for progress. The informal discussion with the deputy head is five times more frequent than the formal discussions recorded in table 4.13. Consensus is important for a majority of these schools and the consensus view would appear to be the innovation that finally emerges as the formal suggestion at the staff meeting. This would suggest one possible reason for the very small number of modifications to the innovations that arose at staff meetings, and it could also explain why none of the suggested modifications proved acceptable to the head teacher. Only five modifications were of sufficient significance to be remembered, but if, as it has already been suggested, the exact boundaries of the innovation had been arrived at in the light of expressed comment and availability of resources, then the consensus innovation would be a reasonable explanation of the low number of modifications. Other reasons for this situation, however, could be:

1   The hierarchical staff arrangement.
2   The innovation was almost totally acceptable, because it had been seen working in other schools.
3   That the only areas of discussion for modification were those of the ways and means of its implementation.

Some measure of its acceptance or otherwise by staff would be the amount and length of time of resistance to the innovation, and resistance could be revealed in various ways. If informal discussion is an important aspect of the implementation of change, then informal discussion should also provide a medium for the expression of views that indicated a continued challenge to the innovation. The question was asked, 'How long elapsed after the change before the staff stopped offering suggestions about modification?' and the answers are given in table 4.16.

Tables 4.16 and 4.17 suggest that innovation may be accepted without any modification being offered, but staff may still have reservations

TABLE 4.16   Length of time before suggestions for modifications stopped

	Junior High Schools	*Senior High Schools*
No time (immediate acceptance)	6	2
Limited (up to the moment of implementation)	1	0
Persisted, still existing	2	3
No evidence offered	1	0

TABLE 4.17   Staff reaction changes after implementation

	Junior High Schools	*Senior High Schools*
Accepted wholeheartedly	4	2
Accepted with reservations	3	2
Accepted against their wishes	2	1
No evidence	1	0

about it that last for a limited period of time. Table 4.16 also suggests that once positions are stated they tend to persist. Of the fourteen changes about which there is any evidence, only two show an alteration in staff attitudes. In table 4.16 only five of the fifteen reserved their position, the others being either for or against. This polarisation may be one of ideology, age or personality, or related to the nature of the change itself, but whatever the basis of the opposition, the only form it took was that of discussion and suggestion. Revolution there was none and the opposition never achieved any measure of modification in the innovation.

The question was also asked, 'What changes did you make once you saw the innovation working?' This change in the original innovation could have resulted from observations of the innovation in practice, or a response to opposition, or encouragement for further extension of the innovation, from parents or teachers or children. No suggestion was made as to the specificity of the modification, but the search for evidence of some modification to the innovation once it had been initiated was thorough. The answers to this question are given in table 4.18.

TABLE 4.18 Modifications to number of innovations

	Junior High Schools	Senior High Schools
None	8	3
None, but change contemplated	2	2

No school had made any modification to its innovation, though four schools suggested that they could well have to make some adjustments. Two of the contemplated adjustments were a reduction in the innovation itself. In one case, the head of department was dissatisfied with the methods and aims of Nuffield science and intended to introduce more 'formality', as it was felt that the needs of the students in the Senior High Schools, and the 'O' level examination, made it desirable for the pupils in this particular Junior High School to have the correct 'basic attitude to learning' (case study 8). In the other it was felt that the demands of 'O' level maths would not necessarily be best met by having a mixture of modern and traditional maths and, if this were so, then potential 'O' level candidates would receive less of the innovation (case study 9). Both these schools were Junior High Schools. In the Senior High Schools both adjustments contemplated were administrative. In one the innovation was now hampered by lack of space, and adjustments would have to be made in classroom use, and in the other school the adjustment was one of timetabling procedures. The total amount of intended change in the innovations for thirteen of the schools is miniscule, and is either a tribute to the effective organisation and aims of the school, or an indication of the nature of the change itself. The organisation of the schools is not generally questioned, expecially if the bureaucratic nature of the school society is accepted. The evidence of table 4.18 would suggest that innovations are successfully introduced and that the success of the innovation is due to extensive formal and informal discussion. The discussion that precedes change is of such length and totality that the resulting consensus innovation is certain of acceptance. If this is so, then innovation is more the result of what is possible than that of what is desirable.

VIII

The immediate reaction of head teachers to the question asking for the source of the initial suggestion of the possibility of change was to reply in effect, ourselves – the head teachers, as is shown in table 4.20 – but discussion and reflection resulted in a different category of answers (see table 4.19, adjusted response). By suitably weighting the adjusted response, it is possible to arrive at some order of importance in the agencies of change in schools. Column '1st' lists the initial source of the suggestion of the possibility of innovation. Column '2nd' lists the

TABLE 4.19   The adjusted response on the main sources of influence for the change

Source	1st	2nd	3rd	4th	Weighted value
Head teacher	3	9	2	1	44
Head of appropriate department	1	1	2	2	13
Colleague in another school	2	0	1	0	10
HMI	0	2	1	0	8
Schools council	1	0	1	0	6
Course attended	6	0	0	0	24
LEA adviser	1	1	0	0	7
Public opinion	1	0	0	0	4
Other members of staff	0	0	2	1	5
Deputy head	0	1	1	0	5
None specified	0	1	5	11	–

NB The weights are as follows: 4, 3, 2 and 1 for columns 1, 2, 3 and 4.

TABLE 4.20   Rank order of influences on the initiation of change

Head teacher's immediate response	Adjusted response
1 The head teacher	1 The head teacher
2 Head of appropriate department	2 Course attended
3 { HMI / Course attended / Other members of staff / Deputy head	3 Head of appropriate department
	4 Colleague in another school
	5 HMI
	6 LEA adviser
	7 Schools council

main reinforcing agency, column '3rd' and Column '4th' the successive supporters for the innovation. The final figure is the weighted value.

Not surprisingly the head teacher emerges as the most important agency of change, not only in their own immediate view, but also in the adjusted view. This is in contrast with the main source of suggestion for change, which was attendance on a course by a member of staff or the head teacher.

A head teacher can actively promote change; or moderate change suggested by some source other than himself. He may, however, merely acquiesce in change initiated by others and these three attitudes or positions to change we have termed instigation, moderation and permissive bystanding. The fifteen studies of change in this investigation divide as shown in table 4.21.

TABLE 4.21   The role of the head teacher as innovator

	Junior High Schools	*Senior High Schools*
The head as instigator	6	5
The head as moderator	1	0
The head as bystander	3	0
Totals	10	5

Case studies 1, 2 and 3 (pp. 153–8), 4 and 5 (pp. 158–61) display the head teacher as an instigator. It would, however, be misplaced to regard all these innovations as the result of educational purpose or contemplation and in case studies 1, 2 and 3 attention has been drawn to baser and less discussed reasons. They display the realisation of non-educational goals, justified on educational grounds.

On p. 176, attention is drawn to the powerful reinforcement that a suggested innovation receives, if it relates in some fairly direct way to a previous happy or successful experience of the head teacher. The expression 'the head as an instigator' implies drive, determination and conviction in the head teacher, but instigation can be the result of happy circumstances; a coming together of opportunity, desire and an accepting climate and the concurrence of these factors is the important generator of an urge for change.

IX

The formal organisation that is found in schools means that nearly all curriculum change is channelled through the head teacher. It has been suggested earlier that change is not initiated unless the head teacher feels that it is likely to succeed, and a measure of this search for the certainty of success is the way in which an innovation becomes an established part of school life. The permanence and stability of an innovation once introduced is given in tables 4.22 and 4.23 which record the replies to the questions:

1. How long has the change lasted?
2. Is the change to continue indefinitely?

Table 4.23 confirms the statement made about the ninety-three innovations recorded on Schedule A, that all these innovations were still

TABLE 4.22 Answers to 'How long has it lasted?'
$N = 15$

Number of terms	1	2	3	4	5	6
Junior Highs	0	3	0	0	6	1
Senior Highs	0	1	0	0	0	4
Totals	0	4	0	0	6	5

TABLE 4.23 Answers to 'Is the change to last indefinitely?'
$N = 15$

	Yes	No
Junior Highs	10	0
Senior Highs	5	0
Totals	15	0

operational at the time of study, with two exceptions. There is change but not decay; and with permanence there is stability. Table 4.7 showed that if the innovation had had to be repeated, given a duplication of the conditions, the heads would repeat it exactly. But the innovation was also exactly the type of innovation the head wanted. The following questions were put to the head: 'Is the change the one you wanted?' and 'Is it exactly the one you wanted?' Table 4.24 records the responses to these questions.

TABLE 4.24 Responses to questions on suitability of innovations

	Yes	No
Is the change the one you wanted?	15	0
Is it exactly what you wanted?	14	1

The one case of the head teacher not getting exactly what he wanted was due to the tactics of the change. The head, in deference to the misgivings of the department's staff, agreed to the change being one of gradual evolution. The head of the department used this arrangement, in the eyes of the head teacher, to delay progress towards the completion of the innovation. It is fascinating to speculate on the possible reasons for head teachers getting exactly what they want, and the possibilities are many; but head teachers undoubtedly, as this study will show later, exercise their power and influence in either allowing innovations that they are persuaded they want to see in the school, or initiating the innovation themselves and tailoring it to the needs, constraints and resources of the situation. Indeed the evidence of this study is that innovation is seen as the art of the practical, and compromises are reached before the innovation is introduced. In this case, therefore, it is not unexpected that the innovation is exactly the one that is wanted. As needs make their presence felt, arrangements to meet the need are introduced at a moment that seems right, because of a change in circumstances or a growing awareness of the necessity to find a solution to the problem. Because the innovation is frequently an answer to need, its permanence is assured and, because the method of answering this need is fully considered in the light of the problem, and the resources to meet it, it is guaranteed stability once introduced. Even the introduction of modern maths, or Nuffield French, is argued on the basis of need, though its appearance in the school curriculum may in fact be due more to a change in fashion than of the requisitions of staff or materials. Case study 9 illustrated this point.

A close examination was made of the ways in which acceptable forms of innovation are arrived at and this involved a detailed search for the source of the impetus for change. The question was asked as to who or what took a leading part in bringing the possibilities of change to the attention of the head teacher, and the immediate answers were recorded. Very often more than one agency was mentioned as playing a prominent part in suggesting the possibility of change, and these answers were recorded so as to give them an order of rank. In the discussion that followed, adjustments, changes and additions were frequently made to this order and a final adjusted order was arrived at.

On twelve occasions the head teacher felt that he had himself been responsible for the initial considerations about the possibilities of change, but in fact on ten of those occasions the idea had come from some other source; and on one occasion the head teacher had thought it to be some other source when in fact it was himself. A number of agencies were mentioned as being responsible for the initial suggestion and, of these, the most important influence was that of courses that had been attended by the head teacher. Such courses were responsible for providing the initial impetus for six of the innovations, but innovation was rarely the result of a single impetus, other agencies often reinforcing the first idea.

The major reinforcing impetus was that of the head teachers themselves, and when evidence was sought as to why an initial impetus should so frequently find a positive response in these head teachers it became apparent that their remembered successful experience, frequently as a class teacher, was an important factor. The initial impetus for change brought to the surface a memory of past success and enjoyment, and this gave the initial impetus a sympathetic response. The evidence for this reinforcement to the initial impetus is given in full in the summary in table 4.25.

TABLE 4.25 Summary of initiating and supporting agencies for innovation

Innovation	Initial impetus	Reinforcement
1 Mixed ability grouping	Public opinion	As a junior head I never streamed and I always felt it was much nicer.
2 Second language (Latin)	Colleague in another school	I enjoyed it [Latin] immensely at school (case study 6).
3 Italic handwriting	Course attended	I attended a course for this some fifteen years ago, and I enjoyed it so much that I went again the following year. I love the style.
4 Social studies	Course attended	This is my subject actually and I taught it for years before I became a head (case study 3).
5 Social studies	Course attended	I did a very similar thing with the early leavers when we were a secondary modern and it was a great success.
6 Modern maths	Schools Council	It's essential to mixed ability teaching (case study 5).
7 Project	Colleague in another school	All my previous experience was in technical colleges . . .
8 Modern maths	Head of maths department	We did it in my previous school and it was very successful.
9 Project work in social studies	Course attended	I had a free hand as head of English in a secondary modern and this method of teaching is marvellous.

In eight of the nine cases listed, previous successful experience strongly reinforced the feelings of the possibility of change created by the initial impulse. It could well be argued that what we have described as the initial impulse triggered off a long held, but dormant, view on the need for change in a particular area in which the head teacher had wide experience. But what is undoubtedly true is that previous successful experience combined with substantial outside support provides sufficient impetus for the introduction of change. On three occasions when the head teachers themselves had been responsible for bringing about reform, the reforms were in that subject area that had formed the main body of previous teaching experience. We would suggest, therefore, that an important element in the introduction of change is previous successful experience in the area of the suggested change itself.

In support of earlier findings table 4.26 summarises the source of the initial suggestions for change in two categories, while table 4.27 lists the major sources of reinforcement.

TABLE 4.26   Sources of suggestions for innovation

	Immediate response	Adjusted response
Impetus from within school	14	4
Impetus from outside school	1	11
Totals	15	15

These summaries confirm the earlier conclusions inferred from the findings on table 4.3 (see p. 143), that the innovations that are allowed to be introduced are those that experience in other schools suggests will be successful. Table 4.26 shows the idea entering from outside the school and table 4.27 shows the idea being taken up within the school

TABLE 4.27   Sources of reinforcement for innovation

	Immediate response	Adjusted response
Source from within school	7	11
Source from outside school	8	4
Totals	15	15

and most often by the head teacher himself. Successful innovation outside the school that can meet a need within the school was shown earlier to be a reasonable interpretation of much of the material obtained on Schedule A. The need is seen as an integral part of the fabric of the school and the innovation highlights the need and the ways of meeting it. Whilst innovation is now conceived of as normal in education, in the schools in this study the prevalent conception was not so much one of the normality of accepting radical change but rather of allowing for modifications of existing structures within well-defined and familiar parameters.

Acknowledgment

The author is grateful to Professor P.H. Taylor of the University of Birmingham for his help and advice in designing and executing the study on which this paper is based.

Handling Innovation
in the Classroom: Two Scottish Examples

David Hamilton

Editor's introduction

As the previous paper showed, decisions to introduce change into a
school may be very far from being simple and clear cut: the nature of
the commitment entered into represents the outcome of complex
accommodations between institutional imperatives and individual
attitudes and needs. But even when the point of introduction is
reached, the actual form that implementation will take still remains
to be decided. Certain restraints will already have become operative,
but those imposed by the necessity of introducing change into the
context of the classroom have yet to declare themselves. Hamilton's
paper traces the response of two Scottish schools to the adoption of
an integrated science curriculum, and describes how '. . . teachers,
students and others interpret and reinterpret the instructional
system for their particular setting', and how the scheme '. . . is
successfully transformed as its wisdom is filtered through the
organizational structure of the school, science departments and
classrooms'.

In the process he raises a wide range of questions, some practical,
some theoretical. Conflicts may arise between the organisational
style of the school – student grouping, departmental structures,
decision-making machinery – and the demands of new curricula.
But underpinning this style is a complex of beliefs and ideologies
about the nature of education, the role of the school, and proper
ways of handling knowledge in the classroom. To understand the
practical problems it is necessary to have ways of thinking about this
infrastructure of norms, values and attitudes. An even more elusive
intellectual problem is how to conceptualise the innovation itself: is

it perfect only in the mind of the original designer, descending thence in a kind of neo-platonist sequence of ever more imperfect simulacra until it arrives in ultimate imperfection in the classroom? Or, as Hamilton suggests, does the only true reality of the innovation lie in its final transaction in the school? (The conclusion that *neither* position is tenable would seem to introduce an unbearable degree of relativism into the situation.) Yet however complex the issues raised, Hamilton's analysis always stays close to day to day events in the schools, and reflects the constant concern with exact observation which must precede imaginative interpretation.

I

Critical examination of curriculum innovations typically begins with a discussion of the pre-specified 'objectives' of the new course, medium or mode under review. Later, the discussion proceeds to an examination of the scheme's impact at college, school or classroom level. When this analytic sequence is used the discussion moves from the pure to the impure; or from an unsullied ideal to a partial and often imperfect reality. Not surprisingly, innovations discussed in these terms become surrounded by an aura of disillusionment and inadequacy.

This account adopts a contrasting theoretical stance to discuss curriculum innovation. It begins with practice rather than precept. It regards the learning milieu as containing the substance of curriculum innovation, not, as is often implied, its pale or distorted shadow.

This paper has two sections. The first part describes the introduction of an integrated science curriculum into two Scottish schools: 'Simpson' and 'Maxwell'. In the event this proved more difficult than previously imagined. In both schools 'integrated' science was organised alongside 'subject-specific' science. Through time, however, each form of organisation developed different social, intellectual and organisational priorities. By linking these priorities to a theoretical model proposed by Basil Bernstein, the account attempts an analysis of the uneasy co-existence between them.

The second part of this paper takes a closer look at Maxwell school and focuses on the classroom rather than the departmental effects of introducing an integrated scheme. In particular it describes the differential impact of the course in four separate classrooms.

The data for this study were collected during periods of participant observation in both schools. Preliminary visits were made in October 1970, the final visits in March 1972. In all, sixteen complete weeks of observation took place. Besides compiling 'field-notes' during the observation I conducted more formal interviews with the teachers and also asked the children to complete six short questionnaires.[1]

Critical to this paper is an understanding of the pattern and history of curriculum development in Scotland. English or transatlantic norms rarely apply. In many respects Scotland can claim to have pioneered 'new' (i.e., post-Sputnik) curricula in Britain. In 1962 – four years before their English counterparts – 'alternative' syllabuses for secondary school physics and chemistry were produced. Although nowadays these schemes would be considered 'string and sealing-wax' affairs, they embodied many of the new ideas current at that time. Nevertheless, in two respects these first generation schemes were strongly influenced by the existing patterns of organisation: they accepted conventional subject boundaries and provided for a similar (i.e., restricted) ability range as before.

Already, however, the schools themselves were gradually moving towards different modes of organisation. In the same year as the alternative science schemes were issued a 'modern studies' examination syllabus was prepared covering an area colonised previously by history and geography. Likewise, comprehensive schools soon began to explore schemes of work suitable for the entire ability range, and for use in 'mixed ability' rather than 'streamed' classes. The preparation of the Scottish Integrated Science Scheme – the subject of this account – represented a fusion of these two educational aspirations.

In 1964 a Scottish Education Department working party was set up to consider the development of science schemes for 'non-academic' pupils (i.e., those not catered for by the 'alternative' schemes). In 1966, however, its remit was changed to take account of the (then) government's plans for universal comprehensive education. The revised remit was for the preparation of a so-called 'common core' science course for the first two years of secondary education, which in Scotland begins at age twelve. Full details of the Scottish Integrated Science Scheme were finally published in 1969. Compared to other novel science curricula developed in the 1960s, the most significant innovatory features of the integrated scheme were its unification of physics, chemistry and biology; its intention that the same teacher should take all the science lessons for any given class; and its suitability for '*all* pupils . . . whether streamed or unstreamed'.[2] According to a national survey, almost 90 per cent of Scottish secondary schools reported they would be following the scheme during the year 1971–2.[3]

The official ideology of the integrated science scheme is contained in a Scottish Education Department report and an accompanying set of 144 worksheets.[4] Curriculum Paper Seven – as the report is popularly known – contains not only a general discussion of the course but also a series of recommendations, a twenty-four page outline syllabus, and 210 specific educational objectives for the fifteen 'thematic' sections of the course. Although the worksheets cover the entire course, they are not intended to serve as its text, but merely as 'props' to support 'discovery methods'. Besides the features already outlined, the Integrated Science Scheme also intends that equal weight be given to biology, physics and chemistry within the unified whole; that the basis of the teaching be 'stage-managed' heurism (or 'discovery' learning); and that multiple choice exams be used for testing the stated objectives of the course.

In these formalised terms (see Curriculum Paper Seven, paragraphs 24, 33 and 45), integrated science is portrayed as a self-contained system or curriculum package: in this case containing a set of pedagogical assumptions, a new syllabus and details of techniques and equipment. Although for most purposes, this blueprint or catalogue description 'stands for' the scheme, it tends to gloss over the diversity of situations which become the focus of its implementation. It merely describes the essence of the Scottish scheme. As an idealised specification, then, it is rather like a genotype or an archetype. To use a term recently proposed, it is an 'instructional system'.[5] (Indeed, if presented in these terms, the Dalton Plan, performance contracting, programmed learning, the integrated day, team teaching, 'Sesame Street' and 'Man: a Course of Study' are also 'instructional systems'.)

Thus, a major concern of this account is the translation of such an instructional system into two real life settings. Central is the idea that when an instructional system is adopted, it undergoes modifications that are rarely trivial. Although it may remain a shared ideal, abstract model, slogan or shorthand, the instructional system assumes a different form in every situation. Its constituent elements are emphasised or de-emphasised, expanded or contracted as teachers, students and others interpret and reinterpret the instructional system for their particular setting. For example, even a cursory glance at the survey figures referred to above, shows that less than 60 per cent of the children described as following the integrated science scheme are, in fact, following a scheme where the biological, chemical and physical sections of the course are taught by the same teacher. Already, the original 'ideal' formulation has, in practice, been the subject of a redefinition process.

In a paper entitled 'On the classification and framing of educational knowledge'[6] Basil Bernstein returns to a theme sketched out in one of his earlier papers: 'Open schools, open society?'[7] His discussion considers the relationship between the gross changes that are taking place in schools, and similar changes that are taking place elsewhere in society. To articulate certain of these ideas Bernstein makes a distinction between what he calls 'integrated-type' and 'collection-type' (i.e., subject-specific) school curricula. This particular distinction – and Bernstein's treatment of it – do much to illuminate events at Simpson and Maxwell.[8]

In Bernstein's terms collection curricula are characterised by a 'closed' compartmentalised relationship between the subjects; integrated curricula by an 'open' relationship. At the level of theory, the integrated idea is sustained by stressing the unity of a subject area, the collection idea by stressing its diversity. Furthermore, Bernstein goes on to argue that these two curriculum types can be linked to a range of distinct sociological and organisational phenomena. That collection types are associated with strong subject loyalties on the part of teachers; a range of different subject ideologies across the collection of subjects in the curriculum; didactic instruction; a hierarchical conception of valid knowledge ('facts' before 'principles'), and oligarchic control (vertical hierarchy of staff) within subjects. And that by contrast integrated types are associated with weak subject loyalties; a common pedagogy, practice and examining style; emphasis on self-regulatory instruction; early initiation into basic principles, and strong horizontal professional relationships among staff.

Much of Bernstein's characterisation of an integrated curriculum matches the intentions of Curriculum Paper Seven, viz.:

Content openness	'Science . . . should be in the form of an integrated study of the various disciplines' (Curriculum Paper Seven, recommendation 4).
Self-regulatory instruction	'The discovery method should be used wherever possible' (recommendation 5).
Common pedagogy, practice and examining style	This is implied by Curriculum Paper Seven's advocacy of worksheets and multiple choice examinations; and its presentation of the behavioural objectives for the course (paras. 33, 44 and 45).
Early initiation into deep structures (ways of knowing)	'A much reduced emphasis on the retention of the factual content of the syllabus. Instead . . . pupils should be exposed . . . to many other aspects of the work of the scientist; . . . the experimental processes of

thought by which he arrives at his conclusions and the language which he uses to
communicate these conclusions to others'
(para. 8).

Strong horizontal   'Science teachers in a school should all be
relationships   free together at least once a week' (recom-
among staff   mendation 32).

Despite these *prima facie* integrated characteristics of the Scottish
Integrated Science Scheme, the Scottish secondary education system
retains, overall, certain of the collection features described by Bernstein.
All Scottish science teachers are necessarily university graduates. (This
distinguishes them from their English counterparts.) After a year's
obligatory subject-based, postgraduate training they are certificated not
merely to teach (as in England) but to teach specified subjects.[9] Throughout, therefore, there is strong subject loyalty induced and strong com-
partmentalisation of established subjects.

Besides a differentiation between subjects, there is also differentiation
between categories of teachers. Although they may be doing identical
work, 'honours' graduates receive higher salaries than 'ordinary'
graduates. Another hierarchical distinction made between honours and
ordinary graduates is that until recently ordinary graduates were
precluded from holding principal teacher (head of department) positions
in senior secondary schools.[10] Thus, the vertical differences between
honours and ordinary graduates within the same subject are widely
reinforced and institutionalised.[11] This clash between the integrated
basis of the Scottish Integrated Science Scheme and the overall collection characteristics of the system is important to the discussion that
follows.

Bernstein's analysis is penetrating. It presents a theoretical basis for
understanding the social, organisational and intellectual differences
between subject-specific and integrated studies. Besides furnishing such
an analysis, Bernstein also discusses a related problem of social order.
He argues that by their very nature (clear boundaries, strong subject
identities, hierarchical authority structure, etc.) the organisation of
collection curricula, relative to integrated curricula, is more clearly
defined and regulated; (given, of course, that those working within the
'collection' accept its value structure). In contrast, Bernstein suggests
with respect to integrated curricula that 'if four conditions are not
satisfied, then the openness of learning under integration may well
produce a culture in which neither staff nor pupils will have a sense of
time, place or purpose' (p. 64). What are these four conditions?

First, Bernstein declares that the integrated idea may only work when there is 'high ideological consensus among the staff' (p. 64). For integration to become a reality rather than an ideal, he argues there should be widespread agreement on its aims and objectives.

Second, he maintains that 'the linkage between the integrating idea and the knowledge to be co-ordinated must also be coherently spelled out' (p. 64). What is meant by this? With any integrated curriculum there is rarely a well-defined body of common knowledge (facts, principles, etc.) which can form a substantive basis for curriculum content (i.e., the syllabus). Rather, to retain the idea of integration, the various contributing subjects must be linked at a higher conceptual or cognitive level. The first three sections of the Scottish scheme are concerned respectively with measurement (rather than, say, 'the metric system'), principles of taxonomy (rather than 'animals and plants'), and energy (rather than 'heat, light and sound'). Although, by and large, these sections are concerned with the same apparatus and experiments, their subject domains are more diffuse and their pedagogical intentions more elevating. They are, therefore, at one remove from the explication of 'mere facts'. In so far as the higher level concepts must emerge from the content of the course, then teachers working under integration should be under no illusion as to the particular high level concept(s) being endorsed.

Third, Bernstein suggests that as evaluation criteria are 'less likely to be as explicit and measurable as in the case of collection' (p. 65) there should be close face to face discussion and feed-back between staff and students.

Fourth, Bernstein points out that if confusion is to be avoided, clear criteria of evaluation (i.e., what is to be assessed and the form of the assessment) should exist.

With regard to these last two *caveats* it is no doubt significant that hand in hand with the development of new curricula has gone a concern for new forms of evaluation and assessment.[12] Curriculum Paper Seven is no exception. For example, its recommendations include the following (emphases added):

'Tests should be designed to assess all aspects of teaching in science; they should not be limited to recall and simple comprehension exercises' (recommendation 7).

'Tests should be used for *other purposes besides* ranking pupils' (recommendation 9).

'Testing should have a limited place in education' (recommendation 10).

'An investigation should be made of what should be tested in science' (recommendation 13).

In each case they reflect a change in the climate surrounding school assessment.

Throughout his paper, Bernstein treats integrated and collection curricula as ideal types; that is, in pure form as analytical constructs. Now I want to return to the murky reality of curriculum development and curriculum change.

II

The essential tension between science and its component parts had a long history in British science education. Throughout, the tension has derived from more than just pedagogic concern. In secondary education 'science' has been a low status subject, taught by poorly qualified 'generalists' in low status institutions to poorly endowed or very young pupils. After the Second World War, recognising the character of this ascription, secondary modern schools rejected 'general science'. Instead, they made considerable efforts to raise their status by presenting science in subject-specific form; that is, as was taught in high status grammar schools.[13] By the 1960s the expression 'general science' was one of the shibboleths of science teaching in Britain. It was scarcely mentioned, rarely advocated. The fact that current variants of general science are now called 'integrated science' or 'combined science' is thus perhaps understandable.

The science departments I studied at Simpson and Maxwell schools had an organisational structure that was essentially subject-specific; that is, each was organised separately for physics, chemistry and biology. When integrated science was introduced at Simpson it was grafted on to the pre-existing subject-specific organisation. At Maxwell – a new school – the two organisational forms were developed side by side.[14]

Simpson school is a large urban comprehensive school that serves an area of predominantly pre-war council housing. Observation took place at the Annexe one and a half miles from the main school. In effect the Annexe was an 'overflow' school which catered only for the first year children. Divided into thirty groups, the pupils (about 500) were taught science for five 35-minute periods per week. Each group contained from sixteen to twenty-one boys and girls drawn from the entire ability range. Up to five groups took science at any one time. (*N.B.* science is considered a 'craft' subject in Scotland and generally taught to half classes. Formally the class size should not exceed twenty pupils.)

There were four science laboratories at the Annexe, and a science hut across the tarmacadam playground. Each lab was similar in design, with rows of fixed teak benches arranged in front of a blackboard and a raised teacher's demonstration bench. In the two labs where observations were recorded, there were sinks and gas taps on the teachers' benches and two sinks on the benches that ran around the perimeter of the room. In one of the rooms there was only one electrical socket other than those on the teacher's bench.

My initial observations at Simpson did not match the picture of integrated science presented by Curriculum Paper Seven. Instead of support materials the worksheets had become *the* syllabus; and, as teacher demonstrations were often substituted for pupil practical work, class teaching had become the dominant activity. Further observation and discussion suggested reasons for this state of affairs.

Although there was only enough teaching for four full-timers, ten people taught science at the Annexe, but only one of them full-time. Most of the remaining teachers commuted from the separate subject-specific departments at the main school – five of them for less than six periods per week. For timetabling reasons, eleven of the thirty groups had more than one teacher. Indeed, one group was taught each week by three different teachers. These factors – school on twin sites, large numbers of teachers, and multiple teaching of classes – were basic constraints on the science teaching.

Conditions were further exacerbated at Simpson by teacher absences; by the relative shortage of apparatus; by the lack of laboratory accommodation appropriate to the needs of Curriculum Paper Seven; and, not least, by the fact that integrated science was only in its first full year of operation at the school.

The essential problem with such a large number of teachers was one of communication. At no time were all ten teachers in the building together. There was no natural opportunity for general discussion of the new scheme or for discussion of pupil progress. For some of the teachers the only channel of communication was a record book kept in the preparation room where each of them indicated the work or work-sheet completed each lesson. At times, unfortunately, this task was forgotten.

When classes were taught by more than one teacher the communication problem was more acute. At Simpson, teachers sharing classes tried to maintain continuous progress through the integrated course. (The alternative strategy was to subdivide the courses – usually along subject lines – with one teacher, say, doing all the 'chemistry' sections.) Thus each teacher was required week by week to begin where the previous one had left off and to finish at a recognisable point. In a situation like this there was little scope for free-wheeling. As one teacher described it, 'All you can do is paddle along.'

For certain demonstrations or experiments there was sometimes only enough apparatus for it to be used by one class at a time. As several groups were taught simultaneously, complicated organisational barter-ing took place to avoid localised shortages. If it was a teacher's turn to use a certain piece of apparatus he had to use it when available or, as sometimes happened, forfeit the opportunity. The fact that some of the apparatus had to be ferried from the main school further added to this difficulty.

Finally, teacher absence was a reality at Simpson school. On such occasions it was customary for the absent teacher's class to be split among the remaining classes rather than to be taken by another teacher. Sometimes teachers did not return from their periods of absences. In the previous year, four science groups had been taught by a succession of five different temporary teachers. When a further teacher left without being replaced, another five groups were distributed among the teachers that remained.

Each of these factors suggests why the teachers were under some pressure to stick to the course. In the circumstances it is reasonable to assume that anyone who had sought to develop his own ideas or even to fulfil the prescriptions of Curriculum Paper Seven was likely to receive little sympathy from his or her colleagues – particularly if it involved their co-operation. As most of the teachers spent so little time teaching at the Annexe, their priorities did not lie with the integrated scheme, but with their own subject courses higher up the school.

De facto responsibility for integrated science at Simpson Annexe was retained by the only science teacher in residence there full-time. The fact, however, that he had no formal authority, nor yet a responsibility allowance, undermined the efforts that he made. Most of his free time was spent easing the organisational workload of the teachers who com-muted from the main school.

Much of the day to day co-ordination was not in the full-time teacher's hands but the responsibility of the laboratory assistant. As she performed the essential task of ensuring the maintenance of entries in the work diary, and as she was the only person at any given time to know where everything was, her position was a key one. Her role belied her designation as 'ancillary'.

Finally, the staffing problems at Simpson school (and particularly at the Annexe) had produced an instability that effectively precluded any long term planning or development of the integrated science teaching. It was public knowledge in the school that the teacher 'in charge' of integrated science was actively seeking promotion.

Maxwell is a new suburban comprehensive school serving an area of mixed private and public housing. Set in its own playing fields, the school comprises a central three-storey building surrounded by smaller satellite blocks serving specialised functions such as craft, home economics and science. The science department is a one-storey block made up of sixteen laboratories built around a central store, lecture theatre, workshop and darkroom. While different in detail, each laboratory had a fixed teacher's bench (not raised) and movable tables for the pupils. Compared to Simpson the provision of sinks and electrical socket-outlets was two to three times more generous. Although integrated science was taught from the time the school opened, eight out of the sixteen labs were architecturally subject-specific. For example, some labs had fume-cupboards (chemistry), others were south-facing (biology).

At the time of the first year's observation there were no pupils in years four to six and only about 700 pupils in years one to three (60 per cent of the final complement for those years). Integrated science in the first and second years was organised around sixteen mixed ability groups in each year. For this number of children there were three heads of department (physics, biology and chemistry), two assistant science teachers and three laboratory staff. No one had special responsibility for science; the heads of department rotated the task termly.

As the school had not been fully opened when the staff were recruited, the new headmaster was assisted by the local science adviser in making his choice of teachers. As the adviser had been very active in the preparation of Curriculum Paper Seven, he had recommended teachers who would be keen to develop integrated science. None of them, however, had previously taught together.

Conscious of their position (working in a 'show' school) and their commitment to implementing Curriculum Paper Seven, the teaching staff at Maxwell recognised many of the problems involved in setting up a new department and running a new integrated science scheme. To meet the difficulties they soon established a sophisticated organisational structure to facilitate the introduction of what, for most of them, was an untried scheme. At weekly staff meetings held after school, strategies were developed for keeping pupil records; for monitoring the use of apparatus; for preparing multiple choice examinations; for making the most economical use of technical staff; and for generally programming the succeeding sections of Curriculum Paper Seven (arranging dates for out-of-school visits, making advance bookings for films and so on).

At the staff meetings (of which I attended the three that took place during the course of the first year's observation) considerable discussion centred on the presentation of the course and the best possible use of the worksheets. Even the content and form of written work was discussed. Needless to say, as a result of this activity, the members of the science department spent a considerable time preparing materials, worksheets and examinations outside school hours. It is obvious in such a situation that the staff meetings played an important part in the organisation of the department. Much of the long term planning of work, and the negotiation of responsibility was performed on these occasions.

In most respects this system functioned successfully. It helped to resolve many of the day to day problems of the integrated course (see below). However, the organisational structure also created a number of problems when it began to exert its own hegemony over the work of the individual teacher. As one teacher put it: 'We're so well organised, at times I don't know what I'm doing.'

One problem that arose concerned the devolution of responsibility. Considerable time was spent at the staff meetings discussing who should be responsible for preparing the succeeding sections of the course; or who, for example, should be responsible for liaison with the laboratory staff. Typically, these discussions revolved around subject loyalties and responsibilities. Was a 'biology' section really a biology section or was it a 'chemistry' section? Was a malfunctioning fish tank the responsibility of the head of biology, the head of science or the person whose room it was in? Who reported it to the lab assistants? Which assistant? In situations like this there appeared to be an organisational tension between the informal parity among the staff and the formal hierarchical structure within the science department. Thus, while the preparation of additional materials was shared out equally among all the teachers, only the heads of department had keys to the science block (which was kept locked outside lesson time).

A second problem arising at the staff meetings concerned timing. In the interests of organisational clarity (and maintenance of a 'common pedagogy') dates were fixed well in advance for the completion of the various sections and for the setting of the multiple choice section tests. However, as various factors usually intervened, time had to be spent at successive meetings rescheduling deadlines fixed previously.

A third problem concerned furthering the aims of the course. However explicitly they are expressed in curriculum papers or teachers' guides, aims and objectives require re-interpretation in practice. Considerable discussion took place at Maxwell around what should be done to fulfil the objectives. In the interests of presenting a unified course, this generally meant seeking agreed common ground rather than allowing divergence of content and method.

By the nature of this research it was possible to take a further look at the organisational structure of Simpson and Maxwell in the following year. (The data for Simpson were collected during a half-day return visit. The data for Maxwell during an eight week observation period.) Not unexpectedly the position at Simpson had changed very little since the first year. If anything, it had moved a little closer towards the integrated idea. In particular, all the staff who taught integrated science now met every six weeks during school time. In two other respects conditions had also changed marginally towards integration. Multiple teaching of single groups had been reduced from eleven to seven groups and no teacher taught at the Annexe for less than five periods. (In the previous year five out of the ten teachers had taught there for less than six periods per week.) Each of these changes enhanced the possibility of integrated science at Simpson gradually beginning to develop an identity of its own.

At Maxwell the position had changed more noticeably. Over the whole school, the numbers of staff and pupils had risen by over 40 per cent (without an equivalent all-round increase of equipment in the science department). The number of first year science groups had risen from sixteen to twenty-four and third and fourth year public examination courses were well under way. The initial response on the part of the teachers to the apparent decrease in apparatus was to reprogramme the sections of the course. To ease the burden on specific items of equipment (e.g., the Van de Graaf generator), sections two ('looking at living things') and three ('energy: the basic ideas'), and sections four ('matter as particles') and seven ('electricity') of the scheme were juxtaposed for half of the twenty-four first year groups. In practice this was only partially successful as section seven leans heavily on ideas supposedly developed in section four.

The response to the increase in staff was to change the committee structure within the science department. General meetings attended by all the staff were replaced by a system of meetings based on four domains of responsibility: (1) meetings of the three heads of department (biology, physics and chemistry), (2) meetings of staff within departments, (3) meetings of all science staff, and (4) meetings for those (usually one teacher from each subject department) concerned with the preparation of the materials and tests used in the various sections of the course.

Since only the departmental and heads of department meetings were scheduled during school time, and since the 'science' meetings took place rarely (none during the eight weeks of the observation), this organisational form served to reinforce a subject-specific rather than an integrated identity within the science department.

A third development in the teaching was that three of the new assistant staff were appointed as subject specialists rather than to teach integrated science. When they began teaching they found to their evident unease that almost 70 per cent of their teaching time was spent on integrated science. While being interviewed they made such comments as 'Teaching biology I'm lost, . . . I feel the chemistry and biology lessons are pretty empty' (physicist); 'I'd rather teach biology . . . I think you should keep it as an integrated course but with different teachers' (biologist); 'I find it difficult teaching other than biology. . . . I don't have enough background. . . . Botany I can talk about off the cuff' (second biologist). In teaching predominantly integrated science, however, they were no different from the other teachers, all of whom spent upwards of 64 per cent of their time similarly engaged (i.e., teaching years one and two).

A final factor which suggested a change of emphasis in the department was that a proposal had been made that subject specialists should teach their 'own' sections of the scheme. Yet, of the eight sections in the first year part of the scheme, only three sections are given unique subject labels by Curriculum Paper Seven. The majority are described as including subject matter from more than one discipline. For example section four, 'energy: the basic idea' is described as including 'physics with chemistry and biology' (see table 5.2, page 195).

From the data presented it is apparent that certain features of the model proposed by Bernstein were exemplified by Simpson and Maxwell. At both schools there was a conflict of interest between the integrated and the collection modes of organisation. At Simpson this conflict was apparent from the outset. At Maxwell this same conflict – though originally latent – increasingly became an important feature of department life as time passed.

In their own ways – as quite different schools – Simpson and Maxwell represent two distinct types. Simpson is a school where a new integrated collection was assimilated and then *redefined* in terms of an older collection curriculum. (Walker and Adelman have aptly named this form of integration 'disguised collection'.)[15] Thus, despite a superficial display of integration (e.g., using the published worksheets), Simpson retained certain important features of a collection curriculum: didactic (factual) instruction predominated; teachers retained their subject identities; and in addition, since horizontal relationships among staff were weak, effective control rested with the only full-time teacher (cf. 'oligarchic control'). As foreshadowed earlier, this general 'collection' effect tended to swamp attempts at introducing the integrated idea.

Maxwell, by contrast, is a school were the opportunity existed for establishing an integrated curriculum. As a new school Maxwell had a hand-picked staff and an abundance of resources. Yet, faced with increased staff and student numbers, and more intense utilisation of resources the science department at Maxwell were having difficulty in fulfilling their aim of implementing Curriculum Paper Seven.

The fact that there were still two or three years before it achieved a 'stable state' (i.e., full quota of staff and students), and the fact that it intended developing collection curricula in years three to six, meant that Maxwell could easily fall back on traditional subject-specific patterns of organisation in years one and two. Clearly, in a school like this, later years present a qualitatively different situation. For the first time the possibility exists for establishing a division of labour and (paid) 'responsibility' based on the integrated science/non-integrated science distinction. Integrated science would become a fourth science subject with its own department, specialists, equipment and laboratories. In this event a polarisation of curriculum identities takes place. At the time of writing (October 1973) this has not occurred at Maxwell since certain countervailing strategies have been deployed. For example, the local authority promotion policy deliberately precludes the appointment of principal teachers of 'integrated science'. Also, the authority actively encourages its teachers to attend 'management' courses which – by using educational simulation exercises – discuss and explore the kind of problems raised at Maxwell.

III

So far this paper has documented aspects of the learning milieu related to the departmental organisation of the Scottish Integrated Science Scheme. In the remaining section I want to look at the classroom impact of two features of the integrated science milieu at Maxwell: the timetable and the testing.

In the context I studied – as will become clear – each of these institutions was taken for granted. That is, it was accepted without comment and did not feature prominently in the perceived business of the department. Here I would like to demonstrate that both timetable and testing were in fact problematic, and that they had a differential impact across the four classes I observed. In each case I shall argue that the public 'reality' sustained at departmental level concealed quite different and sometimes opposing 'realities' within each science class. This section also serves to demonstrate how an instructional system like the Scottish Integrated Science Scheme is successively transformed as its wisdom is filtered through the organisational structure of the school, science department and classrooms. Throughout, a number of 'interference' 'boundary' and 'mediating' effects can be discerned.

At Maxwell the school day began formally at 08.50 hours when the children assembled in their house blocks. Then, divided into nine 35-minute periods, it continued through morning break (20 mins) and lunch (55 mins) until 15.50 hours. Generally, the teachers remained on their home territory and the children moved from department to department and from room to room. To someone coming from outside, each day would appear just the same as any other except that the last two lessons on Wednesday and Friday were set aside for extracurricular 'leisure' activities (sports, outdoor pursuits, visits, chess, etc.). On these occasions up to 50 per cent of the children were occupied away from the main school.

Each of the four classes I observed during the second year of fieldwork had the same amount of time set aside for science: five periods per week. The classes differed, however, in the way their time was allocated. One class, for example, had one treble period and one double period; others had their science time broken down into smaller units. Some double periods were uninterrupted; others had the morning interval

TABLE 5.1   Distribution of first year science lessons of four classes at Maxwell school

	Monday a.m.	Monday p.m.	Tuesday a.m.	Tuesday p.m.	Wednesday a.m.	Wednesday p.m.	Thursday a.m.	Thursday p.m.	Friday a.m.	Friday p.m.
Mr Spencer's class		2					3			
Mr Darwin's class	2*		1							2
Mr Rutherford's class	2					2	1			
Mr Dalton's class				2*	3*					

* Lesson split by mid-morning break.

halfway through. In addition each class was taught by a different teacher (see table 5.1). Within this broad framework the teaching and the course work were disseminated day by day.

In accordance with the structure laid out in Curriculum Paper Seven, first year course work in science at Maxwell was divided into eight sections (see table 5.2). Theoretically, the teachers could follow them in any order they wished. However, as the integrated course was very much a departmental concern, a number of factors – emanating from departmental decisions – affected its classroom organisation. These decisions did not always map neatly onto the timetable. As a result, a series of 'interference' effects became apparent.

TABLE 5.2 Summary of the integrated science first year

Section	Title	Subject matter	Recommended number of periods
1	*Introducing science*	Physics + chemistry + biology	16
2	*Looking at living things*	Biology	12
3	*Energy: the basic idea*	Physics with chemistry + biology	8
4	*Matter as particles*	Physics + chemistry	18
5	*Solvents and solutions*	Chemistry with biology	24
6	*Cells and reproduction*	Biology	22
7	*Electricity*	Physics	24
8	*Some common gases*	Chemistry with biology	24

Source: Curriculum Paper Seven, Appendix 1, table 3.

First, the science department's 'notes for the guidance of staff' contained an integrated science 'calendar' that gave suggested dates for the completion of each section, and included the following among the 'duties' of each course planning subcommittee:

(b) allocate the content, period-by-period if possible, but within the overall time allocation suggested in CP7.
(c) write down specific teaching objectives with suitable experiments and workcards to fulfil them. . . .

    (d) compare these prepared objectives with the more general ones in CP7. This list may be longer and should be more precise than that in CP7. . . .

    (i) prepare a homework schedule for the section on the basis of an average of one written exercise per fortnight. . . .

    (j) prepare suitable revision and summary material. . . .

    (m) as it is important to keep everyone informed, each section group must duplicate the results of their discussions under headings a, b, c, e, f, g, h, i, j above and these will be supplied to every teacher concerned.

These directives – each concerned with time and content – sought to promote a uniform pacing and patterning of the integrated scheme throughout the department.

Second, as noted above, it was decided that half of the twenty-four first year classes should do section seven of the scheme while the other half did section four. When the work in the sections was completed, the 'twinned' classes were to exchange their equipment. Thus, to facilitate a uniform departmental change-over from section to section, each teacher was asked to pay close attention to the time allocation for each of these sections.

A third influence prompting a lock-step effect was the fact that the tests which punctuated the sections were scheduled to take place across the department as close as possible to a given date. As will become apparent later this was to render the test results comparable. (The phasing of testing was to ensure the teaching time for each group was equivalent.)

A fourth and final influence was that each teacher was required to complete three sections of the integrated science course by a certain date. This was to comply with a school request for 'grades' to enter in school reports.

These departmental decisions were based on the assumption that the teaching time for each class was the same. Although in principle this was true, in practice there were a number of important discrepancies between the classes.

For example, 'twinned' sections which were conducted over the same period of time should have been equivalent in length. But, as shown in table 5.2, the recommended time for section seven was 33 per cent more than that for section four. Not only did this affect the pacing of teaching, it also affected the manner in which the teachers presented their lessons.

Towards the end of my observation – having tried to conceptualise and codify the teaching I had seen – I made the following comments in my field notes: 'Style of teaching depends on the time available. Have noticed that each teacher skates [over the work] when in a hurry. If the bell has gone the teacher is more directive and more curt in calling to order.' Earlier I had noticed further examples of this phenomenon (examples taken from different teachers):

Inclement weather. [Teacher] dictating names of trees (rather than allowing children out onto the school grounds to find out for themselves – as was the original intention). Also wants to get finished and have section 2 tests before half-term.

Emphasis or de-emphasis [of content] is used in certain sections.

Mr Darwin has missed a number of lessons. He is hurrying through this section. Assumed that the kids had done more energy experiments than they had. Only two groups had done more than two (out of a possible five).

Besides being affected in this way by the vagaries of time (and weather), the distribution of teaching time within each week also had its effect on the overall pattern of teaching:

Mr Dalton raised the question of having a split double period the day before a treble [see table 5.1]. He said it created problems of (a) continuity, (b) bittiness and (c) organization. Said he would have to treat the split doubles as two singles.

Mr Dalton raised this issue without any prompting. He was referring to the fact that he had only one true double period. He also pointed out that this double lesson came at the end of his week's teaching with that group (he did not see them again for another six days). Mr Dalton felt that each of the first three lessons on his timetable was too short to launch any new work satisfactorily. (Essentially, he regarded them as too brief for any large scale practical work of the kind that typically began each integrated science worksheet.)

The distribution of lessons within each week also affected Mr Darwin's teaching. He too had three single lessons early in the week together with a double lesson on Friday afternoon. As Mr Darwin was also 'head' of the science department at that time he missed lessons through being absent at various meetings both in and out of school. Thus, when he was able to take his classes he was under pressure to make up time. For example, compared with the other teachers I observed (who took upwards of four lessons) Mr Darwin covered the classification system of animals in a double period on Friday afternoon. At that time the increased amount of work required by Mr Darwin caused the following comment in the field notes: 'This was a fascinating lesson as Mr Darwin *attempted to cover* classification. He began with the variety of life and worked up to subdivisions within the vertebrates [emphasis added].'

Although the departmental lock-step effect resulted from a concern with promoting a common pedagogy, it tended, in fact, to exacerbate the differences between the classes. Certain teachers were always trying to keep up to schedule, whereas the others were (not officially) encouraged to 'mark time' by deviating from the prescribed course or providing additional revision materials. Equally, the constant pressure of successive deadlines precluded the 'slower' teachers from adopting a long term strategy for overcoming their difficulties (for example, by totally re-ordering or re-programming the course work for their classes). The science department (led by the respective heads of physics, biology and chemistry) tried to implement a mode of organisation which, publicly, was intended to provide equal opportunities for all the teachers and children. Privately, however, this machinery appeared to abrogate much that it was intended to promote. The mismatch between the instructional system and the learning milieu produced a number of organisational stresses. Some of these could be accommodated within the classroom but others had an impact that reverberated throughout the department and even the school. For example, as noted earlier, the mismatch between expected and actual completion dates for sections was a recurrent item on the agenda of departmental meetings.

While in Curriculum Paper Seven and at the departmental level the equivalence of teaching time was taken for granted, it was manifestly problematic at the classroom level. Like Curriculum Paper Seven, the departmental notes became a 'Bible' (a term actually used for the former). Both represented some kind of handed down wisdom. Despite being prepared by the members of the science department themselves, the notes were objectified and became a departmental prescription – a local instructional system. Depending on their private commitment, however, the teachers accepted, modified or ignored such wisdom. Indeed, the different and diverging standpoints taken by the teachers were reflected in the behaviour of their pupils. This can be more clearly seen in the way that testing and assessment were handled.

As already indicated, the development of new curricula has been associated with a concern for evaluation and assessment. Curriculum Paper Seven reflects this concern: seven of the eleven recommendations specific to the integrated scheme explicitly make reference to 'tests' or 'testing'.

In its general discussion, Curriculum Paper Seven attempts to devalue traditional assessment procedures. It decries, therefore, the 'learning of many associated facts'; the use of test scores for 'making fine distinctions' or 'ranking'; and the examination of the 'correct use of English' as a primary function for tests (paras 41–2 *passim*). Instead, it attempts to point out new directions:

> In this orientation period the only people for whom test results will have any importance will be the school and the pupil himself. Any examinations set should be such that this syllabus is taught as it ought to be; tests should be constructed to examine practical techniques, design of experiments and ability to solve problem situations either by experiment or by describing the experiment in words. *When* written answers are required they should not be long essays about remembered details; instead, questions of the multiple choice and one-word answer type should be used. If the pupil is being required to communicate scientific knowledge he should have the opportunity to do this without being asked to write at length correct English in proper logical sequence at the same time. It should not be supposed from this statement that we minimise in any way the need for the teacher of science to teach the correct use of English. We see language as a very important part of any scientist's training but we see it as *one* aspect. We would certainly want to test for satisfactory verbal communication of scientific information and ideas but we see it as *one* aspect of a test, not something which pervades all of every test [para. 41; initial emphasis added].

Two paragraphs later Curriculum Paper Seven goes on to recommend:

> That any necessary testing at this stage should be only of the informal classroom type discussed above, and that this should be administered at an appropriate stage in the development of the course used, at the end of a section, say, rather than at some prearranged time such as the end of a term [para. 43].

At this point, however, Curriculum Paper Seven neglects its statement that 'tests should be constructed to examine practical techniques, design of experiments and ability to solve problem situations' and, instead, devotes the remainder of its discussion to considering assessment solely in terms of multiple choice tests. The problematic features associated with testing at Maxwell derive from this one-sided emphasis already present in the instructional system.

Overall, Curriculum Paper Seven uses an 'objectives'-based approach to curriculum design. That is, it attempts to specify the 'outcome(s) of learning' in 'behavioural terms' which are 'observable and measurable' (para. 20). It advocates a similar framework for assessing pupil learning. However, despite the fact that the 'general objectives' of Curriculum Paper Seven cover 'knowledge and understanding' as well as 'practical skills' and 'attitudes', discussion of pupil learning is restricted merely to the first of these. By default, therefore, multiple choice testing of knowledge and understanding became the dominant mode of assessment for the integrated scheme.

At Maxwell the one-sided nature of this emphasis in Curriculum Paper Seven went unnoticed. In fact, as can be seen from the following excerpt from the 'notes for guidance of staff', it became heightened. Interests, skills and attitudes became ancillary aspects of the testing programme:

> What is our interpretation of continuous assessment?
>
> Our syllabus contains 15 sections of varying length covering 300 periods in the first two years. During this time we shall conduct between 15 and 20 separate small attainment tests of the pupil's factual knowledge and reasoning based on the content of, and administered at the conclusion of, each of these 15 sections.
>
> At half-yearly intervals, or thereabouts, we should also like to give revision tests, covering all of the work up to that point of time.
>
> We shall also try to assess the pupils' awareness, interest, skills and progress, together with their attitudes to science and to their work in general.

Within this definition of assessment, the use of multiple choice tests at Maxwell did not reflect the prescriptions of Curriculum Paper Seven. The tests deployed were 'norm-referenced' and 'discriminatory' rather than 'criterion-referenced' and 'diagnostic' as intended. That is, they were used to discriminate among children on the basis of the total distribution of marks rather than to provide an indication of whether each child had achieved a certain standard.[16]

A number of other critical comments could be made about the tests and their use. In the context of this account, however, such criticisms are as irrelevant as they are true. Here, these data are being presented not to suggest that the teachers are (unknowingly) 'wrong', but to make a different point: that the assessment procedures envisaged by Curriculum Paper Seven were severely modified at Maxwell when translated into practice.

The fact that these procedures involved a range of complex assumptions (e.g., a knowledge of the difference between criterion-referenced and norm-referenced testing) which were not fully apprehended by the teachers at Maxwell (nor indeed fully spelled out by Curriculum Paper Seven) meant that their implementation was problematic.

Needless to say, a range of unintended effects flowed from the teachers' misinterpretation. As already discussed, the setting of tests simultaneously (to ensure comparability of classes) prompted a lock-step effect in the department. In addition, such an approach promoted invalid discriminations between classes (and teachers) and produced what one teacher called a 'local hit-parade of results'.[17] In addition, since no account was taken of the poor reliability of such tests or of statistical artefacts (e.g., regression effects), they were used to make (statistically) invalid discriminations among individuals. None of these effects was implied by Curriculum Paper Seven.

Finally, some of the pupils picked up the idea that the tests performed a discriminatory (rather than a diagnostic) function. For example, in completing the sentence: 'The main reason we have science tests is that . . .' different children wrote

'the teacher has to give us a mark for our report cards.'
'he has to find a mark for our report cards.'

Certain of this group of children also read a selective function into the assessment procedures, e.g.:

'So the teacher can put you in groups.'
'Maybe we will go to a higher or lower class and it depends on the mark we get.'

It could be argued, of course, that ideas such as these were picked up outside the science department. However, the fact that there is a real difference between the classes reduces the impact of this objection. Unlike the others, Mr Spencer's class did not see the tests as providing their teacher with discriminatory information (see table 5.3).

TABLE 5.3   Number of children in each class who gave 'discriminatory/ selective' responses to an open-ended question about the purpose of testing.*

No. of children who gave discriminatory responses		Total in class
Mr Darwin's class	11	20
Mr Rutherford's class	10	21
Mr Dalton's class	9	19
Mr Spencer's class	1	22

* The children were assigned to this group if they referred specifically to 'assessment', 'reports', 'marks' and 'grades' or to being put into different 'groups' or 'classes' ($\chi^2 = 14.35$; p. $<$ 0.01, d.f. $= 3$).

When observation and interview data are taken into account an explanation can be offered for the differential distribution of the responses. Mr Spencer quite clearly played down the examinations – not only among his colleagues but also in front of the children. My field notes record the following: 'Discussed objective tests with Mr Spencer.

He was "against" them. [Said he preferred] written work, essays.' One day, as he gave out an exam, he commented to the children: 'If the questions look a bit crazy to you they look a bit crazy to a few other people.' Mr Spencer reiterated his views during a formal tape-recorded interview. He noted a conflict between the aims of testing at Maxwell:

> The purpose of the tests has never been established. There have been discussions in science departmental meetings about whether they are designed to see whether pupils have attained the objectives. That's one aim that has been put forward for them. But in distinction to that there's been this other aim that they're to select our pupils so that we can give an assessment mark. . . . These are two confusing aims, but they've never been resolved. When I personally write an exam or even when I give it I, er, well, I don't know what I'm doing. . . .
>
> When I set them [the tests] I told the pupils why we set exams. And I've discussed it with them and they all say it's for their sake, to be selected, and things like that. . . . I always try to put forward a teacher's viewpoint: that the teacher's trying to test himself and to see what he's missed out, see what's been badly taught. . . . I think they've got this more flexible attitude now. . . .

From these various sources it can be seen that the (expressed) opinions and demonstrated feelings of Mr Spencer were perceived by the children. Like him they placed relatively little emphasis on examinations as discriminatory devices.

Whether, however, they were able fully to appreciate his viewpoint (that tests are to test the teacher) is not clear. One girl in Mr Spencer's class wrote that a reason for having science tests is that 'the teacher knows we understand what he has taught'. No one else gave a reply that suggested the tests were a means whereby Mr Spencer obtained feedback on his own teaching rather than on pupil performance. In every class I observed the children saw the tests as providing the teacher with information about themselves. The distinctive feature, therefore, of Mr Spencer's class was simply that only one child saw the tests as a discriminatory/selective device. (His comment was: 'Maybe we will go to a higher or lower class and it depends on the mark we get.') The remainder of Mr Spencer's class gave reasons which referred to the tests being used in a diagnostic rather than a discriminatory mode, e.g.:

'The teacher wants to know if we are learning anything.'

'The teacher can find out if you understand or listen to him.'

'The teacher can find out if you were listening all the time or not.'

Compared to Mr Spencer, Mr Darwin elicited the greatest number of discriminatory/selective responses. This was not surprising since he appeared to take the tests more seriously. Field notes taken on different days illustrate this idea:

> (Addressing class) 'Remember, your folders will be taken in and given a grade for neatness.'

> Mr Darwin gives out tests on the previous section. Two boys lost two marks each for talking during the test. . . . Mr Darwin spent a few minutes marking the tests and then read out the marks for each child. Finally, the children called out their marks and Mr Darwin entered them in his mark book.

> 'What I'm worried about is whether you've got a grade 1, 2 or 3 [for effort].'

> 'You'll be given out tests (pupils: 'aaah') in a few weeks.'

During the interview Mr Darwin outlined in some detail how he used the tests. In both replies quoted here he described how he used them to draw comparisons between children and classes:

OBSERVER: Where do you feel you get the most help from examinations? In what areas?

MR DARWIN: It's very noticeable in the first year where after the first assessment test you get the kids who perhaps haven't done well and they've been told they've been given a D and also been given a 3 for effort. And nine times out of ten there's a marked improvement.

OBSERVER: The fact that the marks are collated, does this help you in any way – looking across the classes?

MR DARWIN: Yes . . . It's interesting. There are two first year classes I teach this year. And the one I teach where you sit in had only one A whereas the other class had four As. . . . Perhaps my teaching is different – or perhaps it is related to the abilities of the kids. My own feeling is that, actually, the other classes are much better. They seem to be much better right through and the marks they get are much better.

Clearly, as a result of the different views of the teachers the aura surrounding the tests in Mr Darwin's class was quite different from that in Mr Spencer's.

IV

In this paper I have based my discussion on case study material drawn from two schools. The early part supports the argument that the introduction of integrated studies is not merely equivalent to introducing a

new syllabus but implies a radical change of emphasis in the organisational context and thinking of secondary education. As a result simple
questions of content cannot be separated from complex questions of
grouping children by ability, from questions of 'responsibility' and
authority, or even from questions of school democracy. That the new
forms of organisation may be in opposition to the old adds further
potency to these questions.

The current co-existence of integrated and collective curricula in
secondary education points, I suggest, to a fundamental dilemma if not
a crisis for the comprehensive school. Until recently the role of the
secondary school was clearly defined. Each in their own way – junior
secondary, secondary modern and senior secondary schools – performed
a purely academic (or vocational) function. In this and other ways they
exemplified a 'collection' paradigm. Today, however, comprehensive
schools are expected to retain this academic/intellectual function while
at the same time paying tribute to new patterns of organisation, new
boundaries of knowledge and new conceptions of education. In short,
they are expected to run collection and integrated ideas side by side.
Thus, teachers are required to be 'inter-disciplinary' *and* subject
specialists; to be concerned with teaching sixth-formers *and* 'slow
learners'; and to be responsible for both the academic *and* social welfare
of their pupils. Some of the tensions that these expectancies promote
have been described in this paper.

The second part of the account serves to illustrate certain other, more
classroom-based phenomena. First, it shows that an initial mismatch
between an instructional system and the learning milieu can create a
number of boundary or interference effects. These become particularly
noticeable where the two systems fail to intersect or overlap uniformly.
In an extreme case such a mismatching can begin as a minor disturbance but, through time, build up into a major (i.e., increasingly acknowledged) issue. An instance of this phenomenon at Maxwell arose from
the minor discrepancies between the departmental schedule and the
individual teacher's time allocation. Eventually, certain teachers were
unable to keep up with the others.

Second, it reminds us how the teacher functions: not as a mere agent
or curriculum technician, but as an active yet selective amplifier and
transmitter of knowledge. The teacher is a critical mediator between the
pupil on the one hand, and the institutional context and the instructional
system on the other. As a result all are modified extensively in the classroom setting. At Maxwell the children in each class reported their views
on testing differently – but in a way that could be linked to the views of
their respective teachers. Thus, in his mediating role, the teacher is not

merely a 'stage manager' in the classroom, but also a director, designer and, very often, a principal actor.

Third, it shows how the implementation of Curriculum Paper Seven was accompanied by a series of transformations which, ultimately, resulted in its serving ends directly opposed to those intended (norm-referenced rather than criterion-referenced testing). This example is an extreme case. But it suggests confirmation of the assertion made earlier that when an instructional system is adopted it undergoes modifications that are rarely trivial.

Finally, it illustrates that while the teacher's influence is potent, his scope for redefining an instructional system is not limitless. He too is bounded by a series of intervening institutional constraints. At Maxwell, for example, Mr Spencer was required to comply with the grading system that operated across the science department. While his efforts to mitigate its influence were – as shown – moderately successful, he was still unable to distance himself entirely from the departmental norm, and it had a recognisable impact on both himself and his pupils. Eventually, Mr Spencer's capacity to sustain his own classroom ethos in the face of conflicting definitions was exceeded. His ideological position (not only on testing and homework, but also on curriculum integration) became more and more isolated from that of the other members of the science staff. Towards the end of the year he applied for a teaching post elsewhere. In September he took up a post of responsibility in another school where he would be teaching and organising integrated science in a manner which reflected his own interests more clearly.

Notes

1 This account is part of a much larger work. For an earlier version of the first part, see Hamilton, 1973a and for the complete study, see Hamilton, 1973b.

2 This quotation is taken from a summary account of the scheme written by one of the original working party (D. Ritchie, 'Anticipating going comprehensive and on using the Scottish Integrated Science Course', *Education in Science*, 8, No. 34, 1969 pp. 25–8; emphasis in original).

3 S. Brown, 'Report on science courses that secondary departments in Scotland expect to offer to SI and SII in 1971–3', University of Stirling, unpublished.

4 *Science for General Education*, Edinburgh, HMSO, 1969. The work-sheets are published by Heinemann Educational Books.

5 This description of an 'instructional system' and the subsequent account of the 'learning milieu' are taken, with minor alterations, from Parlett and Hamilton, 1972.

6 See Young, 1971, pp. 47–69.

7 *New Society*, 14 September 1967.

8 A comprehensive analysis of the complex ideas expressed in Bernstein's paper is considered to be beyond the scope of this paper.

9 For the relevant Scottish teaching regulations, see *Memorandum on Entry Requirements and Courses*, Scottish Education Department, 1971.

10 In times of teacher shortage this regulation has been breached by placing 'non-qualified' science teachers in charge of the various departments but, of course, without the status or salary of principal teachers. A recent SED discussion document, *The Structure of Promoted Posts in Secondary Schools in Scotland* (1971), has 'suggested' that this honours/ordinary distinction be abolished and that all promoted posts be open to qualified teachers. This has now been ratified (i.e., since the observation took place). Despite such an important change qualification by subject still remains.

11 Such distinction begins while the students are still in training. In at least one Scottish college of education, honours and ordinary graduates – even though they may end up in the same school with equivalent timetables – are trained separately.

12 See, for example, M.C. Wittrock and D.E. Wiley, eds, *The Evaluation of Instruction: Issues and Problems*, New York, Holt, Rinehart & Winston, 1970; and B. S. Bloom *et al.*, *Handbook on Formative and Summative Evaluation of Student Learning*, London, McGraw-Hill, 1971.

13 The expression 'general science' seems to derive from the idea of 'science for all': the title of a Science Masters' Association pamphlet prepared at the request of the government committee to 'Inquire into the Position of Natural Science in the Education System of Great Britain' (1916, also known as the Thomson Committee). When the committee reported in 1918 it advocated a general course of science for all pupils up to the age of sixteen. Subsequently, 'general science' became substituted for 'science for all' and developed as a scheme for elementary rather than grammar schools.

14 All the organisational features at Simpson and Maxwell have been presented in the past tense. This is deliberate and is an attempt to emphasise the reality of educational change. Since the data collection was completed, important changes have, and are, taking place at both schools.

15 See R. Walker and C. Adelman, *Towards a Sociography of Classrooms*, Research Monograph, Centre for Science Education, Chelsea College, University of London, 1972.

16 Each child was awarded a grade (A–E) on the basis of the distribution of the marks across the department: 10 per cent received grade A, 20 per cent grade B, 40 per cent grade C, 20 per cent grade D and 10 per cent grade E. Had the grades been criterion-referenced, it would have been possible for a large number of the children, if not all, to get grade A (instead of only 10 per cent). In the criterion-referenced case 'success' is based on achieving a certain standard, not on the overall distribution of the marks.

17 An analysis of the pupil test scores for the first three section tests of that year was conducted. Although class means differed by up to six marks, the associated wide variation of marks meant that results could have been produced by the operation of chance factors.

6 The Diffusion of Keynesian Macroeconomics through American High School Textbooks, 1936–70

Herbert W. Voege

Editors' introduction

Since it is generally held that curricula are mainly concerned with the transmission of knowledge, it is perhaps surprising that so little attention has been devoted to the growth and decay of areas of interest, of valued skills and concepts, and to studying how their life cycles as elements of the curriculum relate to their careers in other academic spheres, or in society at large. All planned curriculum change takes place against a backdrop of shifting emphases, of new discoveries, of reappraisals of knowledge of which we are sometimes acutely, but sometimes only dimly aware. In areas where dramatic discoveries are unusual, changes in fashion may be so imperceptible that even the expert is barely conscious of them. Yet this backdrop is part of the reality of curriculum change – over long periods perhaps *the* reality when the best efforts of planners and designers have made their brief mark and been superseded by the next project or a newer fashion.

Voege concentrates on the textbooks used by teachers and students rather than on the social and institutional processes which are the primary focus of other contributors to this collection. Taking his example from the field of economics, he tries to draw out some notions of how knowledge is diffused from one level of thought and action to another, and from one level of the education process to another, and hence to sketch out ways of understanding how knowledge, the stuff of which curricula are made, offers itself for inclusion in school programmes. He suggests that the time required for the entry of a leading idea into the high school curriculum may be as much as twenty-five years, and in so doing raises numerous

questions of great theoretical and practical interest. What are the
factors which determine the shape and extent of the life cycle of an
idea in the school curriculum ? What accounts for the differences in
the life cycle of ideas at various levels of the educational system ? On
what grounds might we judge whether a twenty-five year lag is
acceptable ? What are the social dynamics which accompany the rise
and decline in popularity of curricular items ? Do the differences in
the life cycles of items of knowledge in schools and in the world
outside carry implications for a proper division of labour between the
school and other educative influences such as the media and the
family ?

Theories of knowledge creation and transmission are of great
intrinsic interest; they are also of practical concern to the
curriculum designer, for they illuminate some of the constraints
which make for resistance to change, and some of the conditions
under which change may become acceptable, or even demanded.
They also remind us that what is an innovation today may
tomorrow become superfluous and unwanted.

In spite of its many unique features, Voege's study impinges on
some broad issues already raised by other contributors; the need to
pay regard to stability as well as change as a leading notion in the
study of curricula, the relationship between general environmental
factors and the propensity to seek for change, and the way change
rates accelerate once a critical point has been passed.

I

Keynesian macroeconomics ranks among the most important additions
to economic knowledge in the twentieth century. Keynes advocated
creation of an economic and social environment in which the automatic
or semi-automatic adjustments and mechanisms of classical economics
can remain in play while, through various gradual or evolutionary
policies, some of the disadvantages of a totally free market – severe
business cycles, unemployment – are avoided. Keynes is willing to
accept the gradual or evolutionary socialization of investment by means
of private, semi-public, and public bodies as well as a heavier reliance
on central controls to bring aggregate supply into balance with aggregate
demand at a full employment level. In this way Keynes hoped to assure
the continuation of some traditional advantages of economic individual-
ism, such as the incentive of self-interest, personal liberty, the widening
of the field of personal choices, variety of styles of life, innovativeness,
decentralization of power and control, and efficiency. His ideas have

come to pervade economic decision-making and, in rising to this position of influence, have generated an extensive and long lasting controversy that has brought them to the attention of the general public as well as of scholars, businessmen and politicians.

The investigation on which this paper is based[1] sought to provide answers to three questions. How long did it take for Keynesian ideas to be accepted in secondary school economics textbooks and the curriculum? To what extent has Keynesian theory entered secondary school economics textbooks and the curriculum in the United States? What were the circumstances surrounding the process of adoption and what were the reasons and factors causing delay or promoting acceptance?

Keynesian theory and doctrine involve a range of economic concepts,[2] many of which are of a degree of complexity which would render them inappropriate for complete or even partial treatment in secondary school texts. For this reason most attention has been focused on one major issue – relative emphasis on macroeconomics – which is agreed to be a leading characteristic of Keynesian thinking and which could well be expected to influence the content of textbooks used in schools. However, account has also been taken of other, simpler criteria than the inclusion of economic concepts in deciding whether a textbook gives evidence of Keynesian influence. Among these criteria are reference to Keynes or his policies, and mention of ideas such as the accelerator which, although not strictly speaking part of the Keynesian system, can, nevertheless, be taken as indicative of its influence. A simple measure of the rate and extent of progress of Keynesian concepts would have required only a selective quantitative analysis of textbooks, or might even have been achieved through a qualitative study; but the investigation was also concerned with the surrounding influences which might have impinged on or had an effect on the rate of diffusion, and with the competing forces which might favor other trends. So, apart from school textbooks, other sources such as college textbooks, writings of educational thinkers, pronouncements of policy bodies, and the published work of researchers in the field of economics education were considered for the evidence they can provide about the ways in which the school curriculum has reacted to Keynesian thought, and the processes through which this reaction has been brought about.

The textbook, however, is the major source of data, and, for the periods of greatest significance to the examination of the diffusion process for Keynesian ideas (1930 through the 1960s), an analysis was made of all major secondary school texts. For this purpose a taxonomy was developed, consisting in all of fifty-six subtopics based on the six categories of production, exchange, distribution, consumption or 'personal' economics, macroeconomics, and introductory or other material.[3] The category 'macroeconomics' to which most attention is given, is set out in table 6.1.

TABLE 6.1 Taxonomy adopted for analysis of textbooks

Macroeconomics
Nature of macroeconomics, definitions, etc.
Aggregate demand, the simple Keynesian model
National income accounting
Business cycles, price levels
Government spending and budget, national debt
Taxation
National growth
Fiscal policy, the complete Keynesian model

Each text was analysed by determining the number of words devoted to each of the subtopics. The word count was then converted into percentages. Generally the convention was adopted of following the author's classification. Only in rare instances, where the heading did not fit the taxonomy, or did not seem to reflect the real contents of a section, was a change made.

It should be noted that the subtopic 'aggregate consumption' would be considered part of the subtopic 'aggregate demand' used to indicate concepts originating from the Keynesian analysis which concentrated on consumption of the entire economy, a subject which had been largely ignored by classical and neo-classical economists. The major category 'macroeconomics' includes traditional topics from the field of public finance, national income accounting, as well as the Keynesian concepts. Following traditional patterns of classification, money and banking and international economics were classified under the major category of 'exchange.' As Keynesian analysis stressed fiscal policy and de-emphasized monetary policy, the traditional classification has the effect of putting Keynesian concepts under the major classification 'macro-economics.'

The data obtained from the analysis were used both to characterize individual texts, and also to present typical profiles for each decade from the 1930s to the 1960s.[4] However, before setting out the results, it is necessary to fill in a little detail on the development of economics as a subject of study in the American secondary school over the period in question.

II

Economics has a somewhat tenuous grip on its place in the school curriculum. A 1965 survey of secondary schools revealed that only 6·1 per cent of students were enrolled in an economics course, although 20 per cent of high school seniors were studying economics as a separate course. Earlier surveys show that this percentage has remained reasonably constant at from 4 to 6 per cent since 1920, though of course the total number of students taking economics has risen along with secondary school enrolments.

The preceding period had been one of steady expansion, the percentage of schools offering courses in economics increasing from 5 per cent in 1892-4 to 20 per cent in 1912, 28 per cent in 1915, and 40-50 per cent in 1920. After 1920 separate economics courses made no further ground until the 1950s, though this static enrolment does not truly reflect changes in the number of students studying economics because during the same period movements were afoot to incorporate economics into integrated social studies courses.

The intellectual impetus for integrated courses came from such writers as Harold Rugg and William Kilpatrick who were at this time extremely influential among professional educators who regarded themselves as 'progressive.' These men and their followers felt that teaching organized around logically arranged subject fields was artificial and difficult for children. They called for teaching in units of lifelike experience, including material thought to be socially useful and providing students with an opportunity to gain experience with a wealth of social situations in which various kinds of knowledge could be used. Since economics entered into many social situations, and since economics could be integrated with such a great variety of other subjects – ethics, history, political science, government, geography, and the like – economics became an attractive vehicle for integrated programs of all kinds. More important numerically were social studies textbook series which attempted to fuse economics with other social studies into an integrated program. The most famous example of this was Harold Rugg's *An Introduction to American Civilization* (1929). This trend probably did not affect very many students, but the cumulative effects of a number of different pressures toward integration were significant.

In addition to the protracted and unresolved dispute among educators concerning the merits of integration and segregation of academic disciplines, economics education was also dogged by disputes over 'personal' versus 'academic' economics. Those who favored personal economics argued that economics should be taught in practical, everyday, or applied terms so that the subject take on meaning, life, useful-ness, and importance for each and every student. Personal economics minimizes theory and abstraction and tries to convey principles in the context of everyday problems of ordinary people in their roles as con-sumers, producers and voters. Academic economics, on the other hand, emphasizes the power and economy made possible by theory and abstrac-tion. It deals primarily with the analysis of economic systems or whole industries.

Against the historical background of the 1930s and 1940s such issues ceased to be a matter of merely academic controversy and speculation. A succession of momentous events – the Wall Street crash, the Depres-sion, the New Deal and World War II – all served in their various ways to instil in the public mind a consciousness of the potency of economic forces and of the increasing overlap between political and economic decision-making. These developments led the many factions and groups advocating or opposing the need for direct government intervention in the economic field to support the introduction of economics into schools as a means of 'educating the public' on these matters.

The recent history of economics education is largely part of the academic reform movement of the 1950s and 60s. In 1955 the American Economic Association, concerned over the teaching of economics, established the standing Committee on Economic Education. In 1959, two years after Sputnik, when the alleged weakness of American schools was being held by many to be responsible for America's world decline, the committee appointed a Special Textbook Study Committee com-posed of thirteen economists. The committee examined twenty-four widely used textbooks of various types and published a list of six criteria by which they should be judged. In that same year the Com-mittee for Economic Development provided the funds for the creation by the American Economic Association of a National Task Force on Economic Education which published its report in 1961 under the title *Economic Education in the Schools*.

The Task Force Report inspired a number of curriculum develop-ment projects in economics at all levels of the school system. One of its central ideas, 'economic literacy,' became a byword for a time and, in the opinion of one active economics educator, acquired a touch of faddism. A major national television series, *The American Economy*, was intended specifically for, but not limited to, secondary school teachers. In addition, the National Task Force established a committee to review the many sets of teaching materials being produced as a result of the post-Sputnik boom in curriculum development, and later established a Committee for Measurement of Economic Understanding which supervised the construction of a 'Test of Economic Understanding,' to be used in schools to evaluate economics programs.

The National Task Force and the efforts it spawned were uncompromisingly academic in their orientation. The committee stated:

> Economic understanding is not to be equated with the knowledge and skills which help men to operate more effectively as buyers and sellers. . . . The call for more and better economics in the schools does not derive from any need for instruction in these matters. Economics is a social science; its concern is society's efforts to 'economize', not with skills to be employed by individuals in making and spending their incomes.

The Joint Council on Economic Education, formed in 1949 with government, business and labor participation, to promote economic education in the schools, took a more eclectic view. Originally, the Joint Council devoted its efforts to summer institutes for experienced teachers. Later, efforts were made to improve pre-service education through the creation in co-operation with colleges and universities of Centers of Economic Education. From 1955 to 1958 the Joint Council directed the Co-operating Schools Project for Curriculum Development and, from 1964 to 1969, the Developmental Economic Education Program. Both programs involved co-operation between the Joint Council and selected school systems to implement concepts of economic education from kindergarten through grade 12. The Joint Council continues to maintain an active publication program for teachers and others interested in improving economics education. Its approach to increasing economic understanding is well illustrated by the following statement by the executive director, Moe L. Frankel:

> Dealing in the area so sensitive to community pressures precludes any one 'right way' or 'one set of materials'. There will be diversity within a broad framework of what the goal may be, whether it be that described by the Task Force or that developed by some other group. The approach must be kept open-ended, because economics or any social science and behavioral science is in constant change.

This, then, is the background against which Keynesian ideas entered the stage in the period since 1936. Conflict with other social studies, commercial education, consumer education, vocational and technical education, federal legislation, disputes over 'personal' versus 'academic' economics, Depression, World War, new and active governmental intervention in the economy, the Sputnik-reinforced academically-orientated curriculum reform movement, the National Task Force and the Joint Council are some of the major factors that shaped economic education in this period.

III

Galbraith has pointed out that on a number of occasions popular ideas have been ahead of conventional wisdom. One such striking example, according to Galbraith, occurred in the Great Depression when practitioners and politicians, such as Hoover and Roosevelt, were urging pump priming and public works to reduce unemployment at a time when economists favored monetary measures to curb the business cycle and to promote the adjustment process. Only after the appearance of Keynes's *General Theory* in 1936 did fiscal measures become more respectable as policy tools acceptable to academic economists.[5] Textbook treatment before Keynes shows awareness of many facets of the problem of economic instability.

Of the texts first appearing in the 1930s (table 6.2) that by Corbett

TABLE 6.2   Bibliographical data concerning the textbooks representing the 1930s

C 35:	CORBETT, JAMES F. and HERSCHKOWITZ, MINNIE L., *Modern Economics*, New York, Macmillan, 1935.
F 32:	FAY, CHARLES R., *Elements of Economics*, New York, Macmillan, 1932.
G 38–55:	GOODMAN, KENNARD E. and MOORE, WILLIAM L., *Economics in Everyday Life*, Boston, Ginn & Co., 1938, 1941, 1943, 1947, 1950, 1952 and 1955.

deals with Fisher's equation of exchange and presents the quantity theory of money and criticisms directed against it. The approach is heavy on monetary theory and devoid of fiscal policy aspects, a circumstance typical of pre-Keynesian thought. Attempts at explaining business cycles are given under the headings: psychological, lack of planning, oversaving (Sismondi, Hobson), overhead costs, monetary and cumulative. The arguments under the heading 'overhead costs' stress the volatility of investment in its effect on aggregate demand and are remarkable for the degree to which they anticipate some of Keynes's explanations. Corbett lists as possible remedies for excessive business fluctuations: stabilization of production, stabilization of currency and credit, unemployment insurance, public works, (better) business statistics, redistribution of income, and economic planning. In terms of practical policies, Corbett's book is remarkably up to date and aware of New Deal measures and motives.

In the introduction, the authors state:[6]

> As new methods and problems of production and distribution arise, the traditional concepts of *laissez faire* can be applied only to an order of things which is fast disappearing. . . . Intelligent citizenship requires an understanding of the conflict which has arisen between a system of *laissez faire* and the necessity of social control because this conflict affects the welfare of the Nation.

In summary, it might be said that the textbook by Corbett and Herschkowitz reveals sensitivity to Keynesian philosophy and outlook, but, as it predates the *General Theory*, one cannot expect technical details originated by Keynes.

Unlike Corbett, Fay treats business cycles in the context of production and marketing rather than in the context of exchange and monetary problems. Possible causes of business cycles are given as: 'the sun-spot theory (Jevons, Huntington), overproduction, overspeculation, socialist explanations, Mitchell's monetary theory.'[7] Possible remedies are listed as the improvement of estimates by businessmen, better statistics, use of public works, and credit control.[8] Fay's work does not appear as sensitive to the problems raised by the Great Depression or at least not as sensitive to the later Keynesian trends and to the New Deal as Corbett's text, but from the standpoint of brief, formal enumeration, Fay's book does not fall significantly behind Corbett's treatment.

An examination of table 6.3 shows that, whereas Corbett and Fay devote respectively 3 and 4 per cent of total contents to business cycles, Goodman allocates only 2 per cent to this topic. The comparable percentages for the major category of macroeconomics for the three authors are: 9 per cent, 10 per cent and 8 per cent. Percentages for the major category 'personal' economics are: 3 per cent, 6 per cent, and 13 per cent. Thus, there could be an inverse relation between macroeconomics and 'personal' economics. To the extent that an author tends to emphasize 'personal' economics, there seems to be a tendency to reduce space given to macroeconomics. The differences in percentages are admittedly too small to draw definite conclusions, but, on the other hand, slight quantitative differences 'on the margin' could be taken to reveal underlying biases.

The development in textbooks in the 1940s which follows certainly adds weight to the observations of the preceding paragraph on trends still in their incipience in the 1930s. Another important factor to be considered is the great success of Goodman's book for seventeen years. This success could, of course, be a reflection of a well-entrenched publisher with a sales and editorial staff geared effectively to the

TABLE 6.3 Percentage allocations of space in secondary school general economics texts of the 1930s

	C	F	G
	35	32	38–55
CATEGORY			
Macroeconomics			
Subtopics			
Nature of macroeconomics, definitions, etc.	–	–	–
Aggregate demand, simple Keynesian model	–	–	–
National income accounting	–	–	–
Business cycles, price levels	3	4	2
Government spending and budget, national debt	1	2	4
Taxation	5	4	2
National growth	–	–	–
Fiscal policy, complete Keynesian model	–	–	–
Total	9	10	8
Production	25	15	16
Exchange	27	37	27
Distribution	9	21	11
'Personal' economics	3	6	13
Introductory and other material	27	11	25
Overall total	100	100	100

secondary school market. On the other hand, one wonders to what extent potential adopters of secondary school economics texts were sensitive to 'personal' economics and welcomed Goodman's emphasis.

Like Corbett, Goodman treats business cycles in the context of exchange and hence of monetary phenomena. His treatment is essentially parallel with that of the other two authors, but limited to three pages. Public works and other possible depression remedies are mentioned. The problem of government planning and control versus *laissez faire* is also treated. A noncommittal or open-ended stance is adopted, that is, the existence of government regulation as a fact of the 1930s is stated, the question of the proper and wise use of such regulation is raised, but an answer or a guide to policy is not given.

The 1940s were the decade of 'personal' economics for the high schools. In 1940 the National Association of Secondary School Principals through the Council for the Advancement of Secondary Education had launched the Consumer Education Study.[9] Since 1935 the first textbooks entirely devoted to consumer economics had emerged. Accordingly, the general economics texts for secondary schools in the

1940s differ from their predecessors of the 1930s mainly in the amount of space and the number of subtopics devoted to 'personal' economics. There are few other changes of equal importance (see table 6.4).

TABLE 6.4   Bibliographical data concerning the textbooks representing the 1940s

---

B 49:   BOODISH, H.M., *Our Industrial Age*, New York, McGraw-Hill, 1949.

C 48:   CLARK, HAROLD F., *Economics*, New York, American Book Co., 1948.

D 45:   DODD, JAMES H., *Applied Economics: Elementary Principles of Economics Applied to Everyday Problems*, Cincinnati, South-Western Publishing, 1945.

F 40:   FAIRCHILD, HENRY P., *Economics for the Millions*, New York, Modern Age Books, 1940.

H 43:   HUGHES, RAY O., *Fundamentals of Economics*, Boston, Allyn & Bacon, 1943.

J 41:   JANZEN, CORNELIUS C. and STEPHENSON, ORLANDO W., *Everyday Economics*, N.Y., Silver Burdett, 1941.

K 47:   KLEIN, JACOB and COLVIN, WOOLF, *Economic Problems of Today*, Chicago, Lyons & Carnahan, 1947.

L 40–9: LUTZ, HARLEY L., FOOTE, EDMUND W. and STANTON, BENJAMIN F., *Getting a Living: the Foundations of Economic Society*, Evanston, Ill., Row, Peterson, 1940, 1941, 1945 and 1949.

P 41:   PATTERSON, S. HOWARD, LITTLE, A.W.S. and BURCH, HENRY R., *American Economic Problems*, New York, Macmillan, 1941.

Table 6.5 shows the percentage distributions for space allocations in the high school general economics texts of the 1940s. An examination of the table shows that all high school authors devote space explicitly to the phenomenon of business cycles. The space allocation varies and hence the depth of treatment which is possible. However, in all instances coverage was found to be conventional. By conventional the present writer means the type of pre-Keynesian treatment in which the phases of the business cycle are explained, and various theories of the causes of business fluctuations are enumerated. Fluctuations of investment and the related accelerator principle are mentioned as possible causes.

Assessments of the effectiveness of fiscal policy as applied to the business cycle differed, presumably with the political and economic biases of the various authors. In order to permit a full discussion of political biases in high school economics texts, reference is made in the following comments to the general economics high school text authored by Fred Rogers Fairchild and Thomas J. Shelly which was first published in 1952, the quantitative analysis of which appears in table 6.7.

TABLE 6.5 Percentage allocations of space in secondary school general economics texts of the 1940s

	B	C	D	F	H	J	K	L	P
	49	48	45	40	43	41	47	40	41
								−9	

CATEGORY									
Macroeconomics									
Subtopics									
Nature of macroeconomics, definitions, etc.	–	–	–	–	–	–	–	–	2
Aggregate demand, the simple Keynesian model	–	–	–	–	–	–	–	–	–
National income accounting	–	–	–	–	–	–	–	–	1
Business cycles, price levels	7	2	1	2	2	1	4	2	4
Government spending and budget, national debt	2	–	4	–	–	3	1	4	–
Taxation	5	3	3	–	–	2	3	2	4
National growth	–	4	–	–	–	–	–	–	–
Fiscal policy, complete Keynesian model	–	–	–	–	–	–	–	–	–
Total	14	9	8	2	2	6	8	8	11
Production	7	22	13	28	34	24	17	10	11
Exchange	13	30	33	19	18	24	33	30	27
Distribution	9	4	22	18	11	16	11	16	8
'Personal' economics	5	21	6	5	7	6	9	12	6
Introductory and other material	52	14	18	28	28	24	22	24	37
Overall total	100	100	100	100	100	100	100	100	100

The book by Fred Rogers Fairchild should not be confused with the book by Henry Pratt Fairchild published in 1940, the quantitative analysis of which appears in table 6.5. The following discussion refers always to Fred Rogers Fairchild. Fairchild seemed to occupy one extreme in holding that pump priming had apparently been ineffective and that dangers of government debt and deficit and of inflation loomed large, and Klein tended to the view that such spending could be helpful, but he did give arguments for the possible dangers of such spending.

A careful assessment of the presentations seems to indicate that no author can be blamed for completely suppressing existing facts, such as public works and the attendant problems. Fairchild, however, did suppress all arguments that would favor the use of fiscal policy in the Keynesian perspective. In other words, while Fairchild did not deny the employment and appearance of public works, he did not give a single argument in their favor, but many arguments against them. In the opinion of the present writer, no other high school author showed the same degree of bias. All other authors stated the facts of public and governmental policy and then proceeded to state a number of arguments for and against Keynesian policy measures. In the process of such enumeration of arguments 'pro' and 'con' the author's own bias might be detectable, but no author other than Fairchild was guilty of suppressing all the arguments on one side of the issue.

The tenor of all authors would be regarded as conservative and cautious as of the time of the present writing. To the current writer, the high school authors showed no reaction different from that of college authors: Keynesian thinking was new, and new ideas are generally treated cautiously not only on the high school, but also on the college level.[10]

From the preceding discussion it should be noted that high school authors described and attempted to assess the practical effects of New Deal policies. Except for one author, there was no mention of Keynes, the multiplier, the accelerator, or any other theoretical concepts attributable to Keynes.

The 1947 edition of Klein's book gave a sympathetic account of New Deal measures, but did not mention Keynes by name. Later editions by Klein in the 1950s always mentioned the British economist and will be discussed below.

The one exception referred to above, is the secondary school general economics text written by Clark, who was then professor of educational economics at Columbia University. Clark states:[11]

J.M. Keynes has written a book on economics that has been very famous in recent years. The title is the *General Theory of Employment, Interest, and Money*. In it he suggested that a negative rate of interest be adopted. This means that if people insist on keeping their money idle, they will not be paid interest but will be charged for keeping it idle.

For decades certain economists had been contending that lack of purchasing power or underconsumption was the primary cause of depressions. Although many had stated this position as early as the nineteenth century, it remained for Keynes to make the doctrine one of high fashion. The governments around the world that have adopted deficit financing as a permanent part of their financial policy have been greatly influenced by the Keynes doctrine.

In general, Keynes holds that depressions are caused by the lack of an adequate amount of effective purchasing power. In that case the solution is obvious. The government is to borrow money and to dispose of the money in ways to increase purchasing power. The doctrine seems so easy and so obvious that many people have said why doesn't the government guarantee permanent prosperity. Seemingly, many people and some economists think the government can and should guarantee adequate effective purchasing power and thereby prevent the possibility of major, prolonged depressions.

While giving the Keynesian argument, Clark does not deny classical economic thinking and states other considerations stressed in connection with the problem of the business cycle. He discusses aggregate demand and the importance of aggregate consumption and investment; he also mentions public works and the various favorable and critical arguments.

An examination of table 6.5 indicates that Clark allocated space much as other high school authors of the 1940s. However, in the area of macroeconomics he is more sensitive to the tide of the future than other high school textbook writers; in fact, his book was published but one year after the first thoroughly Keynesian introductory college textbook, that by Tarshis.[12] The textbook by Sayer in 1950 (see table 6.6) and the editions by Klein in 1953 and 1956 give short accounts of Keynes and his ideas, much in the capsule fashion of Clark. While Clark, Sayer, and Klein generally do not name, define, and carefully explain theoretical Keynesian concepts, their treatment does constitute a transition in high school texts from the conventional pre-Keynesian treatment to the more detailed exposition of some texts published after 1959. Other high school texts do not allude to Keynesian ideas as distinguished from practical policy measures prompted by Keynesian economists and politicians.

A comparison of the secondary school general economics texts of the 1950s (tables 6.6 and 6.7) with those of the 1940s reveals no pronounced

TABLE 6.6 Bibliographical data concerning the textbooks representing the 1950s

---

B 51:   BAGLEY, WILLIAM C., JR and PERDEW, RICHARD M.,
          Understanding Economics, New York, Macmillan, 1951.

D 51:   DODD, JAMES H., *Applied Economics: Introductory Principles
          of Economics Applied to Everyday Problems*, 4th ed.,
          Cincinnati, South-Western Publishing, 1951.

D 56:   DODD, JAMES H., *Applied Economics, Introductory Principles
          Applied to Everyday Problems*, 5th ed., Cincinnati,
          South-Western Publishing, 1956.

F 52–65: FAIRCHILD, FRED R. and SHELLY, THOMAS J., *Understanding
          Our Free Economy*, Princeton, N.J., Van Nostrand, 1952,
          1956, 1962 and 1965.

G 57   GOODMAN, KENNARD E. and MOORE, WILLIAM L., *Today's
and 60:   Economics*, Boston, Ginn and Co., 1957 and 1960.

222 *Case Studies in Curriculum Change*

H 54   HOLT, SOLOMON, *Economics and You*, New York, Charles
and 56:   Scribner's, 1954 and 1956.
K 53:   KLEIN, JACOB and COLVIN, WOOLF, *Economic Problems of
Today*, Chicago, Lyons & Carnahan, 1953.
K 59:   KLEIN, JACOB and COLVIN, WOOLF, *Economic Problems of
Today*, Chicago, Lyons & Carnahan, 1959.
S 50:   SAYER, ALBERT H., COGEN, CHARLES and NANES, SIDNEY,
Economics in our Democracy, New York, McGraw-Hill,
1950.
S 50   SMITH, AUGUSTUS H., *Economics for Our Times*, New York,
and 53:   McGraw-Hill, 1950 and 1953.

shifts, so that the decade of 'personal' economics extended its influence
also over the 1950s as far as the high schools were concerned.

However, there are indications that new microeconomic developments which were causing a surge in the major category of production
in the college texts of the early 1940s were being reflected to a slight
extent in the high school books of the 1950s. If this observation is true,
one might conjecture that influence of innovations on high school texts
follows college introductory texts by about ten years, inasmuch as the
Keynesian influence did not become operative on the high school level
until the 1960s but had shown itself in college texts of the late 1940s.
This conclusion would be reasonably well in line with Paul Mort's
estimate of a lag of twenty-five years behind best practice and Bushnell's
estimate of twenty years.[13]

Turning to the detailed analysis of the texts (table 6.7), that authored
by Sayer in 1950 gives a short account of Keynes. On the whole, Sayer
follows the conventional pattern of treatment. He includes a section on
national income accounting. In dealing with the causes of business
cycles, the underinvestment theory is mentioned. The possible disparity
of intended savings and intended investment is described and illustrated
by a cartoon copyrighted in 1945 by the Newspaper PM, Inc., which
makes the fallacy of composition a departure of humor. An irate father
demands to know why his son is about to smash his piggy bank. His son
answers: 'But, Pop, if savings exceed investments, a whole downward
cycle is set in motion.'[14]

Keynes's name or other theoretical Keynesian concepts are not stated
in this connection, but Keynes's name, the idea of compensatory
spending, deficit spending, and pump priming are mentioned in connection with the treatment of New Deal measures. The presentation is
limited to one page.[15] Theoretical concepts, such as the multiplier,
accelerator, consumption function, marginal propensity to consume,
marginal efficiency of investment, liquidity preference, etc., are not
used or named.

TABLE 6.7   Percentage allocations of space in secondary school general economic texts of the 1950s

	B 51	D 51	D 56	F 52 -65	G 57 & 60	H 54 & 56	K 53	K 59	S 50	S 50 & 53
CATEGORY										
Macroeconomics										
Subtopics										
Nature of macroeconomics, definitions, etc.	–	–	–	–	–	–	–	–	–	–
Aggregate demand, simple Keynesian model	–	–	–	–	–	–	–	–	–	–
National income accounting	5	–	–	–	–	–	3	2	1	–
Business cycles, price levels	6	–	1	3	2	5	2	2	7	3
Government spending and budget, national debt	2	4	4	2	3	3	2	2	3	2
Taxation	3	3	3	7	3	3	3	3	1	3
National growth	–	–	–	–	–	–	–	–	–	–
Fiscal policy, complete Keynesian model	–	–	–	–	–	–	2	2	3	–
Total	16	7	8	12	8	11	12	11	15	8
Production	18	15	17	20	13	21	19	19	18	16
Exchange	26	24	24	30	27	25	32	29	16	32
Distribution	8	20	18	12	11	16	11	13	11	16
'Personal' economics	11	15	12	2	18	12	7	8	9	11
Introductory and other material	21	19	21	24	23	15	19	20	31	17
Overall total	100	100	100	100	100	100	100	100	100	100

Whereas treatment of macroeconomic problems in Klein's 1947 edition followed conventional lines, his 1953 and 1959 editions mention Keynes explicitly and discuss policy and practical measures. Theoretical Keynesian concepts are not spelled out, but are hinted at.[16]

John Maynard Keynes, an English economist, formulated a theory of budgeting called deficit spending. According to this theory governments are justified in periods of depression in borrowing in order to spend for the purpose of creating employment. Government expenditures help to make up or to compensate for the lack of employment in private industry. If such spending causes an increase in production the rise in national income is much greater than the cost.

John Maynard Keynes, a great English economist, claimed that if private savers do not wish to lend and private investors fail to buy capital goods, the government must undertake *compensatory* purchase of capital goods. This will increase employment in the capital goods industries and increase the demand by their workers for consumer goods.

Keynes had a great influence on the remedies adopted by the Roosevelt Administration during the depression of the 1930s.

Klein's pertinent statements have been quoted in full to indicate that the multiplier and accelerator concepts and the disparity of intended savings and intended investment are implied or hinted at, but not expressly labeled or highlighted for students. In all other respects the treatment of business cycles, government spending, and taxation by Klein is conventional. Klein does have a section on national income accounts.

As is evident from table 6.7, the text by Bagley shows the highest space allocation to macroeconomics. Nevertheless, Bagley's textbook is conventional in the sense in which this term was used previously, that is, New Deal measures, problems and theories of the business cycle are discussed, but theoretical Keynesian contributions or even the name of the British economist are not mentioned. An innovation of some books of the 1950s over those of the 1940s is the inclusion of national income accounting data, such as the now familiar circular flow chart of national income. Bagley is among the first high school authors to present this material, bearing out once again that the lag from first innovative publication to inclusion in a secondary school economics text is about twenty years or more. This would assume that innovation of social accounting by the Department of Commerce and other agencies is dated about 1931. It is difficult to date, but 1931 would appear to be a reasonably good choice when one considers that work prior to that time was limited to certain sectors of the national income accounts, such as foreign trade, and was a rather esoteric professional endeavor. The Great Depression certainly contributed to public awareness and acknowledgement of the importance of this economic tool.

Bagley discusses deficit financing and surplus financing.[17] The practical New Deal policy measures and public works seem to recede somewhat in importance, and the practical aspects of Keynesian thought seem to be in better focus in his text than in those of the 1940s. However, this in no way gives the student Keynesian theoretical concepts.

TABLE 6.8   Bibliographical data concerning the textbooks representing the 1960s

A 68:	ALEXANDER, ALBERT, PREHN, EDWARD C. and SAMETZ, ARNOLD W., *The Modern Economy in Action: an Analytical Approach*, New York, Pitman, 1968.
B 68:	BROWN, JAMES E. and WOLF, HAROLD A., *Economics: Principles and Practices*, Columbus, Charles E. Merrill, 1968.
C 68:	CALDERWOOD, JAMES D. and FERSH, GEORGE L., *Economics in Action*, New York, Macmillan, 1968.

D 69: DAUGHERTY, MARION R. and MADDEN, CARL H., *The Economic Process*, Glenview, Ill., Scott, Foresman, 1969.

D 62: DODD, JAMES H., KENNEDY, JOHN W. and OLSEN, ARTHUR R., *Applied Economics: Introductory Principles Applied to Everyday Problems*, 6th ed., Cincinnati, South-Western Publishing, 1962.

D 67: KENNEDY, JOHN W., OLSEN, ARTHUR R. and DODD, JAMES H., *Applied Economics: Introductory Principles Applied to Everyday Problems*, 7th ed., Cincinnati, South-Western Publishing, 1967.

F 58–66: FEIER, RICHARD, *Economics for Modern Living*, New York, College Entrance Book Co., 1958, 1960, 1963 and 1966.

G 63 and 66: GOODMAN, KENNARD E. and HARRISS, C. L., *Economics: an Analytical Approach*, Boston, Ginn, 1963 and 1966.

G 67: GORDON, SANFORD D. and WITCHEL, JESS, *An Introduction to the American Economy: Analysis and Policy*, Boston, D.C. Heath, 1967.

H 59 and 63: HECKMAN, HARRY W., *The Economics of American Living*, New York, Rand McNally, 1959 and 1963.

H 62 and 64: HOLT, SOLOMON, *Economics and You*, Chicago, Follett, 1962 and 1964.

H 62 and 64: HURWITZ, HOWARD L. and SHAW, FREDERICK, *Economics in a Free Society*, New York, Oxford Book Co., 1962 and 1964.

L 68: LEITH, HAROLD R. and LUMPKIN, R. PIERCE, *Economics U.S.A.*, New York, McGraw-Hill, 1968.

L 59 and 62: LINDHOLM, RICHARD W. and DRISCOLL, PAUL, *Our American Economy*, New York, Harcourt Brace, 1959 and 1962.

L 64: LINDHOLM, RICHARD W. and DRISCOLL, PAUL, *Our American Economy*, New York, Harcourt Brace, 1964.

M 64–9: MORTENSON, WILLIAM P., KRIDER, DONALD T. and SAMPSON, ROY J., *Understanding Our Economy: Analysis, Issues, Principles*, Boston, Houghton Mifflin, 1964, 1967 and 1969.

S 69: SILK, LEONARD S. and SAUNDERS, PHILIP, *The World of Economics*, New York, McGraw-Hill, 1969.

S 59: SMITH, AUGUSTUS H., *Economics for Our Times*, 4th ed., New York, McGraw-Hill, 1959.

W 65: WARD, RICHARD J., *Economics: its Principles and Means*, New York, W.H. Sadlier, 1965.

W 64: WRONSKI, STANLEY P., DOODY, FRANCIS S. and CLEMENCE, RICHARD V., *Modern Economics*, Boston, Allyn & Bacon, 1964.

Treatment of macroeconomic topics both in the 1951 and the 1956 editions by Dodd is entirely conventional and shows little change from his earlier editions. This qualitative judgement is borne out by the quantitative data which are limited to the traditional macroeconomic topics of business cycles, government expenditure, and taxation. The

TABLE 6.9 Percentage allocations of space in secondary

	A 68	B 68	C 68	D 69	D 62
CATEGORY					
Macroeconomics					
Subtopics					
Nature of macroeconomics, definitions, etc.	–	–	–	–	–
Aggregate demand, simple Keynesian model	3	–	4	–	–
National income accounting	6	4	2	6	4
Business cycles, price levels	3	7	8	5	4
Government spending and budget, national debt	2	3	7	3	4
Taxation	3	5	–	–	3
National growth	6	3	17	15	–
Fiscal policy, complete Keynesian model	3	1	5	3	–
Total	26	23	43	32	15
Production	11	10	13	16	16
Exchange	12	32	16	19	30
Distribution	9	8	–	4	15
'Personal' economics	–	–	3	4	10
Introductory and other material	42	27	25	25	14
Overall total	100	100	100	100	100

pronouncements just applied to Dodd's editions also hold for the textbook by Fairchild.

In the preface to his 1957 edition, Goodman acknowledges the influence of the Council for the Advancement of Secondary Education and states that his text is designed to assist students with economic and consumer problems of their daily lives and to enhance their civic understanding.[18] Goodman limits his treatment of macroeconomics to the three traditional topics. Business cycles are discussed but briefly and along conventional lines. Government spending and taxation are mentioned as possible tools to stabilize the business cycle along with the tools of monetary policy, that is, changes in the interest rate and credit controls.[19] Arguments are given for and against public works. Keynesian theoretical concepts are not mentioned.

The treatment by Holt is also conventional. Business cycles are defined, and their phases, such as prosperity, crisis, depression, and recovery, are discussed. There is also the usual consideration of the usefulness or futility or public works.[20]

The 1953 edition of Smith's general economics text for secondary schools is also entirely conventional with respect to macroeconomics. Possible remedies or means to reduce the severity of business cycles are listed as the stabilization of production, public works programs, better school general economic texts of the 1960s

D 67	F 58 –66	G 63 & 66	G 67	H 59 & 63&64	H 62 & 64	H 62	L 68	L 59 & 62	L 64	M 64 –69	S 69	S 59	W 65	W 64
–	–	–	6	–	–	–	–	–	–	–	2	–	–	–
–	–	–	7	–	–	–	–	–	–	–	5	–	–	–
3	1	3	3	2	–	–	6	6	6	4	5	3	3	3
3	2	3	11	2	5	3	5	2	2	4	5	7	1	4
4	1	4	3	11	3	4	4	5	5	2	2	3	5	3
2	4	4	6	–	3	3	4	5	5	4	–	3	–	–
–	–	2	–	–	2	–	2	–	–	–	2	–	8	–
–	2	3	–	2	–	–	2	2	2	1	2	–	1	–
12	10	19	36	17	13	10	23	20	20	15	23	16	18	10
15	16	9	7	13	21	12	14	19	18	18	11	22	12	16
32	31	29	20	32	22	18	35	15	14	24	26	19	29	21
15	12	12	14	9	15	11	15	17	14	7	5	14	13	12
8	16	12	7	–	13	12	2	7	7	11	–	10	–	13
18	15	19	16	29	16	37	11	22	27	25	35	19	28	28
100	100	100	100	100	100	100	100	100	100	100	100	100	100	100

business information, and control of credit. Doubt is expressed as to the efficacy of the New Deal public works program.[21] The 1959 edition by Smith showed Keynesian influence and in a sense ushered in the more Keynesian treatment of macroeconomics by texts of the 1960s. For this reason, the analysis of Smith's 1959 edition appears in Table 6.9 and is treated together with similar texts of the 1960s.

The 1960s were the years of macroeconomics for secondary school general economics texts (see table 6.8). As mentioned previously, even consumer economics texts on the high school level were affected by the surge to macroeconomics though to a lesser extent. Total space allocated to macroeconomics in secondary school general economics texts went from a range of 7 to 16 per cent in the sample of the 1950s to a range from 10 to 43 per cent in the 1960s (table 6.9). Macroeconomics gained at the expense of distribution which went from a range of 8 to 20 per cent in the 1950s to a range from 0 to 17 per cent in the 1960s and at the expense of 'personal' economics which went from a range of 2 to 18 per cent in the 1950s to a range of 0 to 16 per cent in the 1960s. The major categories of production and exchange remained fairly stable from the 1950s to the 1960s.

Comparison of the macroeconomic content of the texts of the high school authors of the sample shows that Gordon advances to the level of the simple Keynesian model and embodies more Keynesian content in his text than any other author. In terms of Keynesian contents, Silk is on the same level as the immediately following authors, but Silk has an up to date, post-Keynesian level of analysis embracing a neo-classical synthesis for high school students which is exceptional and ahead of all other secondary school authors.

The following writers are oriented to Keynesian thought and explain Keynesian terminology by verbal discussion generally without use of graphs or algebra. A few of them use one or two pictorial illustrations or numerical tables: Alexander, Brown, Calderwood, Daugherty, Goodman, Leith, Dodd and Smith.

Feier and Heckman are in line with the treatment of the preceding authors except for the brevity of their statements which hinders as full an exposition. Feier has a good account of the roles of intended savings versus intended investment in their effect on business fluctuations. While not ignoring Keynesian ideas, Mortenson does give less attention to them than all preceding authors. However, he contrasts classical and Keynesian thought.

Hurwitz, Lindholm, and Ward have a bias to classical economic ideas and show relatively little Keynesian content, perhaps because of their leanings to classical economic thought. Holt and Wronski give least evidence of Keynesian influence and present texts in line with the con-ventional treatment of public finance customary in secondary school textbooks of the 1950s.

In summary, ten of the eighteen textbook writers of the sample of the 1960s do consider and present Keynesian thought with some of its theoretical terminology and implications in contrast with the textbooks of the 1950s which were primarily concerned with the practical evidence of New Deal measures and limited themselves to conventional, pre-Keynesian theories of the business cycle.

To what extent did Keynesian analysis enter the secondary school economics text of the 1960s? Space allocation to the major category of macroeconomics increased, as we have seen, from a range of 7 to 16 per cent in the 1950s to 10 to 43 per cent in the 1960s. To the extent that emphasis of macroeconomics can be considered to express a Keynesian influence, the 1960s would give evidence of the trend. Only four of ten high school editions of the 1950s treated national income accounting as an explicit subtopic of macroeconomics; in the 1960s only Holt and Hurwitz did not make a specific allocation to the subtopic.

High school authors did not emphasize monetary policy to the exclusion of fiscal policy or vice versa. Many mentioned that monetary policy is more effective in an inflation, fiscal policy in a deflation. The possibility of an underemployment equilibrium was brought into focus only by Gordon and Mortenson. Authors stated that fiscal and monetary policies were being used to produce general and price stability. Their attitude to such government intervention was cautiously positive although some, such as Hurwitz, Lindholm, Ward, and perhaps Mortenson, appeared noncommittal.

IV

How long did it take until Keynesian ideas appeared in secondary school economics texts ?

Keynes's *General Theory* was published in 1936. The first college level economics text to show Keynesian theoretical concepts was the one by Tarshis published in 1947. Samuelson's[22] first edition of 1948 was also Keynesian. On the college level the first adoption occurred after about eleven years.

Secondary school textbooks by Clark in 1948, Sayer in 1950, and Klein in 1953 do mention Keynes's name, but few, if any, theoretical Keynesian concepts. The first secondary school text to give Keynesian theoretical terminology and some explanations was the one by Smith published in 1959. Later ones with Keynesian concepts were: Dodd in 1962, Goodman in 1963, Mortenson in 1964, and many others after 1965. The adoption period on the secondary school level was about

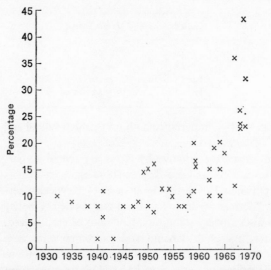

Figure 6.1   Percentage of space allocated to macroeconomics in American high school textbooks, 1930–70 (based on tables in text)

twenty-three years. This finding is in reasonably good agreement with those by Mort and Bushnell (see note 13) to the effect that schools tend to adopt ideas about twenty to twenty-five years after they first become available.

To what extent were Keynesian ideas reflected in the texts? In the textbook samples of the current investigation, percentages of total space allocated to the major category of macroeconomics ranged in the 1930s from 7 to 16 per cent on the college level, from 8 to 10 per cent on the high school level; in the 1940s from 7 to 18 per cent on the college level, from 2 to 14 per cent on the high school level; in the 1950s from 14 to 53 per cent on the college level, from 7 to 16 per cent on the high school level; in the 1960s from 18 to 42 per cent on the college level, from 10 to 43 per cent on the high school level (see figure 6.1).

Thus, college and high school texts did not differ materially in their allocation of total space to macroeconomics during the 1930s and 1940s. It was in the 1950s that macroeconomic allocation surged in college texts, but did not change significantly on the high school level. The quantitative analysis bears out the finding concerning the adoption period (see table 6.10): college texts embraced macroeconomics and Keynesian ideas after 1947; high school texts did not move in this direction until after 1959. The quantitative measures indicate that macro-

TABLE 6.10 Percentage allocation of space to the major category of macroeconomics in textbooks

Decade	College	High school
1930s	7–16	8–10
1940s	7–18	2–14
1950s	14–53	7–16
1960s	18–42	10–43

economics did gain in relative importance both on the high school and college levels.

Whereas treatment of macroeconomics by secondary school authors prior to 1959 was conventional and pre-Keynesian, of eighteen authors after 1959 at least ten included verbal discussions of Keynesian terminology and ideas. Matters pertaining to fiscal and monetary policy such as built-in and discretionary stabilizers, tended to be emphasized. Multiplier, accelerator, aggregate demand and its components were explained verbally. Graphic, numeric, and algebraic presentations tended to be avoided; models were not used in a technical sense except by Gordon and Silk.

V

What circumstances surrounded the innovative process and what theories and hypotheses can help to explain what occurred? A number of holistic and singularistic theories of change and innovation might be invoked to assist in understanding the Keynesian case.

Successive-stage theories

Successive stages may be the phases of one and the same life cycle, or they may be phases of different cycles. Successive-stage theorists claim to discern clusters of similar phenomena which permit ordering, systematization, and clarification for purposes of building theories and gaining insights.[23]

In the present investigation, decades were used as units of analysis or as stages. Frequently there were no marked changes from decade to decade, so that separate labels did not suggest themselves. However, in college level texts, the 1940s could be called the decade of production and the 1950s, the decade of macroeconomics; with respect to secondary school level texts, the 1940s could be labeled the decade of 'personal' economics, the 1960s, the decade of macroeconomics.

Four measures tend to justify the labels given: a pronounced rise in the percentage of total space allocated to the major category in question; an increase in the number of subtopics covered within the major category; an introduction of new concepts and a change in emphasis in the major category recognized by qualitative judgement and frequently due to a major innovation; and parallel shifts in emphasis in course outlines, research literature, and policy statements of the decade involved.

Cyclical theories

The present investigator feels that one of the most important hypotheses if not the most important, proceeding from the current study is that curricular innovation is only part of a longer life cycle of an element of the curriculum. Undoubtedly, this is not a new hypothesis either in the school setting or outside.[24]

Categories of knowledge and subtopics may change in terms of content, so that they rejuvenate themselves and remain in the curriculum with new labels and new terminology. Therefore, it may be improper to speak of a life cycle of an entire subject field. The idea of a life cycle can probably be much better defended and empirically determined with respect to a specific concept or term, for example, consumer and producer co-operatives, conservation, ecology, pollution, aggregate demand, multiplier, syndicalism, etc. Unfortunately for this purpose, the present study is not directed to concepts other than Keynesian ideas. These have been in the ascendancy in the period under study, so that a life cycle might be inferred primarily from its expansionist phase.

High school texts of the last half of the 1960s tended to show high allocations of space to macroeconomics and conversant use of Keynesian concepts. Low space allocations to macroeconomics and limited use of Keynesian terminology in the 1960s tended to characterize revised editions of books originating in the 1950s. However, in the judgement of the present writer, the text by Silk constitutes an exception. With 23 per cent of total space given to macroeconomics, the allocation may be considered modest for the last half of the 1960s. In terms of content, there is a post-Keynesian, neo-classical synthesis which, to the present writer, breaks new ground in a direction that is not Keynesian in the sense of contemporary texts. If so, the text of the future may show a decline in Keynesian terminology and an increase in post-Keynesian topics and concepts.

Even if sufficient empirical evidence for the life cycle of a term can be submitted, which the present study cannot, opponents of a life cycle theory may indicate that such empirical evidence goes to linguistic and terminological matters and says little about the life of an idea, but studies by Bronfenbrenner and Stigler[25] support a rising and waning of interest in economic topics in the professional literature and in research. Similarly, the present writer has found that land, labor, and entrepreneurship gradually fell into disuse as explicit subtopics of production in college texts, and conjectures that this had to do with the emergence of modern microeconomics which tends to classify material by states of the market rather than in the historical Ricardian scheme.

Accounting in a business context became an explicit subtopic of production in high school and college texts only in the 1950s and 1960s. Before the emergence of national income accounting and of Keynesian economics, entity accounting had apparently been considered a topic outside the accepted boundaries of the discipline of economics.

Questions of corporation finance, of stocks and bonds, and of stock exchanges had declined in interest in college texts in the 1940s and 1950s and were not considered as an explicit subtopic in college texts of the 1960s. The topic continued, however, in high school texts.

Questions of personal saving and investment, a subtopic of the major category of exchange, were covered explicitly by college texts of the 1940s and 1950s, but at no other time. One wonders whether this was with some lag in response to the Great Depression. High school texts show continuous coverage of this subtopic.

Analysis of high school texts before 1930 indicates that the subtopic 'transportation' had gained explicit treatment which continued unabated until the 1960s when a decline was registered. This subtopic had appeared last in some college texts of a sample of the 1940s. Such a development tends to support a hypothesis that the life cycle of topics (and concepts) on the high school level may be lagged about ten to twenty years behind the corresponding college cycle.

In the taxonomic context of the current study, the subtopic of aggregate demand was employed for the theoretical concepts involved in the so-called simple Keynesian model, such as aggregate consumption, aggregate investment, aggregate government expenditures, multiplier, accelerator, average and marginal propensities to consume, marginal efficiency of capital. It is interesting to note that this subtopic is the last Keynesian subtopic to be treated by high school texts. In other words, once again it is apparent that practical and more visible policy aspects, such as fiscal policy and national income accounting and reporting, tend to be recognized ahead of theoretical concepts. In this sense high school texts appear to reflect what occurs in society at large: New Deal and Keynesian policy measures of depression relief preceded publication and public debate of the *General Theory*. This bears out Kushner's[26] ideas of malleable or technological traits as distinguished from persistent traits as well as the idea of culture lag expressed by Chapin[27] and others.

Normative functionalism

Theories by Parsons and Shils[28] lay emphasis on the concept of equilibrium and on the social importance of common values or common culture elements. In the opinion of the present writer, theories involving inventories of culture elements or configurations differ from successive-stage and cyclical theories in manner and language of interpretation rather than in the nature of the phenomena observed. Waves, cycles, or fluctuations result from limitations imposed on inventories or spaces of knowledge; the composition and nature of culture inventories or spaces is determined by fluctuations and cycles of social interest and participation, in a word, there are reciprocal relations between motions of change (the diffusion and discontinuance of innovations) and the culture content of a society.

It is in the nature of limitations imposed on textbooks and in the nature of percentage analysis that an increase in one area must be offset by decline(s) in other areas. Nevertheless, an expanding field can grow

at the expense of *all* other fields or at the expense of only one or two
other fields. The present analysis of textbooks in economics indicates
that sometimes a discernible trade-off occurs, that is, that the decline
of one or two categories *alone* accounts for the increase in the emerging
or expanding category. From the standpoint of pedagogical orientation,
such trade-offs are probably as significant as changes on the margin as
they provide the historian with a relatively unbiased clue concerning the
main social or educational thrust of a period.

Conflict theory

Theories by writers such as Dahrendorf and Rex[29] consider an understanding of the goals, interests, and motivations of conflicting groups
within society as the best way of assessing the direction of social change
and the diffusion of innovations. Economic education has been the
arena for many confrontations, such as rigor and analysis versus description, emphasis on macroeconomics versus emphasis on microeconomics,
social versus personal economics, classical orthodoxy versus New Deal
or Keynesian economics.

To what extent did such conflicts, particularly of a political type,
impede or accelerate the diffusion of Keynesian concepts ? As the present
investigation concentrated on textbooks, course outlines, and related
research, any answer is predicated on these sources.

With the exception of Fairchild, secondary school authors of the
1950s wrote textbooks which are middle of the road and reasonably well
balanced in presenting liberal and conservative positions as expressed
in 1951 by McKee and Moulton:[30]

> In general the authors of these [most widely used] texts were favorable
> to the private enterprise system, though most of them felt that the
> government had a considerable role to play. One author puts it thus:
> 'Too much government regulation of business would be as damaging
> as *laissez-faire*. The great problem is to find the correct balance.'

By contrast McKee and Moulton stated that college textbooks were
more inclined to stress what the college text authors considered to be
the necessity and inevitability of government interference and control
in the economy. McKee and Moulton saw the high school books as a
little more biased towards *laissez-faire* than were the contemporary
college texts.

The AEA Textbook Study published in 1963, but conducted in 1959–
1960, was critical of secondary school economics texts, but political or
social bias was not among the many criticisms expressed. However, the

AEA-Textbook Study did find that treatment of aggregates and of the government were submerged:[31]

> The emphasis in all of these books is on microeconomics, with only one book dealing at all seriously with aggregative economics and the problem of instability. The one exception offers a good chapter on the measurement of national income and the circular flow of economic activity. But even this treatment of instability and its causes impressed all members of the subcommittee as inadequate. In other books, fiscal policies and central banking policies receive even less attention.
>
> The neglect of the aggregative approach and of the problem of instability has the added consequence that the role of government in the economy is discussed in only a very limited sense. The functions of government and the manner of financing public services are described in each book, but little or no mention is made of shifting, incidence, and effects of taxes, and public borrowing and its economic effects are almost completely ignored. The role of the government as a regulator is not handled well and there is a clear tendency to avoid such roles as (i) maintaining stability and helping to establish and enforce 'the rules of the game'; (ii) furnishing services which cannot be provided efficiently by private enterprise; (iii) supplying services – or added services – that are or could be furnished by the free market but where 'public policy' demands larger or different provision than would be accomplished by the market; (iv) modifying the real income distribution by 'welfare' expenditures and by nonproportional taxation; (v) establishing and achieving national goals that extend beyond the horizon of most individuals and firms.
>
> Factors which determine the economic role of governments are also neglected and efforts to evaluate the effects of governmental action against established economic criteria such as the efficient allocation, full utilization, and conservation of resources are noticeable by their absence. The subcommittee is agreed that the effects (good or bad) of governmental action merit more extended and analytical treatment than is offered by any of these books.

Thus, while the AEA Textbook Study does not find overt bias, there is an implication of bias by omission. The present textbook analysis is in agreement with the judgement expressed by the AEA Textbook Study to the effect that aggregative or Keynesian economics, particularly in its analytical and theoretical presentation, was absent from the secondary school texts of the 1950s, but it is also true that the judgement of the AEA Textbook Study could have been applied, with modifications, to the college texts of the 1940s. The difficult and crucial question which remains is whether the ten year lag on the secondary school level is inherent in the academic diffusion of innovations from the graduate school downwards or whether political biases operated more strongly on the secondary school level than on the college level.

There is reason to believe that probably both factors were operative. Mort's and Bushnell's lag of twenty to twenty-five years for educational practice behind the best available practice is reasonably in line with the findings of the current investigation which would tend to support an argument for the natural impediments to the diffusion of educational innovations. This was the position taken by the chairman of the AEA questionnaire study of 1950 who inferred that teachers are influenced by standards and topics prevailing in graduate schools at the time of their attendance.

Texts by Holt and by Wronski of the 1960s are in effect textbooks of the 1950s with a publishing date in the 1960s. These two texts exemplify the lag due to the slowness of the educational diffusion process. On the other hand texts by Hurwitz, Lindholm, and Ward (table 6.8) are examples that a bias to classical economics tends to be positively correlated with low space allocations to macroeconomics and relative absence of a presentation of Keynesian ideas.

Other reasons in the delay of the diffusion of Keynesian ideas may have been caused by conflicts between analysis and description, 'personal' economics and socio-civic economics, macroeconomics and microeconomics. Socio-civic economics and macroeconomics might have a tendency to facilitate and favor the diffusion of Keynesian concepts.

For instance, would the diffusion of Keynesian concepts have occurred in the 1960s to the extent that it did without the National Task Force Report of 1960 and the involvement of the professional economist? Texts by Feier and Smith, first published in 1958 and 1959 respectively, did give attention to Keynesian economics before the National Task Force Report, but certainly not on the scale and to the extent as the textbooks oriented to macroeconomics published after the report.

Singularistic studies in the diffusion of innovations

Some parallels can be seen between the development of economic education and various models discussed by Clarke[32] concerning the institutionalization of innovations. Endeavors of the business community and of the Joint Council on Economic Education were promoting and improving economic education outside the systems of formal education on the secondary and college levels and were comparable with patterns inherent in the (English) extra-university growth model. University centers of economic education and chairs of economic education were in line with the (German) inter-university diffusion model and the

(American) intra-university differentiation model of the institutionalization of innovations. It must be assumed that the progress of economic
education in the decades under discussion also enhanced the diffusion
of Keynesian concepts.

Important events, such as the Great Depression, World War II, the
Full Employment Act of 1946, and the Cold War, probably influenced
not only textbook writers and publishers, the primary focus of concern
in the current investigation, but also teachers, students, teacher-
education institutions, superintendents, and other supervisory personnel. Present evidence suggests that the Great Depression stimulated
emphasis of 'personal' and consumer economics, whereas later events
tended to call for more and more attention given to macroeconomics.
This circumstance had an important bearing on the diffusion of the
Keynesian ideas on the secondary school level.

The current investigation supports findings of other studies in the
field of educational innovation not only with respect to the period of
adoption, but also with respect to the pattern of adoption. There are
relatively few early adopters, leaders, or pioneers, but once the process
of innovation or the life cycle is in its increasing phase, a greater number
of early and late followers adopt the innovation.

To the present writer one of the most promising lines of research
both in educational as well as in other areas of innovation would be to
determine the period of discontinuance as well as the period of adoption,
so that the study of the diffusion of innovations can be more firmly
established as a component of studies in the life cycle of culture elements
or configurations. Such studies might utilize textbooks or other media
to date and observe the process.

Another line of investigation would be to look at the diffusion process
with respect to other important innovations in economics, such as the
Chamberlin-Robinson monopolistic competition analysis, Leontief
input-output matrices, or growth models. An investigation dealing
primarily with college materials would probably necessitate the development of taxonomies more suitable for that purpose. Such taxonomies
may throw light on some of the questions with respect to college texts
which were not a primary concern in the present study.

Studies in specific school systems or colleges involving teachers,
students, and teaching materials could aid in extending the findings of
the present study. For example, though the comparison of course outlines with textbooks, pronouncements of writers and policy bodies
pointed to a definite correspondence of contents in textbooks with contents as taught in the classroom, only specific empirical evidence can
support dependable conclusions on this point.

Notes

1 For a more detailed treatment, including extensive reference to other aspects of Keynesian theory, see Voege, 1972.

2 These would include stress on aggregate demand and the creation of social accounting; denial of Say's law; recognition of a consumption function; emphasis on the importance of investment as the critical and volatile factor in creating necessary aggregate demand (also use of the multiplier); denial of the classical concept of the interest rate (assertion that intended investment does not necessarily equal intended saving); emphasis on fiscal policy and concurrent use of monetary policy, whereas the neo-classical school of economics advocated use of monetary policy almost to the complete exclusion of fiscal policy; belief that there can be an underemployment equilibrium, particularly, but not solely, when wages are rigid; assertion that the labor market and national income do not necessarily determine consumption, investment, interest rates and prices, but that the reverse may be the case. There is a general consensus among post-Keynesian economists that these points embody the major content of *The General Theory*, though there is controversy over their relative weightings (see, for example: Gardner Ackley, *Macroeconomic Theory*, New York, Macmillan, 1961; Thomas F. Dernburg and Duncan M. McDougall, *Macroeconomics: the Measurement, Analysis and Control of Aggregate Economic Activity*, New York, McGraw-Hill, 1960; Alvin H. Hansen, *A Guide to Keynes*, New York, McGraw-Hill, 1953; Edward Shapiro, *Macroeconomic Analysis*, New York, Harcourt Brace, 1970; Warren L. Smith, *Macroeconomics*, Homewood, Ill., Irwin, 1970).

3 The categories will be recognized as reflecting, to a large extent, those put forward by John Stuart Mill, whose typology can be traced into many economics textbooks of the nineteenth and twentieth centuries and into many research studies. For a full discussion, see Voege, 1972, pp. 130–8.

4 For some account of the texts of the period before 1930, see Voege, 1972, pp. 141–63.

5 John Kenneth Galbraith, 'Producer persuasion versus public desire: should consumer be king again?,' *Toledo Blade*, March 22, 1970, section B, p. 1.

6 Corbett and Herschkowitz (see table 6.2), p. v.

7 Fay (see table 6.2), pp. 185–9.

8 Ibid., pp. 191–3.

9 Association for Supervision and Curriculum Development, *Educating for Economic Competence*, National Education Association, Washington, 1960, p. 76.

10 For a detailed analysis of college level texts, see Voege, 1972.

11 Clark (see table 6.4), pp. 47, 50.

12 Lorie Tarshis, *The Elements of Economics: an Introduction to the Theory of Price and Employment*, Boston, Houghton Mifflin, 1947.

13 Margaret Bushnell, 'Now we're lagging only twenty years,' *School Executive*, LXXVII (October 1957), pp. 61–3; Paul R. Mort, *Principles of School Administration*, New York, McGraw-Hill, 1946, pp. 199–200.

14 Sayer (see table 6.6), p. 637.

15 Ibid., p. 644.

16 Klein (see table 6.6), pp. 534, 558.

17 Bagley (see table 6.6), pp. 415–19.

18 Goodman (see table 6.6), 1957, p.v.

19 Ibid., pp. 511–13.

20 Holt (see table 6.6), 1954, pp. 285–309.

21 Smith (see table 6.6), 1953, p. 444.

22 Paul A. Samuelson, *Economics*, New York, McGraw-Hill, 1948, 1951, 1961 and 1970.

23 See, for example, Malinowski, 1945; White, 1959.

24 The most elaborate statement of the position is probably that by Sorokin, 1937.

25 Martin Bronfenbrenner, 'Trends, cycles, and fads in economic writing,' *American Economic Review*, LVI (May 1966), pp. 538–52; George J. Stigler, *Essays in the History of Economics*, University of Chicago Press, 1965.

26 Gilbert Kushner, M. Gibson, J. Gulick, J.J. Honigmann and R. Nomas, *What Accounts for Sociocultural Change? A Propositional Inventory*, Institute for Research in Social Science, University of North Carolina, 1962.

27 F. Stuart Chapin, *Cultural Change*, New York, Century, 1928.

28 Talcott Parsons, *The Social System*, Chicago, Free Press, 1951; Talcott Parsons and Edward A. Shils, eds, *Toward a General Theory of Action*, Cambridge, Mass., Harvard University Press, 1951.

29 Ralf Dahrendorf, *Class and Class Conflict in Industrial Society*, Stanford University Press, 1959, pp. 231–6; John Rex, *Key Problems of Sociological Theory*, London, Humanities Press, 1961, p. 196.

30 C. W. McKee and Harold G. Moulton, *A Survey of Economic Education*, Washington, Brookings Institution, 1951, p. 3.

31 Special Textbook Study Committee, 'Economics in the schools,' *American Economic Review*, LIII (March 1963), Supplement, 3 and 4.

32 Clarke, 1968.

7 The Changing Curriculum: Theory and Practice
William A. Reid

Editors' introduction

This paper does not attempt to sum up the case studies; they are
well able to speak for themselves, and do so in their own unique ways.
Its purpose is rather to sketch in an account of the broad field to
which they contribute – the theory of curriculum design and diffusion
– and to consider a basic problem to which they point – the gap
between theory and practice, between the ideal and the norm. All
the studies owe at least part of their interest to the mismatches they
demonstrate between what currently popular models would assume
or predict, and the ways in which curricula are actually designed and
implemented. This finding is not altogether surprising when it is
considered that theories of curriculum development owe relatively
little to descriptive studies of actual practice, and that, although the
argument is less easy to make, similar problems of congruence with
empirical data seem to exist with theories of curriculum
implementation.

The discussion begins with a separate consideration of these two
areas of theory (though it is argued that it is precisely this separation
which has been the cause of many of the difficulties which beset
thinking about curriculum planning). Next, some factors are reviewed
which must be taken into account by any design theory which is
intended to be consonant with the practical constraints encountered
in implementation. Finally, the case studies are drawn upon to suggest
some features which a wider ranging theory of curriculum design
would need to exhibit.

I

Ever since attempts began to be made to construct a theoretical foundation for curriculum design, the dominant concern has been with
elaborating logical mechanisms which proceed from axioms, through

rational processes based on these, to a finished specification, much in the way that one might set about designing a bridge, a ship or an assembly line. The argument in all these cases seems logically impeccable: first you must know what you want to achieve – learning outcomes, performance specifications, traffic flows, production schedules; once these have been stated they will guide the choices you must make between alternative design decisions; finally it remains to make a synthesis between these decisions and check that it enables you to meet the objectives, standards or targets which were initially decided upon.[1] The argument seems particularly persuasive in the case of the curriculum. Presumably the whole purpose of engaging in processes of education or instruction is to bring about desired outcomes and the curriculum is the instrument for achieving these. Once the desired outcomes have been defined they will provide the axioms for the design process. This was the position taken by early theorists such as Bobbitt and Harap.[2] A model of such evident rationality was attractive to someone whose declared aim was 'to lift [teachers] out of the grooves of routine traditional thinking – or rather out of an imitation which is not thought' and to 'so obliterate the grooves that their minds will be free to think out new problems':[3] it seemed to fit the purposive nature of education as an activity, and to offer the promise of security, respectability, and ease of explanation. Moreover, as Kliebard[4] has pointed out, in the early years of this century American society as a whole was fascinated by the possibility of devising ever more efficient techniques of production, and it was natural that education, like other endeavours, should come under the spell of the 'scientific management' movement of which Frederick W. Taylor was the high priest.[5] 'The institution of schooling was simply that vast bureaucratic machinery which transforms the crude raw material of childhood into a socially useful product.'[6] The thought, and the optimism which engenders it, echo through Bobbitt's words:[7]

Human life, however varied, consists in the performance of specific activities. Education that prepares for life is one that prepares definitely and adequately for these specific activities. However numerous and diverse they may be for any social class, they can be discovered. This requires only that one go out into the world of affairs and discover the particulars of which these affairs consist. These will show the abilities, attitudes, habits, appreciations and forms of knowledge that men need. These will be the objectives of the curriculum. They will be numerous, definite and particularised. The curriculum will then be that series of experiences which childhood and youth must have by way of attaining those objectives.

The response to the call was impressive; hundreds of studies were carried out in an attempt to establish empirically what it was that people had to do as citizens and workers.[8] To this extent the early theorists of curriculum design were not merely carrying out a prescriptive exercise. It was their intention that their paradigm should have a sound basis in data about the real world – though these data were to be confined to the daily life of adults and not extended to include the behaviour of teachers, students or curriculum designers. However, it was precisely this empirical prop, slender as it was, that was to prove something of a handicap to the rational model of curriculum planning. It soon became apparent that the critical task of educators was to equip children for an uncertain future and, consequently, that the central concern of curriculum planning must be to foster and facilitate change and not to refine instruments which tended to perpetuate the *status quo*. This realisation led in the 1930s to a temporary eclipse of the ideas of the Bobbitt school of thought, in favour of a more pragmatic and humanistic 'progressive' approach to the curriculum inspired by the writings and example of Dewey. However, in spite of the criticisms which were levelled at it, there were powerful forces at work which preserved the rational model of curriculum planning as an alternative to be reckoned with. The United States, beset by the need to secure some unity of standards over the schools of a whole sub-continent, and stimulated by the problems of selecting and training personnel in World War II, devoted increasing resources to psychological measurement, the implicit models of which have a natural affinity to 'hard-headed' approaches to curriculum design. After the war this trend was further reinforced by the demand for more extensive counselling services, and by the need to provide data on which to make decisions about entry to the fast expanding higher education sector.[9] Consequently, when a swing of fashion led to disenchantment with 'progressive' ideas about how to plan the work of schools, and this disenchantment was compounded by the now legendary panic over the Sputnik launching in 1957, it was not some entirely new approach that began to lay claims to recognition, but, in a refurbished form, the rational curriculum planning model of forty years earlier.[10]

The critical factor in the climate of opinion which led to the resurgence of the rational model was that the demand for curriculum renewal arose from general public concern, and not merely from trends in the private world of the educator; and the expression of public concern through the investment of State and Federal funds led inevitably to calls for the adoption of strict criteria for evaluating development proposals and for measuring the effectiveness of their products. This was the signal for the educationalists, who had seen the initiative in the early wave of national curriculum projects pass to scholars and subject specialists, to reassert their command of the field. The means for doing this lay to hand in ideas developed in the early post-war years by the adherents of the Bobbitt tradition. It was, in fact, a former pupil at Bobbitt's at Chicago, R.W. Tyler, who was responsible for producing the most influential statement of these ideas. Tyler's claims for his book[11] were modest and its positive suggestions couched in singularly tentative language. It was, he said, 'not a manual for curriculum construction', but simply outlined 'one way of viewing an instructional program'.[12] Nor was he disposed to advocate a highly rigorous and analytic approach to the formulation of objectives: 'I tend to view objectives as general modes of reaction to be developed rather than highly specific habits to be acquired.'[13] But Tyler's work was more important for the logical extensions which it invited than for what it specifically recommended, and for what was conspicuously omitted than for what was included. Little or nothing was said about the constraints on curriculum planning, and, in spite of his insistence that there must be many sources of objectives (and not just the task analyses proposed by Bobbitt), problems of choice and of achieving consensus were ignored. Those who later wished to elaborate the paradigm along lines which it logically invited were faced with no brake to their speculations, and, where Tyler led, many eagerly followed. Tyler's proposal that many sources of objectives be consulted removed the unwanted conservatism that had attracted criticism in the earlier form of the model. But, more important, the switch of focus from the definition of objectives was accompanied by a much greater stress on using objectives as criteria for evaluation, and it was the theme of evaluation which, through the 1960s, became dominant in the writings of curriculum theorists. A powerful alliance was forged between curriculum planners and the psychometricians who would provide the instruments for implementing evaluation procedures; an alliance which has proved so potent that the evaluation tail now seems to be wagging the design dog in a flowering of accountability legislation and objectives exchanges.

This is not the place to trace in detail the ways in which the logical theory of curriculum development has been elaborated in recent years through work on behavioural objectives, taxonomies, programmed learning, and the refinement of evaluative procedures. Renewed interest in it, both in the United States and Great Britain, coincided with an upsurge of concern about the adequacy of school curricula, and with recognition of the need for large scale development projects backed by ample funds. Given this, the institutionalization of the model was assured. It provided administrators and funding bodies with criteria against which to judge proposals and procedures; it provided a readily communicable rationale for curriculum workers, and it appealed to scientists in whose fields the major curriculum concerns were being felt. As new curricula have been disseminated and discussed the model has acquired such visibility and respectability that the few curriculum projects that have set their faces against it have done so with a deliberation and a concern to propound theoretical justifications which have marked very clearly their consciousness of departing from an established orthodoxy.[14] But since Tyler imparted a new life and a new direction to it, the model has become essentially prescriptive. In spite of all the work which has gone into its elaboration, little or no effort has been devoted to showing how it relates to the actual behaviour of curriculum designers, or what constraints might limit its usefulness in practice. The price of abandoning its original links with task analysis has been the sacrifice of any explicit connection with the world of real human activities. This is not to say that it does not have something of positive value to contribute to curriculum design, but merely to point out that it falls short of taking into account all the factors which a design theory needs to accommodate.

II

Theories of curriculum implementation have tended to be discussed independently of theories of curriculum design, and they have a more complicated ancestry. But here too, as Giaquinta argues in his recent survey of the field, there is no substantial basis in descriptive theories for propositions about how the process should be carried out.[15] Whereas curriculum design can be seen as a more or less unique activity, having few, if any, close parallels, curriculum implementation has been treated by many writers as a sub-category of the more general question of how to introduce and establish innovations,[16] and comparisons have been freely made with strategies for change in other fields. One branch of theory stems from the 'human relations' movement in management study which first assumed importance in the late twenties with the work of Elton Mayo.[17] Writers who follow his perspectives[18] tend to regard social relations, and particularly the dynamics of informal groups, together with communications, as the key issues in the acceptance of innovations, and to adopt a hypothesis testing approach to defining the conditions under which successful implementation will take place. Another closely related strand of theory is that offered by social psychologists interested in group processes,[19] who advocate preparation of the ground for innovation through techniques aimed at developing favourable attitudes in those who will be affected, and at increasing their receptiveness to information.

A further theoretical tradition has been developed by organisational analysts.[20] Though varying in details, their conceptualisations of organizations tend to include categories such as goals, technologies, social systems (or task groups), and values and beliefs. These are seen as mutually interdependent, and the reaction to innovation is held to depend on the degree to which the consequent reordering of relationships within and between the categories is tolerable in terms of the benefits likely to accrue. The utility of such a mode of analysis for studying curriculum change seems self-evident, given that curricula cannot be considered apart from the institutions through which they are provided. However, few attempts have been made to consider curriculum change in this light.[21]

Finally, anthropological approaches obviously lend themselves to the study of change. Almost any kind of innovation can be seen in a cultural perspective, and one may therefore speculate about the extent to which cultural forces influence the acceptance or rejection of new curricula. In many ways the anthropologist is cultivating the same ground as the organisational analyst, but his preoccupation with stable behaviour patterns and the contexts which sustain them give his work its special flavour. He is less prone to reify innovation and then to ask questions about whether it is accepted or rejected; he is more likely to be interested in the interaction of new practices and established cultures, and in subtle reactions to change which cannot be simply categorised as acceptance or rejection. This mode of enquiry, like the last, would seem to be very appropriate to the study of curriculum change and, after a period of almost total neglect, it is beginning to command attention.[22]

Both organisational analysts and anthropologists have favoured a case study approach to problems of innovation, rather than one based on hypothesis testing so that, to this extent at least, some basis exists for the development of descriptive theories.[23] But it still remains true that most of those who have been engaged in innovation as a field of study have been looking for recipes to ease the path of those wishing to propagate innovations. By being too close to the practical concerns of the administrator they have tended to ignore or to deny complexity rather than to recognise it as an essential given of the situation. Too often innovations have been implicitly regarded as having clearly specifiable properties, as being both durable and desirable, and only rejected through human ignorance and obstinacy. As Giaquinta reminds us, 'resistance continues to be treated primarily as a practical difficulty of organisations that requires a remedy and not as a social phenomenon requiring systematic inquiry and explanation'.[24] Not only have the problems of the administrator remained unsolved but little progress has been made towards providing a secure foundation for lasting insights into the nature of change and innovation.

One type of enquiry which seems to have been unjustly neglected in the study of curriculum change is that which regards processes of planning and introducing curricula as having strongly political characteristics.[25] Yet this too would seem to be of potentially great importance. Sieber, for example, in analysing the reaction of schools to change, identifies four critical features which need to be taken into account: vulnerability to the social environment, values of personnel, diffuseness of goals, and the need to co-ordinate and control, within the bounds of the school, the clients and employees of the system.[26] All of these problematic areas would seem to be ones in which political processes could have a crucial role to play. The innovative school might well be the one which has the appropriate structures for allowing political accommodations to take place between clients and employees, for developing consensus on goals, for permitting adjustments to outside pressures, and for enabling change to be implemented without undermining the values of those concerned.

However, even taking into account the limitations which have been referred to, one may claim that the models of curriculum implementation which we have are in better shape than the currently available theories of curriculum design, in that they offer a variety of perspectives, pay regard to descriptive data, and allow for some degree of subtlety and complexity. What must be regarded as thoroughly unsatisfactory is that such a gulf should exist between the two areas of theory. That it does exist would seem to be a pointer to shortcomings in theories of curriculum development. The gaps between theoretical formulations and the conventional wisdom of schools and teachers are, it would seem, more attributable to inadequacies of the former than the lack of sophistication of the latter. If implementation models of a very different character from the proposed design models have to be considered, this is a strong indication that the practical constraints which should be catered for by planning theory are not, in fact, being accommodated by it. But, in any process where human, social and institutional complexities impose themselves, they need to be accommodated in the design stage as well as the implementation stage – in fact, the attempt to distinguish two different stages of activity may itself be a mistake – a kind of analytical aberration brought about by a belief that being scientific means denying the humanness of human activities. Such conclusions are beginning to impose themselves in areas far less obviously subject to constraint than the implementation of curricula; ships and bridges become environmental catastrophes rather than marvels of engineering, and rationally planned production lines engender alienation, mental stress and loss of production through strikes and absenteeism. But in planning curricula we are very obviously and directly concerned with aims and values, and the resources for implementation must be personal and institutional rather than mechanical and actuarial. The problem, then, is not one of building more sophistication into existing theoretical formulations, but of developing wider ranging theories which respond to the realities of curriculum planning as well as offering systematic approaches to problems of design.

III

Before considering in more detail what characteristics such theories should exhibit, it is necessary to specify what is meant by 'realities of curriculum planning'. Without going into niceties of definition it can be agreed that the curriculum is a set of activities involving teachers, learners and materials, and that these activities are provided through permanent institutions. (Those who would maintain that the curriculum is a written schedule of these activities, and no more, hold a perfectly tenable position, but would presumably have already lost sympathy with the argument. My own view would be that to confine curricula to the drawing-board is eccentric if not irresponsible.) An interesting fact about curricula, and one often overlooked by theories, is that *they are there anyway*. Even without the intervention of theorists, planners, designers and evaluators students go to school and to college and what they experience there is a curriculum. So, before devising schemes to make things different we might pause to ask how they got to be the way they are. In other words, studies of stability might tell us a lot more than studies of change.[27] This simple but important insight forms the basis of the analysis by McKinney and Westbury of secondary schools in Gary, Indiana, and it also lends significance to Voege's investigation into economic textbooks. Both studies avoid the adoption of simplistic notions of the nature of curriculum change by directing their attention to periods of several decades, requiring for their understanding firstly an appreciation of forces tending to preserve the *status quo* as well as those making for change, and secondly a recognition that change involves the abandonment of practices as well as their adoption. This study of stabilising forces is of especial importance when, as in the case of the curriculum, the system they sustain is a highly complex one involving several levels of action and decision. Even when attention is directed solely to the level of the classroom the relationships and behaviours which must be accounted for are of a daunting degree of intricacy; to describe even a brief episode is a demanding task, as the many miles of audio tape, video tape and transcripts collected by researchers into classroom interaction abundantly testify. Yet, in spite of this, the results of a number of studies show that many similarities exist between the curricula which are enacted in different schools when comparisons are made within nations, internationally and over time.[28]

How then are the behaviours of the actors in these very diverse situations regulated? Or, to use Barker's[29] terminology, how is the programme of the setting determined? Such studies as we have[30] would seem to indicate that the three main determinants are the values, beliefs and expectations of teachers, the way classrooms are organised, and the nature and availability of outside support. (This is not intended as a complete list; students, for example, must be an important influence on the nature of classrooms, but one suspects that, if theirs were indeed one of the most powerful influences, more diversity of practice might exist than seems to be the case.[31] But to lengthen the list reduces still further the room available for influence from curriculum guides, teaching materials, training courses, conferences, and all the other artifacts and activities aimed at shaping the curriculum through deliberate policy and planning.)

The case for regarding the teacher as one of the main sources of curriculum stability is perhaps the one which has the most support both from research studies and from a general consideration of the nature of educational systems. Teaching is one of the few trades or professions whose central activities are at some time visible to every member of the community, because all must attend school. But it is not a profession like medicine or the law which generates its own knowledge.[32] Becker[33] has shown how becoming a doctor involves unlearning what one thinks he already knows about the way a doctor behaves. In the case of teaching, what might have to be unlearned is the result, not of a few isolated encounters, but of over a decade of close, formative contact. Hamilton's paper provides some good illustrations of the difficulty that teachers may have in departing from practices hallowed by tradition. He shows how the ideology of testing subscribed to by teachers in Maxwell School overrode that advocated in the Integrated Science Curriculum Paper, and how the one teacher whose beliefs were consonant with the demands of the innovation, or were flexible enough to be adapted to them, had ultimately to choose between conforming to the local ideology or moving elsewhere. Education for teaching simply proffers alternative models of behaviour, rather than making acceptance into the profession conditional on rejection of the 'lay' model; and the alternatives tend to be relatively uninfluential, partly because, as McKinney and Westbury point out 'education has characteristically been unable to evolve procedures or methods that point to or evaluate single clusters of behaviour which might, or must be modified, in the interests of more effective, or qualitatively different teaching'.[34] The educator's models, therefore, tend to lack authority, and to be discarded rapidly in face of teachers' needs to adjust to the value systems of the schools where they must shape their careers. Hence teachers tend to promote stability rather than to challenge it.

Apart from its importance as an influence on how they see the process of educating, what teachers have themselves experienced at school, college and university will also condition their attitudes to curriculum content. This experience imparts to them notions of what should be properly included in the curriculum of children of a particular age or ability, and also defines for them what it means to have a specific topic as part of a curriculum. To take what may be an extreme case, simple and unexplicated phrases in English sixth form syllabuses[35] like 'history of the United States from 1783 to the present day', 'the regional geography of Africa', 'Jane Austen, *Persuasion*', or 'wave and corpuscular theories of light' are not unambiguous definitions of what has to be done; they are signals to the teacher which set off a repertoire of acquired behaviours. Teachers, in planning their lessons, can predict with a high degree of certainty what these behaviours will entail in the way of classroom activities, materials to be used, time to be spent and the work to be required of students. This kind of fixed expectation was another problem for the teachers at Maxwell. Some teachers were 'subject specialists' denying any competence to handle material with which they were not already familiar, and finding that suggested work schedules conflicted with their preconceived notions of what it meant to teach the kinds of topics included in the Integrated Science Curriculum.

The existence among teachers of stable bodies of ideas about how and what to teach is not something to be deplored; without such knowledge schooling would be impossible. No curriculum planner could conceivably spell out in total detail what a teacher had to do and show him how to do it successfully *in his own school*. Every curriculum project, however complete its range of materials and teacher's guides, would fall to the ground but for the existence of this common pool of accumulated skills and beliefs. As Bridgham nicely puts it, 'New curricula can be thought of as trajectories through pedagogic space; they are properly defined not by single lines but rather by envelopes containing an infinite set of "allowed" solutions to the problems envisaged by the curriculum designers.'[36]

But the curriculum is also influenced by the ways in which schools organise classrooms and teaching groups. There is a tendency to see organisation as a variable that can be manipulated with relative ease. (Educational thought seems to move in cycles between seeing children or educational environments as fixed. Advocacy of 'open classrooms' proclaims the child as the immovable object.) But unless we abolish schooling altogether, in which case the notion of curriculum becomes redundant, there will always be some sense in which learning has to be organised, and therefore to take on enduring characteristics imparted by institutional arrangements. And it remains the case, both in Great Britain and the United States, that most teaching is conducted in formal classrooms. Westbury, in a recently published article[37] has tried to spell out the links between classroom context and teacher response – to answer the question posed by Hoetker and Ahlbrand, 'Why does the recitation persist?'[38] He argues that

> we can only come to terms with the paradoxes raised [by Hoetker and Ahlbrand] if we see the classroom we know as an environment that contains demands (and, therefore, implied tasks for the teacher) and constraints that are inherent in its nature, given existing goals, structures and resources. The interaction between the demands on the classroom and the constraints within it cause it to be a social setting that has only a limited potential for manipulation by teachers. The recitation is a teaching strategy that permits teachers to deal, in at least a minimally satisfactory way, with the tensions that this interaction between demands and constraints creates.

He goes on to show that the present level of knowledge about the conditions under which new sets of relationship might be created between teachers, learners and instructional materials is very low; there is, in fact, a yawning gap between educational slogans about open classrooms and child-centred learning and the development of the technologies of teaching which might turn them into a reality.

Finally, beyond the school and the classroom, are the supportive agencies which provide those resources for mounting curricula which schools cannot, except in unusual circumstances, supply for themselves: trained teachers, curriculum materials and equipment and general financial provision, as well as the less tangible resources of ideas about what to teach and how to teach it, and of legitimation for the role of the school as a public institution. The study of the Gary schools amply documents the part played by outside bodies in preserving an equilibrium of initiating successful or abortive attempts to change the curriculum. The conclusions drawn attack the notion that innovation is the antithesis of stability, and that, since stability depends on enduring supportive structures, innovation should try to get off the ground through levitation in order not to compromise its principles. They question the tendency of innovators either to appeal to the logic of their position and believe that a demonstration of the error of their ways will cause people to change, or to invoke an ideological commitment in the belief that innovation can be wrought by declarations of faith.[39] In fact, where logic prevails in human affairs it is usually because major institutions have been enlisted on its side, and the spread of ideologies owes more to their success in setting up efficient bureaucracies than to the unaided power of their dogmas. Similarly, when the evolution of the curriculum is studied over a long time span, it is seen that the initiation of successful change is, to a very large extent, dependent on the creation or enlistment of enduring supportive structures. For, as McKinney and Westbury express it, the curriculum is 'an *idea* that becomes a thing', and '. . . development and renewal are only meaningful notions in so much as they are embedded in structures'.[40] A new science curriculum demands that agencies be available to provide teachers having the requisite skills, general advice and support, and curriculum materials rich enough in information to convey an unambiguous message about what they are intended to achieve, and by what means this is to be brought about. The alternative proposition, that innovation in the curriculum should have the character of ultra-protestantism, denying the authority of central agencies, and encouraging each individual school to follow its own path of salvation, is an invitation to a succession of heady ephemera, lapsing into confusion and sterility. The problem is not how authority, whether in the shape of government, administrators or subject disciplines, can be thwarted, but how it can be used as a resource to help schools develop courses appropriate to them and their students. For without the intervention of 'authorities' no system embracing thousands of schools and millions of students can be purposefully deflected from the path to which overriding constraints commit it.

IV

Given that this outline of some factors making for stability characterises the realities with which curriculum planning and implementation have to deal, what might be the desirable characteristics of curriculum theory designed to respond to them, and what pitfalls should it avoid ? First of all it should not proceed on the assumption that curriculum design inhabits a different universe from curriculum implementation. The fundamental concern for any curriculum planner, or planning body, should be – What actually happens in the classroom? It is not a case of being able to offer an instrument with known performance specifications (much as many evaluators would like this to be so). The purpose of curriculum planning should be to see how skills in design, communication and organisation can be used to change the inertial forces controlling the curriculum in order to deflect it into a new path. To achieve this purpose it is necessary to devote at least as much attention to the context within which the curriculum is to be implemented, as to the design of the product itself.[41]

> If we seek to have an enterprise which can attain a goal formulated in advance, but whose structure and mechanism is that appropriate to an organism whose goals are formulated only with hindsight, then our managerial task is one of *organizational design*.

Such a conclusion is inescapable if we agree with Hamilton in regarding 'the learning milieu as containing the substance of curriculum innovation, not, as is often implied, its pale or distorted shadow', or if we consider the implications of Dickinson's portrayal of the way in which head teachers field the balls carelessly thrown to them by curriculum projects and then use them to play their own games.[42] Secondly, any unified curriculum theory which refuses to subscribe to a dichotomy between design and implementation should avoid the adoption of a concept of innovation entirely divorced from the wider question of how curricula generally are sustained and how they evolve over time. To focus too closely on the concept of change is perhaps to miss some of its essential attributes which only show up in a broader context. It is both theoretically mistaken and practically unhelpful to see innovation as unidirectional, as 'good', as 'resisted or implemented', rather than as cyclical or subject to shifting fashions, as functional in some circumstances as leading to processes of negotiation and adaptation. Voege's paper suggests that it is more realistic to see the claims of new ideas and practices on the curriculum as being transitory, and therefore as demanding a flexible, relativist stance on the part of planners, but he also suggests that the life cycle of successful innovation is to be measured in decades, implying a need for patient nurturing rather than attempts to force instant conclusions. To try to deny this complexity and to see curriculum change as something which can be conceptualised in simple, mechanistic terms, is not merely to invoke an alien theory, it is also to import a rigid and antipathetic dogmatism into an activity which, our case studies suggest, depends for its effectiveness on consensus, negotiation and deliberation. The denial of complexity is, as Burkhardt maintained, the essence of tyranny and, ours, as he foretold, the age of the great simplifiers.[43] To build a greater degree of sophistication into the rational model does not entirely answer the problem. It is basically flawed if it dogmatically assumes that the determination of ends can always precede the specification of means, that criteria for the selection of means can rest upon statements of aims and objectives, and that constraints can be taken into account in an incidental way, or be the concern of other agencies, and need not figure as a major component of the model. The 'means-end' approach tends to belittle the contribution that the 'conventional wisdom' of teachers and administrators can make to curriculum planning, and to oppose to it a rationalistic formulation of such incompatible characteristics that only a schizophrenic could identify himself at one and the same time with planner and practitioner. Theory should attempt to encompass the behaviours of both, not by elevating conventional wisdom to the status of theory, but by formulating models to which practitioners can subscribe without renouncing all their previous works. Walker's study makes an important contribution to defining how this might be achieved, in that he shows the actual behaviour of curriculum developers to be susceptible to analysis in theoretical terms which can then provide the elements of a prescriptive model for curriculum design. Through building themselves on studies of practice new models could afford to aspire to slightly humbler pretentions than their predecessors, contenting themselves with the achievement of small but significant advances, and foregoing sweeping but often illusory promises of wholesale reform.

The most urgent need is for curriculum theory that will help us to make good use of human resources. The studies by Walker and Shaw indicate that a thorough-going means-ends approach is likely to be counter-productive in this respect. They show that both curriculum projects and educational administrators operate in a situation of unclear preferences, that the parts played in decision-making by aims and constraints are difficult to disentangle, and that statements of objectives are only one of many devices for guiding discussion, defining decision points and adjudicating between alternatives. The problem has been noted before, but often in terms of a defect to be remedied rather than a reality to be grappled with, or even built upon. Smith and Keith, for example, remark that they are[44]

> struck with the difficulties that even bright people have when they try to make sense out of the interrelationship among ideas such as curriculum objectives, learning experiences, course content, and the like . . . the time and the thought that this requires . . . might well be

beyond the resources of the school personnel themselves, and, perhaps, of the district.

Yet the notion that it is of doubtful utility to try to set aims apart from other considerations which govern planning is, in fields other than the curriculum, far from new:[45]

> Those constraints that motivate the decision maker and those that guide his search for actions are sometimes regarded as more 'goal-like' than those that limit the actions he may consider or those that are used to test whether a potential course of action he has designed is satisfactory. Whether we treat all the constraints symmetrically or refer to some asymmetrically as goals is largely a matter of linguistic or analytic convenience.

Only by casting aside as irrelevant the notion that the curriculum planner *must* be concerned with implementation, and therefore with organisation and social structure, can aims be elevated to be the prime determinants of action. Even a simple admission that curricula need people to implement them should alert us to the necessity of questioning how far human activities can or should be planned solely around aims, goals or objectives.

In the curriculum project some of the constraints are removed through the creation of a temporary system within which people can feel securer in their rejection of traditional solutions, and can be exempt from the necessity of shaping their actions in accordance with the demands of an institution. Here the planning process might be thought to exist in a purer form, yet Walker shows that, even in this context, it fails to conform to the rational model. Decisions arise from an interplay between abstract ideas or notions and concrete practical considerations. Far from proceeding systematically, the project was to be compared to 'an amoeba . . . [which] . . . lurched forward by extending the very stuff of its life – its deliberations – in localised forays into the territory ahead'. Yet these deliberations were analysable, and therefore understandable. With understanding their quality might be raised, the process become more controlled and explicit. The skills needed to achieve this outcome will not be learned from a textbook, neither will they depend on mastering formal, logical operations; they will, to use Schwab's term, be 'practical'[46] – concerned with judgment and with intuitive responses to the ebb and flow of argument, exposition and reflection. The knowledge required will include a study of the relationships between the composition of curriculum groups in abilities and allegiances and the likely outcomes of their deliberations, in terms of both design and implementation. For if what Walker describes as 'the value-laden aspects of practical action' cannot be confined to an initial stage of selecting desirable objectives, then the question of *who* deliberates assumes major importance. If the interaction of value systems is to continue throughout the whole design process, a delicate balance must be held between allowing antagonisms to develop which may hinder the establishment of consensus (or lead to the pseudo-consensus which represents the victory of one party over another), and limiting the interests represented so that failure may arise from not incorporating a sufficient diversity of skills and experience.[47]

When curricula are planned within institutions, or when institutions implement the work of outside planning groups, then the deliberative process takes on a different character. Perhaps, with Shaw, we should call it 'negotiation' rather than 'deliberation'. But the change is not fundamental. Although conducted in a context in which a political dimension assumes heightened importance, negotiation, like deliberation is basically concerned with achieving consensus, with devising solutions which respond to needs but respect constraints, and with securing commitment to these solutions. Constraints, however, take on greater significance. Existing skills and stocks-in-trade must be accommodated, curriculum decisions must be congruent with organisationa decisions about finance, staffing and equipment. The implications of curriculum decisions for the distribution of power and influence must be scrutinised:[48]

> The primary characteristic of viable systems is that they try to optimize a whole set of conflicting objective functions at once . . . their method of control is essentially one of contriving a balance, and not of seeking some unique maximum.

As the studies by Dickinson and Hamilton demonstrate, the more we insist that curriculum planning is rational and not political, and the more we emphasise aims at the expense of constraints, the more certain we make it that the end of our endeavours will bear little resemblance to the high hopes with which we began. Not that such an unpalatable conclusion will be forced on our attention. Implementers are never eager to tell the initiators of plans any news which they think they may not welcome, and, as Dickinson shows, schools are 'success systems', always ready to avert failure by a masterly show of 'innovation without change'. Part of the answer is to make sure that curriculum planning is itself to a degree political, thereby preventing it from being subject to an entirely different set of considerations from those that govern implementation. For the 'value laden' aspects will always be there, whether we recognise them or not.

Prescriptive theories of curriculum planning which are grounded in descriptive data about the process to which they relate will not be tidy and well-ordered, for they must reflect an activity which thrives on flexibility and redundancy. But if claims to operate in the same intellectual and theoretical territory as the physical scientist or mathematician must be set aside, this does not imply a flight from rationality. Curriculum development, as Walker observes, 'is a genuinely creative endeavour, but one governed by a rational consideration of the merits of the things created'.[49] The rationality to be cultivated is one geared to a context which is, in Simon's term, 'artificial'.[50]

> The artificial world is centered precisely on [the] interface between the inner and outer environments; it is concerned with attaining goals by adapting the former to the latter. The proper study of those who are concerned with the artificial is the way in which that adaptation of means to environments is brought about – and central to that is the process of design itself.

Theory which responds to this type of concept of the design process cannot be elaborated through abstract thought alone. Just as medical theory is extended and refined through treating patients, so curriculum theory must be built through teaching students. Indeed, planning itself should take the form of an educational experience.[51]

> We have usually thought of city planning as a means whereby the planner's creative activity could build a system that would satisfy the needs of a populace. Perhaps we should think of city planning as a valuable creative activity in which many members of a community can have the opportunity of participating – if we have wits to reorganise the process that way.

With suitable adaptation such a motto might profitably guide the thinking of those who plan the curricula of our schools.

Notes

1 For a contrasting point of view, see B. Klein and W. Meckling, 'Application of operations research to development decisions', *Operations Research*, 6, 1958, pp. 352–63.

2 F. Bobbitt, *The Curriculum*, Boston, Houghton Mifflin, 1918, and *How to Make a Curriculum*, Boston, Houghton Mifflin, 1924; H. Harap, *The Technique of Curriculum Making*, New York, Macmillan, 1928.

3 Bobbitt, 1918, p. 284.

4 H.M. Kliebard, 'Bureaucracy and curriculum theory', in Association for Supervision and Curriculum Development, National Education

Association, *Freedom, Bureaucracy and Schooling*, Washington, DC 1971, pp. 74–93.

5 F.W. Taylor, *The Principles of Scientific Management*, New York, Harper, 1911.

6 Kliebard, op. cit., p. 75. Compare also M.L. Seguel, *The Curriculum Field: its Formative Years*, New York, Teachers College Press, 1966, p. 80.

7 Bobbitt, 1918, p. 42. See also E.W. Eisner, 'Franklin Bobbitt and the "Science" of Curriculum Making', *School Review*, 75, 1967, pp. 29–47.

8 See Harap, op. cit., *passim*.

9 See M.S. Schudson, 'Organising the "meritocracy": a history of the college entrance examination board', *Harvard Educational Review*, 42, 1, 1972, pp. 34–69.

10 The idea that a new alternative might have been fastened upon is not fanciful. Possible sources lay to hand in, for example, the work of Lindblom on policy making, or the cyberneticians on open system management (Lindblom, 1958a, 1958b and 1959; Wiener, 1948; Beer, 1959).

11 Tyler, 1949.

12 Ibid., p. 1.

13 Ibid., p. 43.

14 The Schools Council Humanities Project, now based at the University of East Anglia, is a case in point. See L. Stenhouse, 'Some limitations on the use of objectives in curriculum research and planning', *Paedagogica Europaea*, Braunschweig, S-Hertogenbosch 1971.

15 Giaquinta, 1973.

16 See, for example, Rogers and Shoemaker, 1971.

17 Elton Mayo, *The Human Problems of an Industrial Civilisation*, New York, 1933.

18 See, for example, F.J. Roethlisberger and W. J. Dickson, *Management and the Worker*, Cambridge, Mass., Harvard University Press, 1949.

19 For some examples of research, see D. Cartwright and A.F. Zander eds, *Group Dynamics: Research and Theory*, Evanston, Ill., Row, Peterson, 1953.

20 See, for example, A. Etzioni, ed, *Complex Organisations*, New York, Holt Rinehart, 1961, or C. Perrow, *Organisational Analysis: a Sociological View*, London, Tavistock, 1970.

21 See, however, H.L. Thompson, *et al.*, 'A hierarchy of basic organisational needs in liberal arts colleges', *Educational Administration Quarterly*, 6, 1970, pp. 56–77, and P.H. Taylor, W.A. Reid and B.J. Holley, *The English Sixth Form: a Case Study in Curriculum Research*, London, Routledge & Kegan Paul, 1974, ch. 7.

22 An approach along these lines is advocated by Sarason, 1971. For some examples of research, see Smith and Geoffrey, 1968, and Smith and Keith, 1971.

23 A tradition set by such classic studies as Selznick, 1949.

24 Giaquinta, 1973, p. 189.

25 The studies which have been made have tended to concentrate on the level of general policy, rather than curriculum decision-making at the 'tactical' level. See Kirst and Walker, 1971, and Young, 1972.

26 Sieber, 1968.

27 The same point is made by D. Hemphill, 'A general theory of innovativeness', *Alberta Journal of Educational Research*, 14, 2, 1968, pp. 101–14.

28 Kirst and Walker, 1971, Hodgetts, 1968 and Hoetker and Ahlbrand, 1969.

29 R.E. Barker, *Ecological Psychology: Concepts and Methods for Studying the Environment of Social Behaviour*, Stanford University Press, 1968, and R.G. Barker and P.V. Gump, *Big School, Small School: High School Size and Student Behavior*, Stanford University Press, 1964.

30 For a summary, see Westbury, 1973.

31 For a development of this point, see L.J. Waks, *Freedom, Morality and the Material Environment of the Schoolchild*, paper presented to the American Education Research Association Conference, Chicago, 1972.

32 Simpson and Simpson, 1969.

33 H.S. Becker *et al.*, *Boys in White: Student Culture in Medical School*, University of Chicago Press, 1961.

34 P. 9 of the present volume.

35 The curriculum in question is based on the study in depth of two or three traditional academic subjects, and the teachers are very homogeneous in outlook and education. See Taylor, Reid and Holley, op. cit.

36 R.G. Bridgham in Eisner, 1971.

37 Westbury, 1973, p. 100.

38 Hoetker and Ahlbrand, 1969. The 'recitation' is the process of rehearsing factual information through rapid questioning on the part of the teacher who is seeking brief, instantaneous replies.

39 For an analysis of this syndrome, see Smith and Keith, 1971: '. . . individuals characterized by true belief and crusading sentiments . . . are highly committed. . . . The commitment, however, [is] to nonexistent structures, that is, to abstract ideas and ideals at best and, at worst, to vaguer more poorly defined personal needs' (pp. 397–8).

40 Pp. 6 and 50 of the present volume.

41 Beer, 1966, p. 380.

42 For further examples of the gap between the intentions of curriculum developers and classroom implementation, see Sarason, 1971, and Eisner, 1971.

43 Quoted from E.F. Kelly, *Curriculum Evaluation and Literary Criticism: the Explication of an Analogy*, paper presented to the American Education Research Association Conference, New Orleans, 1973.

44 Smith and Keith, 1971, p. 295.

45 H.A. Simon, 'On the concept of organisational goal', *Administrative Science Quarterly*, 9, 1, 1964, p. 20.

46 Schwab, 1969, 1971, 1973.

47 See Schwab, 1973, and S. Fox, 'A practical image of "the practical" ' *Curriculum Theory Network*, No. 10, fall 1972, pp. 45–57.

48 Beer, 1966, p. 99.

49 P. 132 of the present volume.

50 Simon, 1969, p. 58.

51 Simon, 1969, p. 75.

Select Bibliography

BEER, S. (1959), *Cybernetics and Management*, London, English Universities Press.

BEER, S. (1966), *Decision and Control: the Meaning of Operational Research and Management Cybernetics*, London, Wiley.

CLARK, B.R. (1970), *The Distinctive College; Antioch, Reed and Swarthmore*, Chicago, Aldine.

CLARKE, T.N. (1968), 'Institutionalization of innovations in higher education: four models', *Administrative Science Quarterly*, 13, pp. 1–25.

COHEN, M.D., MARCH, J.G. and OLSEN, J.P. (1972), 'A garbage can model of organisational choice', *Administrative Science Quarterly*, 17, pp. 1–25.

DAHLLÖF, U.S. (1971a), *Ability Grouping, Content Validity, and Curriculum Process Analysis*, New York, Teachers College Press.

DAHLLÖF, U.S. (1971b), 'Relevance and fitness analysis in comparative education', *Scandinavian Journal of Educational Research*, 15, pp. 101–121.

DREEBEN, R. (1970), *The Nature of Teaching; Schools and the Work of Teachers*, Glenview, Ill., Scott, Foresman.

EISNER, E.W. (ed.) (1971), *Confronting Curriculum Reform*, Boston, Mass., Little, Brown.

FENSHAM, P.J. and HOOPER, D. (1964), *The Dynamics of a Changing Technology: a Case Study in Textile Manufacturing*, London, Tavistock.

GIAQUINTA, J.B. (1973), 'The process of organisational change in schools', in F.N. Kerlinger (ed.), *Review of Research in Education, I*, Itasca, Ill., F.E. Peacock, pp. 178–208.

GOODLAD, J.I. *et al.* (1966), *The Changing School Curriculum*, New York, Fund for the Advancement of Education.

HAMILTON, D. (1973a), 'The integration of knowledge: practice and problems', *Journal of Curriculum Studies*, 5, 2, pp. 146–55.

HAMILTON, D. (1973b), 'At classroom level: studies in the learning milieu', unpublished Ph.D thesis, University of Edinburgh.

HARRIS, C.C. (1969), 'Reform in a normative organisation', *Sociological Review*, 17, 2, 1969, pp. 167–85.

HICKSON, D.J., PUGH, D.S. and PHEYSEY, D.C. (1969), 'Operations technology and organization structure: an empirical reappraisal', *Administrative Science Quarterly*, 14, pp. 378–97.

HODGETTS, A.B. (1968), *What Culture? What Heritage? A Study of Civic Education in Canada*, Toronto, Ontario Institute for Studies in Education.

HOETKER, J. and AHLBRAND, W.P. (1969), 'The persistence of the recitation', *American Educational Research Journal*, 6, pp. 145–67.

JACQUES, E. (1951), *The Changing Culture of a Factory*, London, Tavistock.

KALLÓS, D. (1973), *On Educational Scientific Research*, Reports from the Institute of Education, No. 36, University of Lund.

KIRST, M.W. and WALKER, D.F. (1971), 'An analysis of curriculum policy-making', *Review of Educational Research*, 41, 5, pp. 479–509.

KUHN, T.S. (1970), *The Structure of Scientific Revolutions*, University of Chicago Press.

LAWRENCE, P.R. and LORSCH, J.W. (1967), 'Differentiation and integration in complex organisations', *Administrative Science Quarterly*, 12, pp. 1–47.

LINDBLOM, C.E. (1958a), 'Policy analysis', *American Economic Review*, 48, pp. 298–312.

LINDBLOM, C.E. (1958b), 'Tinbergen on policy making', *Journal of Political Economy*, 66, pp. 531–8.

LORTIE, D.C. (1969), 'The balance of control and autonomy in elementary school teaching', in Etzioni, A. (ed.), *The Semi-Professions and their Organisations; Teachers, Nurses, Social Workers*, New York, Free Press, pp. 1–53.

LUNDGREN, U.P. (1972), *Frame Factors and the Teaching Process; a Contribution to Curriculum Theory and Theory on Teaching*, Stockholm, Almqvist & Wiksell.

LYNTON, R.P. (1969), 'Linking an innovative subsystem into the system', *Administrative Science Quarterly*, 14, pp. 398–416.

MALINOWSKI, B. (1945), *The Dynamics of Culture Change; an Inquiry into Race Relations in Africa*, New Haven, Conn., Yale University Press.

PARLETT, M.R. and HAMILTON, D. (1972), *Evaluation as Illumination; a New Approach to the Study of Innovatory Programs*, occasional paper No. 9, Centre for Research in the Educational Sciences, University of Edinburgh.

ROGERS, E.M. and SHOEMAKER, F.F. (1971), *Communication of Innovations: a Cross-Cultural Approach*, New York, Free Press.

SARASON, S.B. (1971), *The Culture of the School and the Problem of Change*, Boston, Allyn & Bacon.

SCHWAB, J.J. (1969), 'The practical: a language for curriculum', *School Review*, 78, 1, pp. 1–24.

SCHWAB, J.J. (1971), 'The practical: arts of eclectic', *School Review*, 79, 4, pp. 493–542.

SCHWAB, J.J. (1973), 'The practical 3: translation into curriculum', *School Review*, 81, 4, pp. 501–22.

SELZNICK, P. (1949), TVA *and the Grassroots*, Berkeley, University of California Press.

SHAW, K.E. (1972), 'Curriculum decision-making in a college of education', *Journal of Curriculum Studies*, 4, 1, pp. 51–9.

SHAW, K.E. (1973), 'A study of organisation in a college of education', unpublished Ph.D thesis, University of Bath.

SIEBER, S.D. (1968), 'Organisational influences on innovative roles in educational organisations', in T.L. Eidell and J.M. Kitchel (eds), *Knowledge Production and Utilization in Education*, Eugene, Oregon, University of Oregon, pp. 120–42.

SIEBER, S.D. (1972), 'Images of the practitioner and strategies of education change', *Sociology of Education*, 45, pp. 363–85.

SIMON, H.A. (1969), *The Sciences of the Artificial*, Cambridge, Mass., MIT Press.

SIMPSON, R.L. and SIMPSON, I.H. (1969), 'Women and bureaucracy in the semi-professions, in Etzioni, A. (ed.), *The Semi-Professions and their Organisation; Teachers, Nurses, Social Workers*, New York, Free Press, pp. 196–265.

SMITH, B.O., STANLEY, W.O. and SHORES, J.H. (1957), *Fundamentals of Curriculum Development*, New York, World Book Co.

SMITH, L.M. and GEOFFREY, W. (1968), *The Complexities of an Urban Classroom*, New York, Holt Rinehart.

SMITH, L.M. and KEITH, P.M. (1971), *Anatomy of Educational Innovation; an Organisational Analysis of an Elementary School*, New York, Wiley.

SMITH, M.P. (1971), 'Curriculum change at the local level', *Journal of Curriculum Studies*, 3, 2, pp. 158–62.

SOROKIN, P.A. (1937), *Social and Cultural Dynamics*, 4 vols, New York, American Book Co.

STINCHCOMBE, A.L. (1965), 'Social structures and organisation', in MARCH, J.G. (ed.), *Handbook of Organisations*, Chicago, Rand McNally, pp. 142–93.

TABA, H. (1962), *Fundamentals of Curriculum Development: Theory and Practice*, New York, Harcourt Brace.

TAYLOR, P.H. (1973), 'New frontiers in educational research', in *Paedagogica Europaea 1973: Assessment and Guidance in European Education*, S-Hertogenbosch, Braunschweig, pp. 17–33.

TYLER, R.W. (1949), *Basic Principles of Curriculum and Instruction*, University of Chicago Press.

VOEGE, H.W. (1972), *The Impact of Keynesian Ideas on Secondary-School Economics Textbooks of the United States, 1936–70*. No. 3, University of Michigan Social Foundations of Education Monograph Series, Ann Arbor, Michigan.

WALKER, D.F. (1970), 'Toward more effective curriculum projects in art', *Studies in Art Education*, 11, pp. 1–13.

WALKER, D.F. (1971), 'Strategies of deliberation in three curriculum development projects', unpublished Ph.D dissertation, Stanford University.

WESTBURY, I. (1973), 'Conventional classrooms, "open" classrooms and the technology of teaching', *Journal of Curriculum Studies*, 5, 2, pp. 99–121.

WHEELER, D.K. (1967), *Curriculum Process*, University of London Press.

WHITE, L.B. (1959), *The Evolution of Culture*, New York, McGraw-Hill.

WIENER, N. (1948), *Cybernetics*, Cambridge, Mass., MIT Press.

YOUNG, M.F.D. (ed.) (1971), *Knowledge and Control; New Directions for the Sociology of Education*, London, Collier-Macmillan.

YOUNG, M.F.D. (1972), 'On the politics of educational knowledge: some preliminary considerations with particular reference to the Schools Council', *Economy and Society*, 1, pp. 194–215.

ZACHARIAS, J.R. and WHITE, S. (1964), 'The requirements for major curriculum revision', *School and Society*, 92, pp. 66–72.

ZALD, M.N. (1962), 'Power balance and staff conflict in correctional institutions', *Administrative Science Quarterly*, 7, pp. 22–49.

Index